The Memoirs of Shah Tahmasp I

The Memoirs of Shah Tahmasp I

Safavid Ruler of Iran

Translated with an Introduction and Commentary
by A. C. S. Peacock

I.B. TAURIS
LONDON • NEW YORK • OXFORD • NEW DELHI • SYDNEY

I.B. TAURIS
Bloomsbury Publishing Plc, 50 Bedford Square, London, WC1B 3DP, UK
Bloomsbury Publishing Inc, 1359 Broadway, 12th Floor, New York, NY 10018, USA
Bloomsbury Publishing Ireland, 29 Earlsfort Terrace, Dublin 2, D02 AY28, Ireland

BLOOMSBURY, I.B. TAURIS and the I.B. Tauris logo are
trademarks of Bloomsbury Publishing Plc

First published in Great Britain 2024
This paperback edition published 2026

Copyright © A. C. S. Peacock, 2024, 2026

A. C. S. Peacock has asserted his rights under the Copyright,
Designs and Patents Act, 1988, to be identified as Editor of this work.

For legal purposes the Preface and Acknowledgements on pp. ix–x constitute an extension of this copyright page.

Cover design: Paul Smith
Cover image: Shah Tahmasp I (1514–1576) Seated in a Landscape c. 1575, Iran. Opaque watercolor and gold on paper. Gift of the John Huntington Art and Polytechnic Trust 1917.1078. Courtesy of The Cleveland Museum of Art, OH.

All rights reserved. No part of this publication may be: i) reproduced or transmitted in any form, electronic or mechanical, including photocopying, recording or by means of any information storage or retrieval system without prior permission in writing from the publishers; or ii) used or reproduced in any way for the training, development or operation of artificial intelligence (AI) technologies, including generative AI technologies. The rights holders expressly reserve this publication from the text and data mining exception as per Article 4(3) of the Digital Single Market Directive (EU) 2019/790.

Bloomsbury Publishing Inc does not have any control over, or responsibility for, any third-party websites referred to or in this book. All internet addresses given in this book were correct at the time of going to press. The author and publisher regret any inconvenience caused if addresses have changed or sites have ceased to exist, but can accept no responsibility for any such changes.

A catalogue record for this book is available from the British Library.

A catalog record for this book is available from the Library of Congress.

ISBN: HB: 978-0-7556-5355-3
PB: 978-0-7556-5356-0
ePDF: 978-0-7556-5358-4
eBook: 978-0-7556-5357-7

Typeset by Newgen KnowledgeWorks Pvt. Ltd., Chennai, India

For product safety related questions contact productsafety@bloomsbury.com.

To find out more about our authors and books visit www.bloomsbury.com and sign up for our newsletters.

Contents

List of Plates	vi
List of Figures	vii
List of Maps	viii
Preface and acknowledgements	ix
Chronology	xi
Introduction	1
Note on the translation	43

Translation of the *Memoirs*

1	Introduction and the affair of Ulama	49
2	A brief account of the affair of Ghazi Khan	89
3	The affair of Alqas Mirza	97
4	The account of İskender Pasha	123
5	The affair of Beyazid	137

Glossary	145
Textual notes	147
Bibliography	151
Index	161

Plates

1 The opening of Tahmasp's *Memoirs* in the short recension, in a manuscript made for Shah 'Abbas in the handwriting of Riza 'Abbasi. National Library of Russia, St Petersburg, MS Dorn 302, fol. 2b
2 Shah Tahmasp and the Ottoman ambassadors. National Library of Russia, St Petersburg, MS Dorn 302
3 Opening of the long recension. British Library, MS Or 5880, fol. 1b-2a. Courtesy of the British Library Board
4 Opening of the long recension in the Calcutta manuscript made for Lumsden. By kind permission of the Asiatic Society, Kolkata, MS PSC 87

Figures

1. Ownership statements on the first page of MS Or 5880, showing the manuscript's presence in a library in Ardabil before it entered the possession of the Safavid prince Abu'l-Fath Sultan Muhammad Mirza in Lucknow in 1212/1797–8. Courtesy of the British Library Board 38
2a,b Colophon of the Calcutta manuscript made for Lumsden from Abu'l-Fath Sultan Muhammad's copy, showing the names of both. By kind permission of the Asiatic Society, Kolkata, MS PSC 87 39

Maps

1 The Safavid Empire in the first half of the sixteenth century   xiv
2 Northern Iran, the Caucasus and north-eastern Anatolia   9

Preface and acknowledgements

This book provides an annotated translation of the important sixteenth-century Persian historical source, the *Memoirs* of Shah Tahmasp. The reign of Tahmasp (1524–76), the longest-reigning Iranian ruler, marks a crucial phase in the history of Iran as the Safavid dynasty (1501–1722) consolidated its control and began the process of transforming the country, giving it its distinctive Shiite identity. Indeed, the territorial identity of modern Iran began to emerge in this period; in particular the reign of Tahmasp, who faced repeated Ottoman campaigns, and his success in withstanding Ottoman attacks was crucial to the survival of the dynasty. The Treaty of Amasya with the Ottomans in 1555 fixed the Safavid border with their western neighbour, and the modern Turkish-Iranian border largely follows its parameters. Meanwhile, the Ottoman-Safavid wars consolidated confessional identities, as the two empires increasingly defined themselves in opposition to each other in stark religious terms, emphasizing their Sunnism and Shiism respectively.

Tahmasp's *Memoirs* offer a unique insight into this period by allowing us an insight into how Shah Tahmasp wished his reign to be understood. They are also of considerable interest to historians of the Ottoman Empire, and indeed, as much of the action described takes place on the current territory of Turkey as it does of Iran. However, as is discussed in more detail in the introduction, the *Memoirs* are far from being a comprehensive autobiography. They omit any discussion of the last fourteen years of Tahmasp's rule, which he spent largely in seclusion in his new capital of Qazvin, while the *Memoirs*' treatment of the earlier parts of Tahmasp's reign is often highly selective. I have tried to indicate in the notes some of the more important omissions and the reasons for them, but the aim of this translation is simply to make the *Memoirs* accessible to English-speaking readers, given both the importance of the text and the general lack of translated Safavid historical texts. It is not intended to offer a detailed study of all aspects of Tahmasp's reign, nor to exhaust all the possible comments that could be made on the text in the light of Ottoman, Safavid and Shaybanid historiography, which would be a monumental task. The interested reader will find guidance to the relevant literature in the introduction and bibliography.

Several individuals and organizations have provided invaluable assistance in acquiring manuscripts and images used in this work. I am especially grateful to National Library of Russia for supplying the images of MS Dorn 302 reproduced in the plate section, and to Olga Yastrebova, Oyat and Rustam Shukurov for their help with facilitating this. I would like to thank the Staatsbibliothek zu Berlin, the British Library and the Asiatic Society, Kolkata, for permitting me to reproduce images of manuscripts in their collections, and to Penny Copeland for the accompanying maps. I am also indebted to Ali Shapouran for his assistance with manuscripts in Iran and help identifying some of the poetry quotations in the text, as well as for his comments on an earlier draft of the translation. I am grateful to Sacha Alsancakli for advice on some questions of Kurdish history. I would also like to thank the Institute of Iranian Studies at the University of St Andrews for providing financial support for the reproduction of images in this book.

Chronology

Events not discussed or only mentioned in passing in the *Memoirs* are in italics.

1334 *Death of dynastic ancestor Shaykh Safi of Ardabil*
1501 *Capture of Tabriz by Shah Isma'il Safavi and foundation of Safavid state*
1511 *Şahkulu's pro-Safavid revolt in Anatolia, Ulama defects to Safavids*
1512 *Accession of Ottoman Sultan Selim I*
1514 Birth of Tahmasp; *Safavid defeat by Ottomans at Battle of Chaldiran*
1516 *Tahmasp appointed titular governor of Khurasan, based in Herat, under the guardianship of Amir Sultan Mawsillu*
1517 *Birth of Tahmasp's half-brother Sam Mirza, and full brother Bahram Mirza*
1518 *Amir Sultan Mawsillu removed as governor of Herat and Tahmasp, recalled to Tabriz*
1520 *Death of Ottoman Sultan Selim I, accession of Süleyman*
1521 *Sam Mirza appointed as titular governor of Khurasan in Herat under guardianship of Durmish Khan*
1524 *Death of Shah Isma'il Safavi*, accession of Tahmasp I; death of Durmish Khan, tutor of Sam Mirza, and his replacement by Husayn Khan
1524–7 Rule of the Triumvirate of Qizilbash Amirs, Köpek Sultan, Div Sultan and Chuha Sultan
1527 *Killing of Köpek Sultan and Div Sultan*, Chuha becomes effective ruler of Safavid state with title of *vakīl*
1530 Herat is surrendered to Uzbeks by Husayn Khan and Sam Mirza, Tahmasp's half-brother

1531 The 'Tekellu calamity'; renewed Uzbek attacks, Ulama defects to Ottomans; Husayn Khan Shamlu appointed by Tahmasp as *vakīl*

1532 Ulama conducts operations with Ottoman support against Kurdish principalities; Uzbek siege of Herat; 'Ali Karaki honoured by Tahmasp with titles of nā'ib al-imām and khātam al-mujtahidīn

1533 *Alqas Mirza appointed governor of Astarabad; accession of Uzbek ruler 'Ubaydallah Khan; death of 'Ali Karaki*

1534 Tahmasp sends campaigns against Uzbeks in Marv and Gharchistan; first Ottoman invasion of Safavid lands led by Süleyman, probably in collusion with Husayn Khan, *in order to put Sam Mirza on the throne*; Ottoman capture of Tabriz. *Tahmasp orders execution of Husayn Khan;* Tahmasp issues first 'Edict of Repentance' ordaining Islamic standards of behaviour throughout his realm

1535 Ottoman retreat from occupied Safavid territories, except Baghdad, which remains in Ottoman hands

1536 Treachery of Ghazi Khan; *execution of Ottoman vizier Ibrahim Pasha on Suleyman's orders*

1536–7 Second Uzbek occupation of Herat, ending with Uzbek evacuation of Khurasan

1538 Alqas Mirza appointed governor of Shirvan by Tahmasp

1540 Death of Uzbek ruler 'Ubaydallah Khan

1544–5 Mughal ruler Humayun takes refuge with Tahmasp, and is supplied with military aid in return for his reluctant (and temporary) conversion to Shiism

1547–9 Revolt of Alqas Mirza; second Ottoman invasion of Safavid lands, briefly capturing Tabriz in 1548, and securing Van, which becomes a major Ottoman base.

1550 Killing of Alqas Mirza in captivity

1552–3 *Safavid attacks on frontier, in particular Van region; execution in 1553 of Ottoman prince Mustafa on charges of colluding with Tahmasp*

1554–5 Süleyman launches third campaign against Safavids, the so-called Nakhchivan campaign

1555 *Safavids sign Peace of Amasya with Ottomans*

1556 *Tahmasp proclaims his second 'Edict of Repentance' ordaining standards of morality for public officials throughout his realm*

1557 *Tahmasp relocates capital from Tabriz to Qazvin*

1559 Ottoman prince Beyazid flees to Qazvin

1562 Ottoman ambassadors come to Qazvin to retrieve prince Beyazid; *execution of Beyazid by envoys in Qazvin on Süleyman's orders*

1563 *First redaction of Memoirs completed no later than this date and sent to Qutbshahis in Deccan*

1566 *Death of Ottoman sultan Süleyman, accession of Selim II*

1576 *Death of Tahmasp*

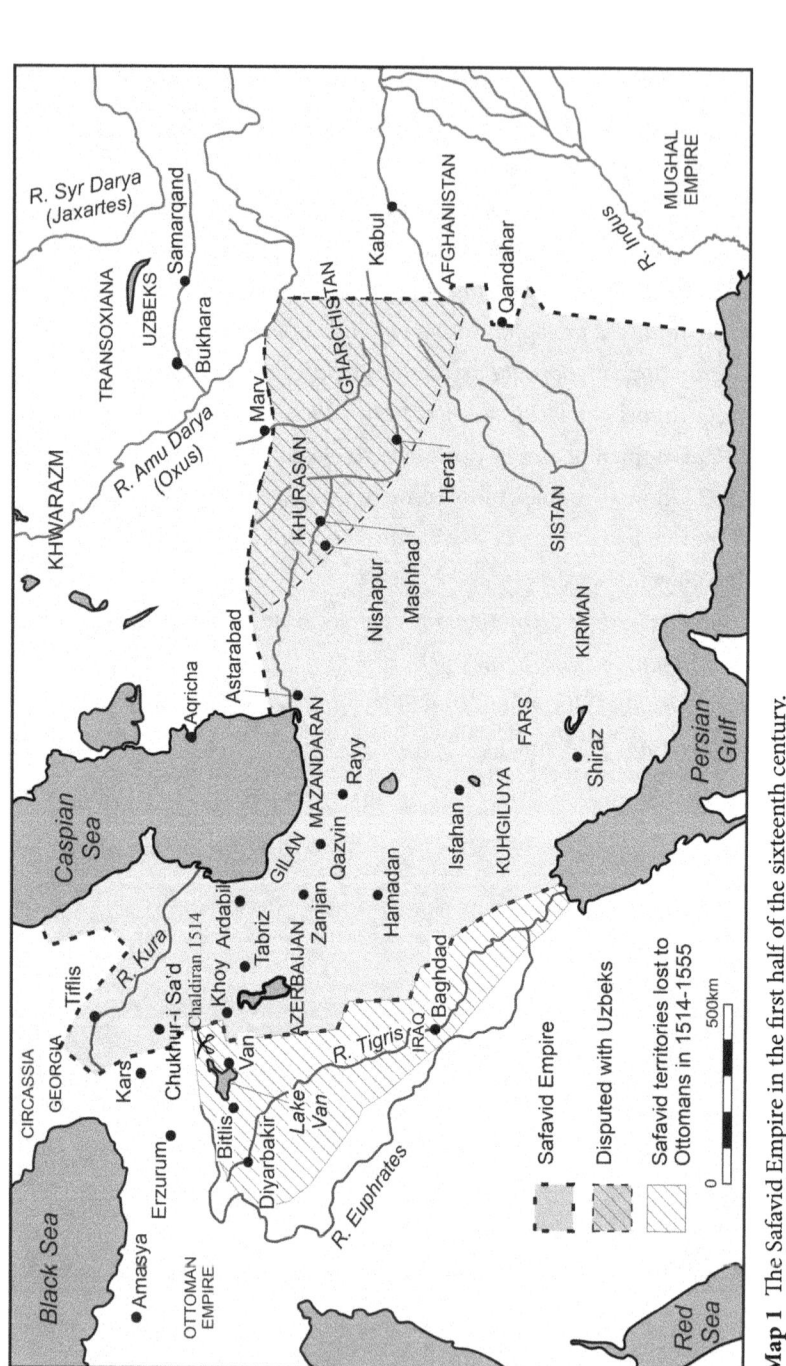

Map 1 The Safavid Empire in the first half of the sixteenth century.

Introduction

Originally composed in 1562, the *Memoirs* of Shah Ṭahmasp (1514–1576, r. 1524–76), second ruler of the Safavid dynasty of Iran (1501–1722), represent an important source for the history of the sixteenth-century Middle East, in particular the Safavids' wars with their neighbours, the Ottoman Empire (c. 1300–1922). As such, the *Memoirs* have been regularly cited in modern scholarship, although not previously translated into English. The text's importance derives from the fact it is a rare first-person narrative by a key participant in these events, showing how Tahmasp wished his previous four decades of rule to be perceived, especially his conduct of wars against the Ottomans, and offering insights into the development of an ideology that justified his reign. The *Memoirs*, then, are a public document, rather than the product of introspection, nor do they reveal much of their author's personal life beyond his religious faith, with their repeated references to aspects of Shiite doctrine. The *Memoirs* were also the source for later Persian chronicles, and represent one of the earliest Safavid prose histories to discuss Tahmasp's reign in detail.[1] Yet the *Memoirs* are a complex text, in which Tahmasp obscures as much as he tells.

To understand the *Memoirs*, their ideological and political function must be appreciated, an aspect to which Tahmasp himself draws attention in his introduction to the text.[2] He wrote that it is 'a memoir (*tazkira*) of my life and deeds, recounting how things happened from

---

1 Among the main Persian sources for Tahmasp's reign are Hasan Rumlu, *Ahsan al-Tawarikh*, ed. 'Abd al-Husayn Nava'i (Tehran, 1384; abridged translation by C. N. Setton as *A Chronicle of the Early Safawis Being the Ahsanu't-Tawārīkh of Ḥasan-i-Rūmlū* (Baroda, 1934), vol. II), composed in 1578, and Khurshah b. Qubad, *Tarikh-i Ilchi-yi Nizamshah: Tarikh-i Safaviyya az Aghaz ta 972 hijri qamari*, ed. Muhammad Riza Hasani and Koichi Haneda (Tehran, 1379), composed around 1563–5. The latter, in particular, explicitly draws on the *Memoirs*. See further pp. 23–4, 33–4 below.

2 A useful introduction to the text is Philip Bockholt, 'Shah Ṭahmāsp and the Taẕkira: A Sixteenth Century Ruler's Justification of His Politics', in Maribel Fierro, Sonja Brentjes

the time of my accession till today, as a lasting memorial (*yādgār*) of me and a manual (*dastūr al-'amal*) for my noble children and beloved people, so that whenever our supporters read it they will remember us with a prayer'. The word Tahmasp uses to describe his text, *tazkira*, here translated as 'memoirs', has a wide semantic range, encompassing the ideas of 'reminding' and of 'biographical account'.[3] The *Memoirs* evade easy categorization as text. As Tahmasp indicates, they were intended not only to perpetuate the Shah's memory, but also to act as a guide for future generations of the Safavid dynasty. In this sense, they might be considered a sort of 'mirror for princes' – a popular genre of text in Islamic courts, providing both edifying and practical advice on kingship, although the *Memoirs* diverge significantly in format and content from other examples of the genre.[4] Neither are the *Memoirs* an autobiography in the modern sense and, as we shall see, Tahmasp in fact sometimes effaces his own role in events; but nor are they a straightforward chronicle, for they omit numerous noteworthy events. To give just one example, the Mughal emperor Humayun, defeated by his enemies, was forced to seek refuge at Tahmasp's court during the years 1544 to 1545. In return for a reluctant conversion to Shiism (subsequently abjured), Tahmasp offered Humayun military support to regain his empire. Given the episode was sufficiently famous to be depicted on the walls of the later Safavid palace of Chihil Sutun in Isfahan,[5] and is treated in detail in almost all other contemporary Persian chronicles, one might expect that the spectacle

and Tilman Seidensticker (eds), *Rulers as Authors in the Islamic World: Knowledge, Authority and Legitimacy* (Leiden, 2024), 635–59.

[3] See, for example, Francis Joseph Steingass, *A Comprehensive Persian-English Dictionary, Including the Arabic Words and Phrases to Be Met with in Persian Literature* (London, 1892) s.v. *tazkira*: 'Memory, remembrance; anything that aids the memory (as a knot tied on the pocket-handkerchief); biographical memoir, biography; a billet, schedule, obligation, handwriting; official note'.

[4] An introduction to the 'mirrors for princes' literature, with translated excerpts from important texts, is Louise Marlow, *Medieval Muslim Mirrors for Princes: An Anthology of Arabic, Persian and Turkish Political Advice* (Cambridge, 2023).

[5] On this see Sussan Babaei, 'Shah 'Abbas II, the Conquest of Qandahar, the Chihil Sutun, and Its Wall Paintings', *Muqarnas* 11 (1994): 125–42.

of this ruler paying homage to the shah would have merited more than the single passing reference that the *Memoirs* gives (see p. 142). Indeed, even Tahmasp's wars with his eastern neighbours, the Uzbeks, over the province of Khurasan, which dominated the first decade of his rule, are only recounted briefly and partially, with no mention of his final triumph over the Uzbeks in 1537.

Instead, Tahmasp focuses on five episodes of cross-border treachery in the Ottoman-Safavid wars of the sixteenth century. This focus derives partly from the exemplary nature of these episodes in providing a warning for future generations of how to deal with duplicitous rebels and the Ottoman enemy; but also from the ostensible origins of the text as a speech given by Shah Tahmasp to envoys from the Ottoman empire in 1562, as will be discussed further in due course. To understand the text, then, it must be borne in mind that Tahmasp's aim is not to provide a full and accurate account of events of his reign, but rather is rooted in the desire to justify his actions, as well as to impart ethical lessons through practical examples of kingship. The emphasis on Safavid-Ottoman hostilities reflects the fact that these had represented an existential threat to the dynasty, but one which, by 1562, Tahmasp could feel confident he had overcome. In what follows, to allow the reader to understand the text, I situate the *Memoirs* firstly in their historical and secondly in their literary context. I then examine the circumstances of the composition and transmission of the *Memoirs*, their audiences and manuscripts.

Tahmasp's *Memoirs* in their historical context

The Safavids take their name from the dynastic ancestor, Shaykh Safi al-Din (1253–1334), a Sufi holy man from Ardabil in northern Iran.[6]

---

6 Useful surveys of Safavid history on which I draw here include H. R. Roemer, 'The Safavid Period', in *The Cambridge History of Iran*, vol. 6 (Cambridge, 1986), 189–350;

Over the fourteenth to fifteenth centuries, through processes that remain obscure, Shaykh Safi al-Din's descendants transformed from being leaders of a Sunni religious order to commanders of an extremist Shiite warband. By the fifteenth century, the Safavids were claiming descent from the Prophet Muhammad via the Shiite Imams, and this status as *sayyids*, as the Prophet's descendants were known, was to become an important aspect of their identity and political legitimacy,[7] and one that is emphasized repeatedly by Tahmasp in his *Memoirs*. They also, however, started to act as not just religious but also military and political leaders. Under Shaykh Junayd (d. 1460) and his son Haydar (1459–1488) Safavid claims to military and political as well as religious leadership were articulated through repeated campaigns against non-Muslims in Shirvan (roughly modern Azerbaijan) and Caucasia. These campaigns also brought the Safavids into conflict with local Muslim rulers, in particular the Turkmen Qaraquyyunlu nomadic federation that dominated the region. To his followers, however, the Safavid leader was not merely a Sufi spiritual guide (*murshid*), but the embodiment of 'Ali b. Abi Talib, the Prophet's cousin who is the subject of particular veneration by Shiites and from whom the Safavids claimed descent, and even of divinity itself. It was Haydar who is reputed to have commanded his Turkmen followers to wear the famous red hat with twelve tassels, representing their loyalty to the twelve Shiite Imams – 'Ali and his

---

Andrew Newman, *Safavid Iran: Rebirth of a Persian Empire* (London, 2006); Rudi Matthee (ed.), *The Safavid World* (London, 2022), brings together essays that provide an overview of Safavid history and society. Specifically on Isma'il and Tahmasp, the most accessible overviews in English are Roger M. Savory and Ahmet T. Karamustafa, 'Esmā'īl I Ṣafawī', *Encyclopaedia Iranica*, VIII/6: 628–36, and Colin P. Mitchell, 'Tahmasp I', *Encyclopaedia Iranica*, available online at https://www.iranicaonline.org/articles/tahmasp-i. An extremely detailed biography in Persian offers the most comprehensive study of Tahmasp's reign, although tends more to narrative than analysis: Manuchihr Parsadust, *Shah Tahmasp-i Avval: Padishahi Azmand, Zirak, Ba Siyasat-i Khas-i Mazhabi* (Tehran, 1377).

7 Kazuo Morimoto, 'The Earliest 'Alid Genealogy for the Safavids: New Evidence for the Pre-dynastic Claim to Sayyid Status', *Iranian Studies* 43 (2010): 447–69.

direct descendants – after which they became known by the Turkish word Qizilbash ('Red-heads').

The Safavid state is conventionally considered as having been founded in 1501, some thirteen years before Tahmasp's birth, when his father Isma'il, the son of Haydar, seized the city of Tabriz in Azerbaijan and made it the basis for a Shiite polity that encompassed modern Iran, eastern Anatolia and parts of Central Asia. The foundation of the Safavid empire is often seen as a watershed in the history of the Middle East, marking the creation of an Iranian nation state that espoused Shiism, and thus providing a direct antecedent for modern Iran.[8] Yet such simplistic parallels are misleading. Isma'il was brought to power by Turkish-speaking military devotees, the Qizilbash, who in the initial years of the Safavid state dominated most senior positions, although in time Isma'il began to dilute their influence by appointing members of the old Iranian bureaucratic elite. There is no evidence to suggest Isma'il saw himself as establishing an 'Iranian' state. While there were certainly numerous influences from the Timurid dynasty (1370–1507) that had ruled Iran and Central Asia, if anything the most obvious antecedent for the Safavid state was the Turkish Aqquyunlu ('White Sheep') Turkmen nomadic confederation (mid-fourteenth century–1501). The Aqquyunlu domains at their height straddled eastern Anatolia and Iran; like the Safavids they had a capital at Tabriz and drew on Turkish military strength, and the Safavids were linked to them by long-standing marriage ties.[9] The Safavids drew on their Aqquyunlu predecessors for many elements of their administrative practice, and indeed many of the same personnel served both dynasties. Cities that might now be considered to be in

---

8 This idea originates in the influential book by Walter Hinz, *Irans Aufstieg zum Nationalstaat im fünfzehnten Jahrhundert* (Berlin, 1936), but continues to resonate in more recent scholarship such as the works of Roger Savory, as well as much modern Persian-language historiography in Iran.
9 Haydar's mother and one of Junayd's wives were both Aqquyunlu women; Shah Isma'il himself was thus of Aqquyunlu descent.

eastern Anatolia such as Erzincan and Diyarbakır, which constituted the Aqquyunlu heartland, comprised part of Shah Isma'il's domains initially. It was above all the early Safavids' religious claims, which were evidently regarded with some embarrassment by later Safavid chroniclers, that set them apart from the Aqquyunlu. Alongside the exaggerated veneration of the Prophet's son-in-law 'Ali b. Abi Talib, elevating him virtually to the status of the divine, that was a hallmark of extremist Shiite movements (*ghuluww*), Shah Isma'il was seen by the Qizilbash as the Mahdi, the saviour Imam whose coming marks the end of time, and himself as at least semi-divine.[10]

Shah Isma'il achieved significant success against his neighbours in the east, the nascent Sunni Shaybanid dynasty or Uzbeks, whose leader Muhammad Shaybani Khan was killed in battle against the Safavids in 1510; Isma'il is memorably said to have turned his skull into a wine cup. While subsequently the Uzbeks made gains at the Safavids' expense in Khurasan, and fighting with them occupied much of the early years of Tahmasp's reign,[11] it was Anatolia that was to prove Shah Isma'il's downfall. Safavid ambitions conflicted with those of the Ottomans, who, over the later fifteenth and early sixteenth centuries, were seeking to extend their authority over most of the peninsula, the early Ottoman Empire having originally been orientated more towards Thrace and the Balkans. Anatolia, however, was precisely the region from which many of the Safavids' Qizilbash supporters originated, and pro-Safavid feelings were widespread among the nomads, who, apart from religious considerations, had little reason to welcome the more centralized administration that Ottoman rule promised.[12] In

---

10 See Willem Floor and Mohammad Faghfoory, 'Shah Esmail, Deputy of the Hidden Imam?' *Zeitschrift der Deutschen Morgenländischen Gesellschaft* 171 (2021): 375–88; also Kathryn Babayan, 'The Safavid Synthesis: From Qizilbash Islam to Imamite Shi'ism', *Iranian Studies* 27, No. 1 (1994): 135–61.
11 See Martin Dickson, 'Sháh Tahmásp and the Úzbeks: The Dual for Khurásán with 'Ubayd Khán 930–946/1524–1540', PhD dissertation, Princeton University, 1958.
12 The most comprehensive study of the role of the Anatolian Qizilbash in the formation of the Safavid state remains Faruk Sümer, *Safevî Devletinin Kuruluşu ve Gelişmesinde*

1511, a large-scale Turkmen rebellion led by a certain Şahkulu (whose name suggestively means 'The Shah's slave') among the Tekellu tribe of southern Anatolia demonstrated the fragility of Ottoman authority even within their own empire. Emerging victorious after a bloody fight for the succession, the Ottoman Sultan Selim I (r. 1512–20) sought to assert himself. Marching eastwards, Selim defeated Isma'il decisively at the Battle of Chaldiran in 1514.[13]

Although Tabriz was briefly occupied by the Ottomans, Selim was unable to sustain a prolonged campaign in Iran, and logistical difficulties would also beset future Ottoman efforts in the region. Instead, Selim turned to the conquest of the Mamluk empire of Syria and Egypt, and the Safavid state endured, albeit with some territorial losses (Map 1). On the borderlands that comprise modern eastern Anatolia and northern Iraq, a number of Kurdish principalities maintained a degree of autonomy, but for the moment remained broadly aligned with the Safavids. This borderland of the east of modern Turkey, the north of Iran and the Caucasus, would, however, remain one of the main bones of contention throughout the first half of the sixteenth century (Map 2). Although the defeat at Chaldiran was an immense blow to the prestige of Shah Isma'il with his claims to divine kingship, remarkably, the coalition of Qizilbash tribes and Persian administrators that was the basis of his power remained largely intact, and the Safavid ruler remained the focus of loyalty (if not necessarily, in practice, obedience).[14] After the defeat, Isma'il seems to have increasingly

---

Anadolu Türklerinin Rolü (Ankara, 1992); see also now Ayfer Karakaya-Stump, *The Kizilbash-Alevis in Ottoman Anatolia: Sufism, Politics and Community* (Edinburgh, 2020); Rıza Yıldırım, 'Turkomans between Two Empires: The Origins of the Qizilbash Identity in Anatolia', PhD dissertation, Bilkent University, Ankara, 2008.

13 Useful surveys of the Ottoman-Safavid wars include Kaya Şahin, *Peerless among Princes: The Life and Times of Sultan Süleyman* (New York, 2023); Ebru Boyar, 'Ottoman Expansion in the East', in Suraiya N. Faroqhi and Kate Fleet (eds), *The Cambridge History of Turkey*. II. *The Ottoman Empire as a World Power, 1453–1603* (Cambridge, 2013), 74–140; Adel Allouche, *Origins and Development of the Ottoman-Safavid Conflict (906-962/1500-1555)* (Berlin, 1983).

14 The rivalries and bureaucratic system are discussed by Roger Savory, 'The Principal Offices of the Ṣafawid State during the Reign of Ismāʿīl I (907-30/1501-24)', *Bulletin*

retreated from day-to-day government, and rival Qizilbash tribes vied with each other and with the Persian administrative elite for power. This is illustrated by the infighting that followed the appointment of the two-year-old Tahmasp as governor of the sensitive eastern city of Herat in 1516, in accordance with long-standing Turko-Mongol tradition of appointing the heir apparent, even if a minor, to an important governorship under the guardianship of a military officer.[15] Tahmasp was firstly given as tutor (*lāla*) the Qizilbash Amir Khan, a member of the Mawsillu Turkmen tribe and a former Aqquyunlu commander who had joined Shah Ismaʿil's enterprise, who thus also served as de facto governor of Herat given the prince's age. Amir Khan's appointment was apparently intended to limit the power of the Shamlu tribe, who had previously held the governorship. However, a local religious scholar, Amir Ghiyath al-Din Muhammad, held the position of *ṣadr*, in charge of Tahmasp's religious education as well as the economically vital religious endowments of Herat. Despite the growing threat from the Uzbeks, Amir Khan Mawsillu and Ghiyath al-Din Muhammad were constantly at loggerheads, with the *ṣadr* eventually executed on Amir Khan's orders. This chaotic competition between rival factions characterized the latter part of Ismaʿil's reign and the beginnings of that of Tahmasp, who succeeded his father at the age of ten in 1524. The following decade is sometimes known as

of the School of Oriental and African Studies 23, No. 1 (1960): 91–105, which remains useful even if its conclusions need to be modified in some respects in the light of subsequent research. See also Roger Savory, 'The Principal Offices of the Ṣafawid State during the Reign of Ṭahmāsp I (930–84/1524–76)', *Bulletin of the School of Oriental and African Studies* 24, No. 1 (1961): 65–85. For a revisionist study of the early part of Tahmasp's reign, see Gregory Aldous, 'The Qizilbāsh and Their Shah: The Preservation of Royal Prerogative during the Early Reign of Shah Ṭahmāsp', *Journal of the Royal Asiatic Society* 31 (2021): 743–58.

15 For the details of these events, see Maria Szuppe, *Entre Timourides, Uzbeks et Safavides: questions d'histoire politique et sociale de Hérat dans la première moitié du XVIe siècle* (Paris, 1992), 87–93; on the system of governorships, see Colin Mitchell, 'Custodial Politics and Princely Governance in Sixteenth-Century Iran', in Rudi Matthee (ed.), *The Safavid World* (London, 2022), 79–110.

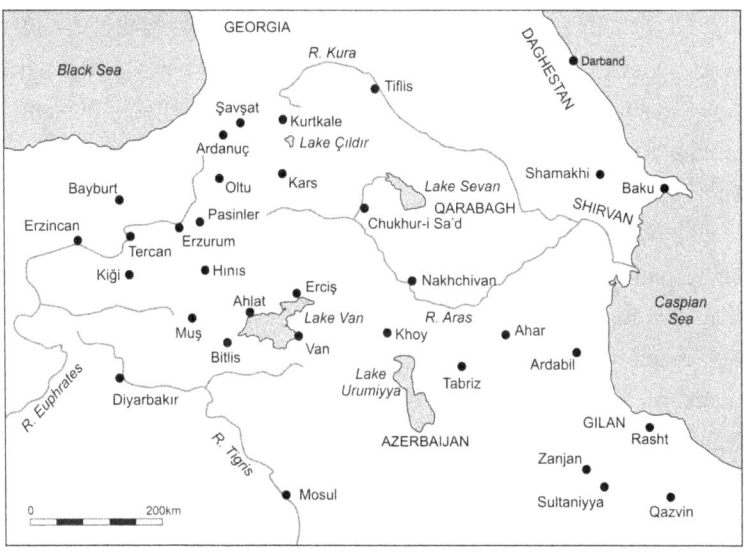

Map 2 Northern Iran, the Caucasus and north-eastern Anatolia.

the 'Qizilbash interregnum' as various factions of Qizilbash amirs contended with each other for control.

The opening of Shah Tahmasp's *Memoirs* describes the battles for power among the three leading Qizilbash, each representing a different tribal group – Div Sultan of the Rumlu tribe, who became Tahmasp's tutor on his accession, Chuha Sultan of the Tekellu and Köpek Sultan of the Ustajlu. A power-sharing triumvirate between these amirs soon descended into open warfare. When Köpek Sultan was removed from power at the behest of the other two amirs, the latter then turned on each other, while the east of the Safavid domains was simultaneously threatened by repeated Uzbek attacks. The *Memoirs* only occasionally hint at Tahmasp's lack of agency during this period; rather Tahmasp portrays himself as actively making appointments and waging war on the Uzbeks from the beginning of his reign. Yet on other occasions when the shah was indeed involved in events, the *Memoirs* often cast a veil of silence over his actions. Thus, while other sources suggest that Div Sultan was eventually killed in 1527 on Tahmasp's orders, or at least with his approval,[16] no direct reference appears in the *Memoirs* to the demise of the shah's once all-powerful tutor. However, Tahmasp notes that it was in this year that he 'properly became shah'.[17] In reality, Chuha Sultan Tekellu became the effective ruler, with the titles of *vakīl*, the 'deputy' of the ruler, and *amīr al-umarā*', 'commander-in-chief'.[18] As remarked by the well informed chronicler Khurshah, who later spent some time at Tahmasp's court, 'nothing more than the name of king and ruler remained to his majesty the shah [Tahmasp]'.[19] Yet, despite Tahmasp's lack of executive authority, it appears that he maintained an important symbolic role, his presence necessary to legitimize Chuha Sultan's actions to the Qizilbash.[20] The *Memoirs* thus on the one hand give a misleading impression of Tahmasp's freedom of action, while on the other obscure events in which the shah was actually involved.

The supremacy of Chuha Sultan and the Tekellu was resented by the other tribes, particularly the Shamlu, led by Husayn Khan, who was governor of Herat and guardian of Tahmasp's brother, Bahram Mirza. Indeed, the rivalry between Chuha Sultan and Husayn Khan repeatedly derailed efforts to fend off Uzbek encroachment in the east, and in 1529–30, and again in 1536–7, Herat was temporarily lost to the Uzbeks. The flight of Husayn Khan to the Safavid court in 1529 precipitated clashes between the Shamlu and Tekellu, in which Chuha Sultan was killed – again a fact veiled by the *Memoirs*. In the *Memoirs*, Tahmasp portrays himself as putting a decisive end to the infighting

---

16 Aldous, 'Qizilbash and Their Shah', 751; Savory, 'Principal Offices during the Reign of Tahmasp', 68.
17 See p. 59 of this volume.
18 Safavid administrative terminology in this period is extremely confused and inconsistent; the titles evidently had a certain significance as they were avidly disputed by Qizilbash amirs, but their precise functions were far from set in stone. For a discussion see Savory, 'Principal Offices during the Reign of Tahmasp', 71–2, 77.
19 '*Az pādishāhī va jahāndārī bi-juz nāmī bar ḥażrat-i shāh bīsh namānd*'. Khurshah, *Tarikh-i Ilchi*, 93.
20 Aldous, 'Qizilbāsh and Their Shah', 752, 754.

by ordering the massacre of the Tekellu. The year of the massacre, 1531, became known in the sources after its Persian chronogram as the 'Tekellu calamity' (*āfat-i Takallū*).

To what extent Tahmasp was able to use the rivalries of the different Qizilbash tribes for his own ends, or was himself merely manipulated by them, remains debatable. In the words of one scholar, 'he ruled by managing the multitude of interests and power relations of which he served as the nexus'.[21] In practice, Tahmasp's ability to exert influence must have varied greatly over the ten-year so-called interregnum; the shah in his late teens was doubtless a different force from the ten-year-old who ascended the throne in 1524. Again, the *Memoirs*, composed nearly four decades later, do not really assist us in understanding such fluctuations. It is clear, however, that Tahmasp wanted to be remembered as having become an effective ruler long before this was actually the case. In reality, the dominance of the Tekellu was replaced by that of the Shamlu tribe, with Husayn Khan becoming *vakīl*. It was only with Husayn Khan's killing at Tahmasp's behest in 1534 that the interregnum is generally recognized to have come to an end. Husayn Khan was murdered for planning to defect to the Ottomans,[22] but despite the concentration of the *Memoirs* on cross-border defection and treachery, his demise is nowhere mentioned.

Thus, on the one hand Tahmasp takes credit for launching campaigns and making appointments in which he in practice had little agency. On the other, he is silent over the demise of each of the main Qizilbash contenders for power, with the exception of Köpek Sultan, whose death in battle is mentioned briefly. Other sources in fact implicate the shah directly in the deaths of Div Sultan and Husayn Khan, while he was probably also present when Chuha Sultan

---

21 Aldous, 'Qizilbāsh and Their Shah', 758.
22 Khurshah, *Tarikh-i Ilchi*, 125; Hasan Rumlu, *Ahsan al-Tawarikh*, III, 1223, trans. Setton, *Chronicle*, 115–16.

was killed.[23] Such omissions underline the fact that the *Memoirs* were composed with certain specific objectives. The first of these was, as Shah Tahmasp indicates, as a 'manual' for his descendants. Tahmasp thus appears acting as a true shah should from the start – campaigning and making decisions – even when in reality he was a child under the control of the Qizilbash. Secondly, the *Memoirs*' treatment of the Qizilbash interregnum implicitly underlines the connection between internal political disorder and external threats. For although the initial sections of the *Memoirs* with their concentration on Qizilbash politics at first seem disconnected from the five main chapters devoted to defectors, in fact they are intimately linked. It was the conflict between the Qizilbash that led to the 'Tekellu calamity'; and it was the Tekellu calamity that brought about the first of the defections – and evidently, perhaps the one that rankled most, for it is referred to repeatedly in subsequent sections. This was the defection of Ulama, a Tekellu who was serving as Safavid governor of Azerbaijan.

Ulama's career illustrates the way in which the Ottoman–Safavid frontier remained permeable, and loyalties fluid, despite the confessional divide between Sunnism and Shiism.[24] Ardabil seems to have been Ulama's home town, but early in his career he was based in Anatolia, participating in Şahkulu's great pro-Safavid revolt of the Tekellu against the Ottomans in 1511, after which he defected to serve Shah Isma'il – facts passed over in silence by Tahmasp and other Safavid chroniclers, but attested in Ottoman sources. Under Shah Isma'il, Ulama served as *yasāvul* (aide-de-camp, responsible

---

23 For accounts of Chuha Sultan's death, see Khurshah, *Tarikh-i Ilchi*, 109–11; Hasan Rumlu, *Ahsan al-Tawarikh*, II, 1199, trans. Setton, *Chronicle*, 108–9; although the shah's presence at the precise time of death is not mentioned, it is specified by Khurshah that it took place in the Royal Precinct (*dawlatkhāna*), and it is clear Tahmasp was in the vicinity at the time. Hasan Rumlu says Chuha was killed in the shah's tent.

24 A survey of Ulama's career, concentrating on the Ottoman evidence, is Géza Dávid, 'Ulama Bey, an Ottoman Office-Holder with Persian Connections on the Hungarian Frontier', in Eva M. Jeremias (ed.), *Irano-Turkic Cultural Contacts in the 11th–17th Centuries* (Piliscsaba, 2003), 33–40.

for ceremonies at royal audiences) and *īshīk-āqāsī-bāshī* (chief chamberlain), and was subsequently appointed by Tahmasp to the governorship of Azerbaijan, an especially sensitive post given this province's location on the frontier with the Ottomans. The reasons for Ulama's flight are reported variously in the Safavid sources. According to the mid-sixteenth-century chronicler Khurshah, who spent some time at the Safavid court and is generally well informed, Ulama had been a protégé of Chuha Sultan and fled to the Ottomans in the wake of Husayn Khan's takeover, fearing the latter's vengeance.[25] Other sources, however, suggest that Ulama had aspired to replace Chuha Sultan as *vakīl*, but his ambitions were thwarted by the promotion of Husayn Khan.[26] Either way, Ulama's defection and attempted takeover of Tabriz in 1531 were in good measure a direct consequence of the 'Tekellu calamity'. Tahmasp devotes extensive space to Ulama's career of treachery among the Ottomans, accusing him of deceiving Sultan Süleyman (r. 1520–66) and his Grand Vizier İbrahim Pasha into attacking the Safavid domains. Ulama subsequently held senior positions not just on the Ottoman frontier with the Safavids, but also in Bosnia and Hungary. For our purposes, however, what is significant is how Tahmasp portrays his role: by making Ulama's treachery a driving force behind Ottoman attacks on the Safavids, the war is represented as a consequence of intertribal Qizilbash rivalry, rather than a clash between Sunni and Shiite powers. In this sense, the story of the Qizilbash infighting during the interregnum and the 'Tekellu calamity' provide a warning to the audience, which must have included Shah Tahmasp's descendants and his courtiers, as to the consequences of letting such tribal tensions get out of hand.

---

25 Khurshah, *Tarikh-i Ilchi*, 112.
26 Hasan Rumlu, *Ahsan al-Tawarikh*, II, 1200, trans. Setton, *Chronicle*, 109; Dávid, 'Ulama bey', 34; Sümer, *Safevî Devletinin Kuruluşu*, 60–2.

However, as noted above, the *Memoirs*, in a slightly different form, were also addressed – at least ostensibly – to another audience, the Ottoman envoys who came to Qazvin in 1562. The version of the text delivered to the envoys had omitted the account of the interregnum and the Tekellu calamity, starting instead directly with the story of Ulama. In other respects, the two recensions are nearly identical, with a couple of exceptions, discussed further below. The omission of the interregnum years means, however, that the story of Ulama is dislocated from its context, and the tale becomes a more straightforward one of disloyal vassals. Here, Ottoman naivety is repeatedly emphasized – Ottoman attacks on the Safavids are portrayed as having been precipitated primarily by the way in which the sultan is misled by his advisors, who in turn are all too credulous of the claims of defectors. Ulama's treachery is followed by the tale of Ghazi Khan, another Tekellu defector to the Ottomans who is depicted as an accomplice of Ulama's. Again, the Ottomans are portrayed as having embarked on a misconceived campaign as they were deceived by Ghazi Khan's claims that Tahmasp's brother Sam Mirza (1517–1566) had rebelled against him. What Tahmasp does not reveal is not just that Sam Mirza did in fact revolt,[27] something glossed over in the *Memoirs*, but also that Ghazi Khan subsequently returned to Safavid service, and was installed in Shirvan as tutor to another brother of the shah, Alqas Mirza (1515–1550), who forms the focus of the third chapter of the *Memoirs*. Ghazi Khan thus forms a crucial link between Ulama and Alqas. Appointed governor of Shirvan by Tahmasp shortly after its conquest by the Safavids, Alqas sought the support of the Qizilbash to establish his own independent rule in 1546–7, apparently at

---

27 Sam Mirza was, however, reconciled after his short-lived rebellion in 1534, which seems to have been instigated by his Qizilbash guardians. On him, see B. Reinert, 'Sām Mīrzā', *Encyclopaedia of Islam*, 2nd edition (Leiden, 1960–2005).

least in part at the instigation of Ghazi Khan's erstwhile followers. Thwarted by Tahmasp's armies and a lack of local support in Shirvan, Alqas fled to Istanbul, where he persuaded the Ottomans to support his attempts to seize the Safavid throne.[28] Again, the Ottomans are portrayed as having been duped by Alqas's unwarranted claims of support among the Qizilbash.

Chapter 4 ostensibly deals with a different cause of strife, İskender Pasha, the Ottoman governor of Erzurum (1550–3), whose attacks on the Safavids' Georgian allies are depicted as provoking a justified Safavid response. The sultan and shah were thus drawn into a wider conflict once more as a result of the actions of such unruly vassals. Even here, the shadowy presence of Ulama can be detected. Ulama had himself served for a brief while as Ottoman governor of Erzurum in 1548 (a fact again not mentioned by Tahmasp explicitly), but despite the fact he was probably in the Ottoman Balkans at this point, where he held a variety of positions before his death in 1556, Tahmasp claims that Ulama's men were sent by the sultan as part of a peace initiative which the shah angrily dismissed. He claims he remarked, 'For why should peace be contingent on Ulama's favour, when he was one of our aides-de-camp (*yasāvul*). Why should he now act as ambassador between us and the sultan?'[29]

The hostilities of the early 1550s resulted eventually in the establishment of peace with the signature of the Treaty of Amasya in 1555 whereby the Ottomans and Safavids recognized each other's right to exist and fixed their borders. The great fortress of Van, around which much of the earlier fighting had revolved, Baghdad and the Shia shrines of Iraq, and most of the Kurdish frontier principalities were all surrendered to the Ottomans, although this

---

28 Alqas's revolt is the subject of a very comprehensive study by Walter Posch, *Osmanisch-safavidische Beziehungen 1545–1550: Der Fall Alḳâṣ Mîrzâ* (2 vols, Vienna, 2013).
29 See p. 129.

was to a large extent a recognition of realities long since established on the ground. The peace negotiations are only briefly mentioned in the *Memoirs*, for the fifth and final chapter deals with a reverse case of defection, that of the Ottoman sultan Süleyman's son, Beyazid. Defeated in his effort to secure his position as heir apparent by his brother Selim (the future Sultan Selim II), Beyazid had taken refuge at the Safavid court, where he was initially well received. Tahmasp's account, which contains many details unknown from other sources, underlines the double-edged nature of Beyazid's treachery. On the one hand, he allegedly conspired to murder his host, the shah; on the other he aimed to forge an alliance with the Ottoman's arch-enemy, the Russians. Beyazid is thus portrayed as the mirror of Alqas, but whereas the Ottomans allowed themselves to be deceived by the latter, Tahmasp does not allow Beyazid to spread discord. Clearly, Tahmasp's account is written with an eye to justifying his handing over of the fugitive Beyazid to the Ottoman envoys in contravention of his explicit promise. The *Memoirs* end quite suddenly with Tahmasp's rather flimsy excuse – he was not breaking his word because he was handing over the prince to Selim not Süleyman, and he had only promised to protect Beyazid from the sultan himself. The tale of Beyazid is evidently meant to contrast Tahmasp's wisdom and statesmanship in not allowing the defector to disrupt relations and cause a breakdown of relations with Ottoman foolishness and aggression. It thus offers an example of how one should deal with defectors, in contrast to the Ottomans who allowed them to become a cause of repeated conflict.

Yet the *Memoirs* articulate little hostility towards the Ottomans. Tahmasp is usually respectful in references to Süleyman. He is invariably described as *ḥażrat-i khudāvandigār*, 'His majesty', and the Ottomans are thus recognized as a legitimate fellow Muslim power. Tahmasp stresses (again possibly disingenuously) how he avoided fighting the Ottomans when Süleyman was absent on one of his numerous campaigns in Europe.[30] Tahmasp's reluctance to attack the Ottomans in part of course stemmed from the geopolitical realities. With the Safavid capital of Tabriz itself repeatedly captured by the Ottomans, Tahmasp would have been all too aware of the vulnerability of the Safavid domains. Nonetheless, the absence of sectarian rancour towards the Ottomans is striking, especially given the well-documented climate of anti-Sunni hostility that Tahmasp actively promoted through the ritual public cursing of the first Caliphs (*tabarra'*). Indeed, *tabarra'* rituals often involved cursing the Ottomans too.[31] Moreover, sectarian anti-Sunni rhetoric features prominently in Tahmasp's correspondence with the Ottomans, of which numerous examples are extant.[32] It is true that in post-Amasya period sectarian propaganda no longer receives the same attention in these royal missives to the Ottomans, and one might interpret the *Memoirs*, ostensibly addressed to the Ottoman ambassadors, as consistent with this policy.[33] Tahmasp's attitude is particularly striking when contrasted with his treatment of another Sunni power, the Uzbek Shaybanid dynasty of Central Asia. The Shaybanid ruler 'Ubaydallah, whose name in full meant 'God's humble slave', is usually contemptuously referred to as 'Ubayd (literally 'little slave'), or occasionally as 'Ubayd the Uzbek. Tahmasp singles out 'Ubaydallah for his vehement anti-Shiite prejudice, whereas no such motives are attributed to the Ottoman sultan. By the time the *Memoirs* were composed, 'Ubaydallah was safely dead, having passed away in 1540, his schemes to seize Khurasan from the Safavids thwarted by Tahmasp, in contrast to Süleyman who was still alive. He was thus a safe target for denigration, especially as the Uzbek state disintegrated into civil

---

30 See p. 71; cf. also p. 132 for a similar religious justification for not fighting the Ottomans.
31 Rosemary Stanfield Johnson, 'The Tabarra'iyan and the Early Safavids', *Iranian Studies* 37, No. 1 (2004): 47–71, esp. 62–3.
32 Colin P. Mitchell, *The Practice of Politics in Safavid Iran: Power, Religion and Rhetoric* (London, 2009), 80–8.
33 Mitchell, *Practice of Politics*, 120–37.

war on death. Indeed, it is striking testimony to Tahmasp's priorities in the *Memoirs* that discussion of the Uzbeks is so limited. Tahmasp says nothing about his final triumph over them in 1537, which freed Khurasan from the Uzbek attacks it had been suffering for most of the previous four decades. Yet ultimately this tale of success is not relevant to Tahmasp's message.

Even if sectarian hostility towards the Ottomans is absent, the *Memoirs* are replete with Shiite piety. Tahmasp's long reign saw the beginnings of the institutionalization of Twelver Shiism in Iran which, till the Safavid revolution, had been largely Sunni. The extent and depth of this Shiitization, as well as the degree to which the Safavids' Shiism was truly Twelver or remained influenced by the extremist religiosity prevalent among the Qizilbash, remains a topic of scholarly debate. The evidence is complex. By the time the *Memoirs* were being written, immigrant Twelver Arab clerics had assumed important roles in the religious hierarchy, although their numbers and influence are disputed, and the Safavid state drew legitimacy from its patronage of great Twelver Shiite shrines such as that of the Imam Riza at Mashhad.[34] Nonetheless, while the apocalyptic and messianic rhetoric through which Isma'il had appealed to the Qizilbash may have diminished, it had not disappeared. Not only did the Safavid dynastic shrine in their hometown of Ardabil continue to play an important role in religious life, receiving extensive patronage from Tahmasp, but the shah himself evidently was still regarded in

---

[34] For a discussion of this process, see Rula Jurdi Abisaab, *Converting Persia: Religion and Power in the Safavid Empire* (London, 2004); for a different view, see Andrew J. Newman, 'The Myth of the Clerical Migration to Safawid Iran: Arab Shiite Opposition to 'Alī al-Karakī and Safawid Shiism', *Die Welt des Islams New Series* 33, No. 1 (1993): 66–112, esp. 94–109, who takes a more sceptical approach to the degree to which sixteenth-century Safavid Shiism was truly Twelver, noting Twelver clerics outside its territories did not accept the regime's legitimacy. Also on religious developments in the period, see Said Amir Arjomand, *The Shadow of God and the Hidden Imam: Religion, Political Order, and Social Change in Shi'ite Iran from the Beginning to 1890* (Chicago, 1984); Babayan, 'The Safavid Synthesis'.

some sense as the chief spiritual guide (*murshid*) of the Qizilbash and, probably, by some, as himself divine. Indeed, the Venetian envoy Michele Membré, who has left us one of the most vivid contemporary accounts of Tahmasp's court, alludes to the shah's continuing interest in the apocalyptic and messianic aspects of Shiism, claiming he kept his sister unmarried as a bride for the Mahdi on his return and a white charger ready for the Mahdi to ride.[35]

It has been argued that the *Memoirs* mark a shift in the religious aspirations of the Safavid shah. Repeatedly, Tahmasp invokes 'Ali b. Abi Talib, who appears to him time and again in dreams, reassuring him, pointing to him how to act and acting as an intermediary of God's favour to the shah. Kathryn Babayan has suggested that this presents a contrast to Isma'il's vision of himself as divine, writing that 'Through his Memoir, Tahmasp rejected his father's role as messiah-God as he cast his own role as saintly-king (*shah vilayāt*) ... He must have wanted to make sure that future generations would judge him and his father in accordance with his own rendering of the two, rather than trusting contemporaneous or future court historians to translate their reigns.' Babayan concludes, though, that 'Tahmasp does succeed in consolidating the way for a (re)interpretation of Isma'il's revolutionary discourse in later Safavi historiography but fails to imprint himself as saint.'[36]

In reality, Isma'il is barely mentioned in the *Memoirs*; Babayan suggests that Tahmasp's 'construction of himself is shaped in contrast to a reflection of Isma'il's holy aura.'[37] Such a contrast could only be implicit, and it is unclear that it would have been evident to the original audiences of the book, who may not have been

---

35 Michele Membré, *Mission to the Lord Sophy of Persia (1539–1542)*, trans. A. H. Morton (Warminster, 1999), 25–6; Newman, 'The Myth of the Clerical Migration to Safawid Iran', 95–6.
36 Kathryn Babayan, *Mystics, Monarchs, and Messiahs: Cultural Landscapes of Early Modern Iran* (Cambridge, MA, 2002), 297–8; compare with ibid., 302–3.
37 Babayan, *Mystics, Monarchs, and Messiahs*, 304.

identical with those of Ismaʿil's poetry. Moreover, the exact nature of the claims that Ismaʿil made is debated; while he was assuredly regarded as at least semi-divine by his followers, it is far from clear that he actually voiced this himself, although there is no doubt about the messianic nature of his propaganda.[38] Yet, in the *Memoirs* on one occasion (p. 92), Tahmasp seems precisely to draw not a contrast but a parallel between his own claims and those of Ismaʿil, suggesting that in a dream a saint had predicted to him his own *ẓuhūr* or *khurūj*, 'appearance' or 'emergence'. These were loaded terms indeed, for Ismaʿil's own rise to power was described by pro-Safavid sources as a *ẓuhūr* or *khurūj*, words which have distinctly apocalyptic overtones.[39] As Tahmasp points out, this is one of the attributes of the Mahdi, and the shah thus seems to suggest that his victories over the Ottomans should be compared to – or in fact are – the victories of the Mahdi at the end of time. In this sense, the old apocalyptic, and messianic, discourse of Ismaʿil lives on in the *Memoirs*, albeit in adapted form.[40]

Tahmasp rarely explicitly discusses the nuts and bolts of his religious policy. Thus he passes over in silence episodes that some modern historians see as the key to understanding the growing role of Shiism in the Safavid state, such as the appointment of the Lebanese cleric ʿAli Karaki as 'deputy of the imam and seal of the mujtahids' in 1532, which, it has been suggested, marks the emergence of a state-sponsored religious hierarchy.[41] Indeed, there is only a short reference

---

38 Ferenc Péter Csirkés, 'A Messiah Untamed: Notes on the Philology of Shah Ismāʾīl's Divan', *Iranian Studies* 52, Nos. 3-4 (2019): 339–95; also Ahmet Karamustafa, 'In His Own Voice: What Hatayi Tells Us about Şah İsmail's Religious Views', in Mohammad Ali Amir-Moezzi, Maria De Cillis, Daniel De Smet and Orkhan Mir-Kasimov (eds), *L'Ésotérisme shiʾite, ses racines et ses prolongements: Shiʾi Esotericism: Its Roots and Developments* (Turnhout, 2016), 601–11.
39 For examples of the use of these terms for Ismaʿil, see Floor and Faghfoory, 'Shah Esmail', 377, 378.
40 For further evidence for such messianic claims made by Tahmasp in other contexts, see Newman, 'Myth of the Clerical Migration to Safawid Iran', esp. 94–5.
41 Arjomand, *Shadow of God*, 133–4.

in the *Memoirs* to this highly influential figure at Tahmasp's court. Yet Tahmasp is at pains to emphasize his own relationship with the divine, through the several accounts of his dreams that feature prominently in the *Memoirs*. While the dreams may seem to a modern audience to be by far the most 'personal' element of Tahmasp's narrative, at the time they would have been understood as communicating political and religious messages. In the pre-modern Islamic world, dreams were seen as divine communications, whether prophetic, revelatory or prognosticatory.[42] If correctly understood, they also served to link the present with the past, and the living with the dead saints, prophets and holy men who regularly featured in them. The interpretation of dreams was especially important in Sufism, and a Sufi aspirant was obliged to tell his spiritual guide (*murshid*) his dreams. A whole genre of literature was devoted to dream interpretation, and other rulers on occasion recorded their dreams. Tahmasp's older contemporary Babur recounts a dream in his autobiographical *Baburnama*, using it, as Tahmasp sometimes does, to indicate that divine favour had blessed his military endeavours, in this case his capture of Samarqand in 1502.[43] However, rulers also sometimes devoted whole books to dreams. The best-known examples are Tahmasp's younger contemporary, the Ottoman Sultan Murad III (r. 1574–94), who wrote down his dreams in a collection of letters,[44] and the south-Indian ruler Tipu Sultan (r. 1782–99) whose Persian 'dream-book', it has been suggested, represented an attempt not just to understand, but also to influence the course of events through divination.[45] Safavid

---

42 For a survey, see Nile Green, 'The Religious and Cultural Roles of Dreams and Visions in Islam', *Journal of the Royal Asiatic Society* 13, No. 3 (2003): 287–313.
43 *The Baburnama: Memoirs of Babur, Prince and Emperor*, trans. Wheeler Thackston (New York, 1996), 20.
44 Özgen Felek (ed.), *Kitābü'l-Menāmāt: Sultan III. Murad'ın Rüya Mektupları* (Istanbul, 2014).
45 Kate Brittlebank, 'Accessing the Unseen Realm: The Historical and Textual Contexts of Tipu Sultan's Dream Register', *Journal of the Royal Asiatic Society* 21 (2011): 159–75.

historians, moreover, regularly included the dreams of Shaykh Safi in their narratives, foretelling the future greatness of his family.[46]

Dreams fulfil multiple roles in the *Memoirs*. They affirm Tahmasp's special relationship with God and 'Ali b. Abi Talib in particular, for it is often 'Ali who appears to Tahmasp in the dreams. They validate his conquests and show they are part of a divine plan, but the dreams also serve as the rationale for Tahmasp's policies. Thus the first 'Edict of Repentance', when Tahmasp banned unislamic behaviour such as drinking in 1534 was, according to Tahmasp, issued directly in response to a dream he had had.[47] Yet as well as recording the dreams, Tahmasp interprets them, thereby asserting his ability to act as an intermediary between the seen and unseen worlds in his waking hours too. *Pace* Babayan, I can find little explicit evidence that the *Memoirs* are meant to document and advertise a new Safavid religiosity with the shah himself as *walī* or saint. That is not to say that Tahmasp did not espouse such a model of sacral kingship, as indeed most of his contemporaries did to some degree,[48] but rather that it is not the focus or objective of the *Memoirs*, which were, as we should remember, written to appeal in the first instance to foreign audiences as much as Safavid ones. The edict of repentance described by Tahmasp was not a revolutionary break with the past: it was quite common for rulers to issue such edicts, just as Babur himself did, when seeking divine favour for conquests or to mark a break with past practice.[49] Indeed, Tahmasp himself issued a second edict of repentance some twenty-four years after the first, in 1556 (again not discussed in the *Memoirs*).[50]

---

46 Sholeh Quinn, 'The Dreams of Shaykh Safi al-Din and Safavid Historical Writing', *Iranian Studies* 29 (1996): 127–47.
47 See the discussion of this in Rudi Matthee, *Angels Tapping at the Wine-Shop's Door: A History of Alcohol in the Islamic World* (London, 2023), 136–8.
48 For a discussion, see Azfar Moin, *The Millennial Sovereign: Sacred Kingship and Sainthood in Islam* (New York, 2012).
49 *The Baburnama*, trans. Thackston, 373–6; see also Matthee, *Angels Tapping at the Wine-Shop's Door*, 114–16, 138–41.
50 For these dates, see Parsadust, *Shah Tahmasp*, 609–13.

Betrayal, war and piety are thus the dominant themes of the *Memoirs*, in keeping with their exemplary purpose. They are far from being a full record of Tahmasp's reign and, even as a factual source, they need to be treated with care, owing to their numerous elisions. However, the *Memoirs* also exist in a broader literary tradition that must also be appreciated to understand them.

The *Memoirs* in their literary context

At first glance, the *Memoirs* may appear to be a literary oddity. The pre-modern Islamic world has a reputation, only gradually being demolished by modern scholarship, for lacking much in the way of autobiographies.[51] However, there was a substantial tradition of including biographical accounts (*tazkira*) in larger historical works under the Timurids, which is undoubtedly one influence on the text.[52] Indeed, the *Memoirs* must be understood in a broader context of historiographical production and writing of biographies and autobiographies in the Islamic east in the period. Like their Ottoman, Mughal and Uzbek neighbours, the Safavid court supported a tradition of literary production, in particular of poetry and historiography. The composition of historical texts, predominantly by members of the bureaucratic and occasionally the military elite, aimed not so much simply to record facts but rather to arrange them in a way that both delivered ethical lessons and supported the political agenda of its dedicatee and the legitimacy of the ruling dynasty more broadly.

---

51 Two important collective volumes on this subject are: Dwight F. Reynolds (ed.), *Interpreting the Self – Autobiography in the Arabic Literary Tradition* (Berkeley, 2001); Louise Marlow (ed.), *The Rhetoric of Biography: Narrating Lives in Persianate Societies* (Cambridge, MA, 2011).

52 Sholeh Quinn, *Persian Historiography across Empires: The Ottomans, Safavids and Mughals* (Cambridge, 2021), 174–201.

Safavid historiography was entirely in Persian, and drew strongly on the models of Timurid historical writing. The principal Safavid historical works dealing with Tahmasp come from the later part of his reign. They include the *Takmilat al-Akhbar*, written by 'Abdi Beg Shirazi in the capital of Qazvin in 1570, and dedicated to Tahmasp's daughter Pari Khan Khanum. Another important source is the *Ahsan al-Tawarikh*, written in 1578 by a senior military officer, Hasan Rumlu, who had accompanied Tahmasp on many of his campaigns, and which was dedicated to Tahmasp's son Isma'il II, shortly after his accession. Also valuable is the history known as the *Tarikh-i Ilchi* by Khurshah b. Qubad, which was written in India for the Shiite Qutbshahi rulers in 1563–5, but contains substantial information about Tahmasp's reign.[53] Other chronicles were composed under Tahmasp, and dedicated to members of the Safavid family, but tended to be universal histories, with relatively little detail on Tahmasp's reign.[54] Two chronicles were dedicated to Tahmasp by Ghaffari Qazvini (d. 1568), but only one of these, the *Nusakh-i Jahan-ara*, treats Tahmasp's reign with an annalistic account of the principal military events of each year down to 1564.[55] Thus, it seems that the *Memoirs*, composed in 1562, represent the earliest substantial prose historiographical work discussing Tahmasp's reign, and passages from it were incorporated verbatim into many of these later texts.

---

53 On Safavid historiography in the period, see Tilman Trausch, *Formen höfischer Historiographie im 16. Jahrhundert: Geschichtsschreibung unter den frühen Safaviden, 1501–1578* (Vienna, 2015); Sholeh Quinn and Charles Melville, 'Safavid Historiography', in Charles Melville (ed.), *Persian Historiography* (London, 2012), 209–57; Dickson, 'Sháh Tahmásp', Appendix II has a useful survey of the major sources for the period, including those composed later.

54 Kioumars Ghereghlou, 'Chronicling a Dynasty on the Make: New Light on the Early Ṣafavids in Ḥayātī Tabrīzī's *Tārīkh* (961/1554)', *Journal of the American Oriental Society* 137, No. 4 (2017): 805–32.

55 Kioumars Ghereghlou, 'Ġaffāri Qazvini, Aḥmad', *Encyclopædia Iranica*, online edition, 2016, available at http://www.iranicaonline.org/articles/ghaffari-qazvini (accessed 1 November 2023).

Tahmasp is at pains to stress that he makes no literary claims for his work, proclaiming in the preface to the second recension that it is 'written without artifice' (*bī takalluf*). In contrast, Timurid and Safavid historiography, with the use of elaborate, bombastic or rhyming prose, allowed the historian to exhibit his literary skills, although it should be noted that there was considerable variation between the works and simpler historical prose narratives that were also produced, especially in Qazvin.[56] One key difference, of course, is that unlike most historians who were seeking a financial reward or appointment as a result of showing off their rhetorical skills, Tahmasp had no need for such patronage.

A further notable characteristic of the *Memoirs*' style is the frequent use of Turkish vocabulary, Turkish remaining the main language of the Safavid army and court,[57] even if Persian was usually – although not always – used for literary and administrative purposes. It was in Turkish that Shah Isma'il had written poems. While some of these famously proclaim Isma'il's divinity and constitute a sort of political propaganda addressed primarily to the Qizilbash, most represent lyrics (*ghazals*) that conform to a longer tradition of Turkish poetry in both Ottoman and, in particular, the Azerbaijani dialects.[58] In addition to the use of Turkish vocabulary, Tahmasp on occasion quotes Turkish poetry, sometimes of his own extemporary composition, and Turkish was doubtless Tahmasp's mother tongue. The fact that Turkish was not used as the medium for the *Memoirs* again underlines the nature of the text as a public document. As well as being the principal administrative and literary language of the Safavid domains, Persian was the main language for diplomatic correspondence, including with the Ottomans, even if the latter generally sent their messages in Turkish (while the literary Ottoman language of the sixteenth century

---

56 Trausch, *Formen höfischer Historiographie*.
57 See Willem Floor and Hasan Javadi, 'The Role of Azerbaijani Turkish in Safavid Iran', *Iranian Studies* 46, No. 4 (2013): 569–81.
58 On Shah Isma'il's poetry, see Csirkés, 'A Messiah Untamed'.

was not identical with the Azerbaijani dialect that was in use in the Safavid lands, the two were close and mutually comprehensible). The choice of Persian as a language is thus consistent with the international audience to whom the *Memoirs* were addressed.

The composition of such a text by the shah should be also understood in the context of courtly literary life. Tahmasp's younger brother Sam Mirza was also the author of a literary anthology, the *Tuhfa-yi Sami*, which brought together biographies of contemporary poets – mainly in Persian, with a few in Turkish. Ottoman rulers frequently composed poetry too, with sultans Beyazid II, Selim I and Süleyman all authors of *divan*s (collections of poetry) – in the case of Selim, in Persian, the international courtly language. The appreciation of literature and poetry was thus as an essential part of a ruler's education, and Tahmasp makes this point himself, both implicitly and explicitly. He frequently cites verses in Persian to underline a moral or to emphasize his point. A particular favourite source is the thirteenth-century moralist Sa'di of Shiraz, whose verse *Bustan* ('Orchard') and mixed prose and verse *Gulistan* ('Rose garden') remain treasured classics of ethical wisdom to this day. Other authors cited include the poets Nizami (1141–1209) and 'Attar (d. 1221), who wrote lengthy didactic epics, and occasionally Hafiz (1325–1390), the great lyric poet of Shiraz. It is striking that at no point does Tahmasp quote from the *Shahnama* of Firdawsi (d. 1010), the great book of kings which was regarded as providing models of ethical conduct, and of which we know Tahmasp himself commissioned illustrated copies, one of which was subsequently sent as a diplomatic gift to the Ottomans on the occasion of the accession of Selim II in 1566.[59] Whatever the reasons for this omission, Tahmasp's choice of verses is not random, but rather is designed to illustrate his mastery not simply

---

59 For a detailed study, see Sheila R. Canby, *The Shahnama of Shah Tahmasp: The Persian Book of Kings* (New York, 2011).

of literary models, but of paradigms of courtly conduct. Criticizing the Ottomans for trusting the defector Alqas, Tahmasp cites a verse from Saʿdi's *Gulistan*:

> It would be a shame if someone on whose advice the king acts should say anything but good.

Tahmasp then comments, 'Yet without probing his intelligence and understanding or his truthfulness or lying, the Ottomans have launched a campaign against us. Showing themselves to be simpletons, the respect and awe in which they were held by the people of every province has been rendered vain and futile; seemingly they never heard these verses and do not read biographies of the Prophet, histories and stories (*siyar va tawārīkh va qiṣaṣ*).'[60] Reading, then, and knowledge of both verse and prose narratives enables a ruler to act with discernment.

Exactly what narratives Tahmasp has in mind is not specified, beyond the exemplary *siyar*, the biographies of the Prophet. However, there were also precedents for his own *Memoirs*, most notably the famous work by his older contemporary Babur, founder of the Mughal empire.[61] Indeed, Tahmasp's account of his accession strikingly mirrors that of Babur, who opened his memoir with the words, 'In the month of Ramadan in the year 899 [June 1494], in the province of Fergana, in my twelfth year, I became king.'[62] After the initial doxology, Tahmasp starts his *Memoirs* in very similar fashion, 'In the year 930 of the hijra, on the morning of Tuesday 19 Rajab [5 May 1524], corresponding to the Turkish Year of the Monkey, I ascended the royal throne at the age of ten.'[63] While there is no

---

60 See pp. 100–1.
61 On this, see Stephen Dale, 'Steppe Humanism: The Autobiographical Writings of Zahir al-Din Muhammad Babur, 1483–1530', *International Journal of Middle East Studies* 22, No. 1 (1990): 37–58.
62 *Baburnama*, trans. Thackston, 35.
63 See p. 51.

direct evidence that Tahmasp had read Babur's *Memoirs*, it is entirely possible, for we know the text was especially valued by Babur's son Humayun,[64] who was Tahmasp's guest from 1554 to 1555.[65] Tahmasp probably would have been able to read the Chaghatay Turkish dialect in which Babur wrote without much difficulty. Royal biography and autobiography were much cultivated under the Mughals. Reminiscences of Humayun were written by his sister Gulbadan Begam, by his chief ewer-bearer Jawhar, and by one of his soldiers, Bayazid Bayat, who was himself from Tabriz.[66] Subsequently, the Mughal emperor Jahangir (1569–1622) wrote his memoirs, mixing reflections on politics, art and family.[67]

Compared to the works by Babur or Jahangir, that by Tahmasp reveals relatively little of his personality, although the Mughal memoirs are certainly far from lacking in artifice, and served to curate the ruler's image for posterity just as the shah intended to, albeit through somewhat different methods. Whereas the *Memoirs* of Babur and Jahangir seem to have originated as diaries which were then subsequently reworked and polished for publication, Tahmasp's do not seem to be based on contemporary notes, as is suggested by the occasional egregious errors in dates (and indeed, Tahmasp also gets his own date of birth wrong).[68] In reality, Tahmasp's *Memoirs* are closest to a common, but perhaps rather seldom discussed,

---

[64] *The Babur-nama in English (Memoirs of Babur)*, trans. Annette Beveridge (London, 1922), xlii; *Baburnama*, trans. Thackston, 11.

[65] On this episode, see Sukumar Ray, *Humāyūn in Persia* (Kolkata, 2002, 1st edn 1948); Mitchell, 'Custodial Politics and Princely Governance', 97–9.

[66] Persian texts and English translations are conveniently gathered in Wheeler M. Thackston (trans.), *Three Memoirs of Homayun* (Costa Mesa, 2009); for a survey of this biographical tradition in the Mughal court, see Stephen Dale, 'Autobiography and Biography: The Turco-Mongol Case: Bābur, Haydar Mīrzā, Gulbadan Begim and Jahāngīr', in Louise Marlow (ed.), *The Rhetoric of Biography: Narrating Lives in Persianate Societies* (Cambridge, MA, 2011), 89–105.

[67] *Jahangirnama: Memoirs of Jahangir, Emperor of India*, trans. W. M. Thackston (New York, 1999).

[68] See pp. 51 n. 10, 85 n. 145.

sub-genre of Persian historiography, chronicles in which the writer himself features prominently in the first person. One such work is the *Tarikh-i Rashidi* by Mirza Haydar Dughlat (1500–1551), a Persian chronicle by a relative of Babur's, the governor of Kashmir, who included plentiful autobiographical information alongside his accounts of the rulers of Mughulistan (roughly present-day Xinjiang) to whom he dedicated the text. Such mixtures of history and autobiography were also composed in the Middle East. Sharaf Khan (1543–1601), the Kurdish ruler of Bitlis (in modern southeastern Turkey), who was himself educated at Tahmasp's court, included a substantial autobiographical appendix to his Persian history of the Kurds, the *Sharafnama*.[69] Another Kurd, Ma'mun Beg, a former prince of Shahrazur in northern Iraq, compiled a Turkish *Memoir* in 1574 which dealt extensively with the Safavid–Ottoman conflict in the region in the 1550s, when he had been ruler, and in particular the Alqas episode.[70] Ma'mun Beg's objective was evidently to introduce himself to the new Ottoman Sultan, Murad III, and to be forgiven and reinstated in his position.

Tahmasp's *Memoirs* thus takes its place among a number of comparable works composed in similar cultural milieus. Like the *Memoirs*, such works tended to be written for political purposes, and to justify the author's part in events. Nonetheless, it is noteworthy that despite the fact that the *Memoirs* evidently were read by later generations of the Safavid family, as we shall see, no subsequent ruler in Iran attempted to produce a similar text. The next remotely comparable effort does not appear until late nineteenth century, when the Qajar ruler Nasir al-Din Shah II (r. 1848–96) undertook journeys in Iran, to Ottoman Iraq, and to Europe, which he recorded in diaries

---

69 On this, see M. Dehqan and V. Genç, 'Reflections on Sharaf Khān's Autobiography', *Manuscripta Orientalia* 21 (2015): 46–61.
70 See the edition of the Turkish text in İsmet Parmaksızoğlu, 'Kuzey Irak'ta Osmanlı Hakimiyetinin Kuruluşu ve Memun Bey'in Hatıraları', *Belleten* 37, No. 146 (1973): 191–230.

that were intended for publication, as a means of strengthening his links with the wider populace of his domains.[71]

The circumstances of the *Memoirs*' composition and the extant manuscripts

Two main recensions of the *Memoirs* exist, as represented in the extant manuscripts, which number at least seventeen currently known.[72] The so-called short recension claims to represent a speech given by the shah on the occasion of the attendance of the Ottoman ambassadors at Qazvin in 1562 to retrieve the fugitive Ottoman prince Beyazid who had been offered sanctuary by Tahmasp after a failed revolt. Its introduction runs as follows:

> The conversation of the envoys of the late Shah Tahmasp with the Ottoman envoys[73]
>
> In the name of God the merciful the compassionate
>
> After limitless praise to his Majesty the Absolute King, the Sovereign of all by right, and felicitous praise upon the Lord of Messengers, the seal of the Prophets, the Messenger of the Lord of Both Worlds, and the immaculate imams, and especially upon

---

71 *The Diary of H. M. the Shah of Persia, during His Tour through Europe in A. D. 1873*, trans. J. Redhouse (London, [1874] 1995, with a new introduction by Carole Hillenbrand).
72 The differences between the two recensions were first noted by V. A. Zhukovsky, in his review of Horn's translation: 'Die Denkwürdigkeiten des Šāh Ṭahmâsp I. von Persien', *Zapiski Vostochnogo Otdeleniia Imperatorskogo Russkogo Arkheologicheskogo Obshestva* 6 (1891): 377–83, further elucidated by Walter Hinz, 'Zur Frage der Denkwürdigkeiten des Schah Ṭahmāsp I. von Persien', *Zeitschrift der Deutschen Morgenländischen Gesellschaft* 88 (1934): 46–54; see also the discussion in Bockholt, 'Shah Tahmasp and the Tazkira'; Zahir Bhalloo, 'Shāh Ṭahmāsp's Narrative of Safavid-Ottoman Relations from 938–969/1531–1562', Unpublished MPhil thesis in Oriental Studies, University of Oxford, 2008. The manuscripts are discussed below.
73 Translated on the basis of the text in *Mukalama-i Shah Tahmasp ba Ilchiyan-i Rum/ Shah-Tamazis Saubari Osmaletis Elchebtan*, ed. K. Tabatadze (Tbilisi, 1976), 3–5. The text of the introduction to this recension is also published in Zhukovsky's review, 381–2.

the strength of the good and pure, his excellency the Commander of the Faithful, the prince of the faith, the leader of the radiant,[74] ['Ali b. Abi Talib], peace and blessings be upon them all: May it be known that the Lord God, great and might are His proofs, in the Noble Book, the Great Qur'an, has said, O Muhammad, call the people to the path of worship and knowledge of their Creator by way of Truth, certainty and advice and fair warning, and dispute with them in the best way.[75] It is well known that God, glorious and exalted is He, commanded his Prophet, peace and blessings be upon him, in this noble verse to propagate the divine laws to all of mankind, both great and lowly. These are upheld in one of three ways: firstly, by the aim being realized through demonstrable premises and conclusive proofs; secondly, by the truth being clarified through sufficient admonition and hypothetical premises; and thirdly, by affirming the claim of the Prophet through well-known and certain premises.

Thus, his imperial majesty, the Lord's vicegerent, may God perpetuate his kingship forever, in emulation of his great ancestor,[76] addressed the messengers and envoys of His Majesty the Sultan in the three aforementioned ways. These had come in 969 [1561–2] to ask for the Sultan's son Beyazid and his sons who had taken refuge with His Imperial Majesty the Shah. He declared in these fair and wise words, 'Several times have we sent an envoy to His Majesty the Sultan, bearing a message from us. Yet His Majesty the Sultan's greatness and arrogance struck them with such awe in their hearts that our envoys forgot what we had told them to say. Since the date that my imperial father passed away and the sultanic throne passed to me till now, which is a period of thirty-nine years, I have always desired that one of His Majesty the Sultan's men should come to

---

74 Read *al-ghurr al-muhajjalīn* not *al-'izz al-muhajjalīn* as per the edition.
75 Qur'an 16.17. In the text, the Arabic is followed by a Persian paraphrase; in the translation I have followed the paraphrase as it indicates how Tahmasp wanted the verse to be understood. The original is slightly more laconic: 'Call to the path of your Lord with wisdom and fair admonition, and dispute with them through that which is the best.'
76 The Prophet Muhammad is meant, alluding to Tahmasp's claim to sayyid status.

us so that I could tell him these tales. Praise be to God that two distinguished men like yourselves accompanied by two hundred of the sultan's slaves and three hundred of your own men have attended on us, so that you can hear these stories and relate them to His Majesty the Sultan. If you do not tell him, certainly one of your men will, and if you cannot tell the sultan himself, tell his pashas and his retinue so that it will reach the sultan in that way. For if these stories are written down, they would fill a book.'

The stories are arranged in five chapters.

The identity of these ambassadors is revealed by the contemporary chronicler Hasan Rumlu, who records how, in 14 Zulqi'da 969/15 August 1562, Hüsrev Pasha, Ottoman governor of Van, and Ali Ağa, a senior aide of the Ottoman prince Selim, arrived in Qazvin accompanied by a small retinue of twenty men (other sources agree with Tahmasp in putting their retinue at two hundred strong). They were received by Tahmasp three days later,

and the lights of royal compassion shone upon them; as Farrukhzad Beg had previously been sent as envoy and had made an agreement with the sultan that any refugee should be returned [to his original country], on this basis, on 21 Zulqi'da [22 August], Sultan Beyazid and his sons were handed over in accordance with the Sultan's request, and they were all strangled.[77]

The *Memoirs* thus ostensibly originated as a speech to these envoys, although the dearth of manuscripts of the work in the Ottoman lands suggest it was never actually disseminated there. It is likely that in fact the written version, while drawing on the oral discourse, represents an elaboration of the speech.[78] The primary manuscript witness of this recension is a lavishly illuminated manuscript now kept in the National

---

77 Hasan Rumlu, *Ahsan al-Tawarikh*, III, 1424 (my translation; compare with trans. Setton, *Chronicle*, 189).
78 Bhalloo, 'Shāh Ṭahmāsp's Narrative', 20–2, 55–8.

Library of Russia in St Petersburg (MS Dorn 302) that was made for Tahmasp's grandson Shah 'Abbas (r. 1578–1629) and was once held in the Safavid dynastic shrine at Ardabil (discussed further below).

It was probably very shortly after this that another, slightly longer, recension of the *Memoirs* was compiled, although we have no unambiguous knowledge of the sequence: it is possible that two recensions with slightly different contents were prepared more or less simultaneously for different audiences. Nonetheless, what we shall call here the 'long recension' differs mainly from that discussed earlier in that at the start of the first chapter, Tahmasp recounts the first seven years of his reign, from his accession in 1524 to the beginning of the affair of Ulama in 1531–2, which is absent from the short recension. Other minor differences between the two recensions seem basically to reflect a tendency to burnish Tahmasp's image in the long recension.[79] Apart from the introduction, the most substantial difference between the two recensions lies in the treatment of the episode of Beyazid. In the long recension, Beyazid is accused of plotting to kill Tahmasp with poisoned confectionary. It has been suggested that this may indicate that the long recension was composed after Beyazid's brutal killing in Qazvin by the Ottoman emissaries, a spectacle that apparently caused widespread public revulsion. The amended text in the long recension may thus have been intended to exculpate Tahmasp for his role in Beyazid's surrender by blackening the prince's character.[80] However, the date such changes were made is unclear. At any rate, manuscripts of both recensions continued to be seen as authoritative, as both the St Petersburg manuscript of the short recension and the Gulistan manuscript of the long recension were made for royal Safavid patrons, in 1601–2 and 1679 respectively, as is discussed further below.

---

79 Bhalloo, 'Shāh Ṭahmāsp's Narrative', 66–72; see for example p. 125 n. 12 below for an example of this tendency.
80 Bhalloo, 'Shāh Ṭahmāsp's Narrative', 72–81.

Our earliest evidence for the circulation of the text dates from around 1563–5, with a mention of the *Memoirs* in the *Tarikh-i Ilchi*, a Persian chronicle composed for the Qutbshahi dynasty of the Deccan in South India by Khurshah b. Qubad (d. 1565), who had himself spent time at Tahmasp's court as envoy. The *Tarikh-i Ilchi* is a valuable source for Safavid history that in several places explicitly cites the *Memoirs*.[81] Khurshah records,

> His majesty the shah, the refuge of the caliphate [Shah Tahmasp] sent Quba Beg the *qūrchī* as his envoy to the court of the Qutbshah, the ruler of Telengana, in 971 [1563]. Shah Tahmasp sent, among other valuable presents, a record of his deeds and experiences (*ḥālāt wa wāqi'āt*) from the beginning of the war with the Ottomans till the aforementioned date [1563], both those in waking hours and his dreams. As the writer of these words was engaged in compiling this short humble work at this time, his majesty God's deputy and shadow on earth (Ibrahim Qutbshah) after reading that noble manuscript, graciously forwarded it to this humble servant (Khurshah) so that he might include in his work some of the events and stories mentioned in it.[82]

The *Memoirs* were thus also intended as a diplomatic gift to Ibrahim Qutbshah (r. 1550–80), the ruler of the other main Shiite state existing in the period, the Qutbshahis of the Deccan, with which the Safavids had close relations. It is possible, but not stated explicitly in the text, that another potential audience was the substantial Iranian émigré

---

81 Khurshah, *Tarikh-i Ilchi*, 126, 160, 180.
82 Khurshah, *Tarikh-i Ilchi*, 115; *Tarikh-i-Qutbi (also known as Tarikh-i Elchi-i-Nizam Shah) of Khwurshah bin Qubad al-Husayni: A Work on the History of the Timurids. Chapter Five*, ed. Mujahid Husain Zaidi (New Delhi, 1965), 25–6, text and translation (modified here). As Zaidi notes, this passage was misunderstood by Rieu in his catalogue of manuscripts in the British Museum. Rieu wrongly believed that the ruler who handed over the *Memoirs* to Khurshah was Tahmasp himself, and this mistake has been repeated in the later literature, which has also therefore tended to grossly overestimate the amount of time Khurshah spent at Tahmasp's court. In fact, Khurshah evidently remained at the court between 1545 and 1547, for about a year and a half (see *Tarikh-i-Qutbi*, 16–22).

community who resided in the Deccan, some of whom retained close links with the Safavid court, serving as emissaries between it and the Deccani kingdoms.[83] Judging from the citations of the *Memoirs* in the text, it seems that Khurshah had the short recension at his disposal.[84] The treatment of the Ottomans in the text of the *Memoirs* may also be related to this Shiite audience in India. The downplaying of sectarian aspects would have the advantage of explaining why Tahmasp had not prosecuted war against the Ottomans more vigorously, and provide an exemplar for coexistence with a powerful Sunni neighbour. This may have been a theme of potential relevance to the Qutbshahis as a Shiite dynasty in a predominantly Sunni world, especially given increasing Mughal expansionism in this period, as well as an acknowledgement of the sensitive religious situation in the Deccan, in which rival dynasties such as the 'Adilshahs and Nizamshahs switched sectarian identity between Sunni and Shiite.

It is clear that the *Memoirs* circulated widely in the sixteenth century, for they are quoted explicitly by the Deccani chronicler Khurshah, and were evidently also used by the Safavid court chroniclers 'Abdi Beg Shirazi (1515–1580) and Qadi Ahmad b. Husayn Munshi Qummi (d. after 1606), the author of the well-known histories, the *Takmilat al-Akhbar* and the *Khulasat al-Tawarikh* respectively. Later, substantial parts of the *Memoirs* were incorporated into an eighteenth-century chronicle written in Lucknow, the *Tarikh-i Tahmasiyya* of Muhammad Mahdi Khan Shirazi, which drew on Khurshah's work.[85]

It is possible that further work on the manuscript history of the text will shed fresh light on the question of the date of the two recensions.

---

83 For these links, see Muzaffar Alam and Sanjay Subrahmanyam, 'Iran and the Doors to the Deccan, *c*. 1400–1650: Some Aspects', in Keelan Overton (ed.), *Iran and the Deccan: Persianate Art, Culture, and Talent in Circulation, 1400–1700* (Bloomington, 2020), 77–103.
84 Bhalloo, 'Shāh Ṭahmāsp's Narrative', 60.
85 On the *Tarikh-i Tahmasiyya*, see C. A. Storey, *Persian Literature: A Bio-Bibliographical Survey*, I.2 (London, 1936), 320.

However, it is clear that the *Memoirs* were not merely intended for the use of Tahmasp's family and followers, as the shah implies in the introduction to the long recension, but also constitute a justification of his reign intended to burnish his credentials among fellow rulers and, given the work's dissemination, among a wider public too. This was very far from being a private memoir, but was rather a public apologia.

Although the *Memoirs* are extant in at least seventeen manuscripts, none of these dates to the sixteenth century, and most to nineteenth century.[86] The earliest surviving manuscript is St Petersburg, National Library of Russia, MS Dorn 302, representing the short recension of the text, which was copied in 1010/1601-2 by the famous calligrapher 'Ali Riza 'Abbasi for Tahmasp's grandson, Shah 'Abbas I, with illuminations made by Zayn al-Din Tabrizi, himself a great-grandson of Tahmasp. The manuscript contains an image showing Tahmasp addressing the Ottoman envoys (Plates 1–2). In 1617, 'Abbas endowed it, along with many other books from the royal library, to the shrine of Shaykh Safi in Ardabil.[87]

The earliest dated manuscript of the long recension was also compiled for the Safavid family. Currently held in Tehran in the Gulistan Palace (MS 831), this manuscript was copied in Sha'ban 1090/September–October 1679 by Muhammad Husayn Damavandi

---

86 Ten manuscripts are listed in C. A Storey, *Persidskaya Literatura: Bio-Bibliograficheskii Obzor*, translated into Russian and revised with additions and correction by Yu. E. Bregel (Moscow, 1972), II, 857–8; Mustafa Dirayati, *Fihristagan-i Nuskhaha-yi Khatti-yi Iran* (Tehran, 1334), 847–8, lists eight manuscripts held in Iranian libraries of which only two are duplicated in Storey-Bregel (Mashhad 7886 and Tehran, Mahdavi 209). To these lists can be added Oxford, Bodleian Library, MS Marsh 84, which includes a copy of the *Memoirs* (with a slightly different preface from the other two recensions) in a collection of official letters compiled in the Safavid period. There are doubtless other extant manuscripts.

87 For a description of the manuscript with reproductions of the images, see Olga Vasilyeva, *A String of Pearls: Iranian Fine Books from the 14th to the 17th Century in the National Library of Russia Collections* (St Petersburg, 2008), 99–103.

'in accordance with the imperial order' (*ḥasab al-amr-i navvāb-i mustaṭāb-i khānī*) as the copyist tells us in the colophon. It thus seems that this manuscript was commissioned by the Safavid ruler Sulayman (r. 1666–94, who also reigned briefly with the title Safi II). The long recension is also represented by a manuscript probably of the seventeenth century, British Library MS 5880, which is undated. This manuscript was in 1136/1724 in the possession of a library in Ardabil, almost certainly that of the dynastic shrine, and in 1212/1797–8 it entered the library of Abu'l-Fath Sultan Muhammad Mirza (1763–1816/7), a Safavid prince who had taken refuge in India in the Shiite city of Lucknow, where a Safavid court in exile was established (Figure 1).[88] The manuscript itself is finely written, again suggesting a royal commission, especially given its earlier association with Ardabil (Plate 3). Or 5880 is the ancestor of two other manuscripts, currently held in the Asiatic Society in Calcutta,[89] which were evidently produced at the Safavid court in exile in Lucknow. The earliest of these, made in 1212/1797–8 (Plate 4), mentions in its colophon the same Abu'l-Fath Sultan Muhammad Mirza, and was apparently made from Or 5880 at the behest of a British officer named Lumsden (Figure 2a, 2b) in the same year that the prince acquired the original.[90] The Lumsden manuscript was probably the source of not just the second Calcutta manuscript, dated 1868, and the Berlin manuscript that was copied on 22 January 1817.[91]

These Indian manuscripts have exercised an important influence on the published editions, and one which is to be regretted as they are mostly rather carelessly written, with numerous mistakes in personal names by scribes who lacked any knowledge of sixteenth-century

---

88 On him, see Giorgio Rota, 'The Man Who Would Not Be King: Abu'l-Fath Sultan Muhammad Mirza Safavi in India', *Iranian Studies* 32, No. 4 (1999): 513–35.
89 See Wladimir Ivanow, *Concise Descriptive Catalogue of the Persian Manuscripts in the Collection of the Asiatic Society of Bengal* (Calcutta, 1924), nos 83–4.
90 Asiatic Society of Bengal, MS PSC 87.
91 Asiatic Society of Bengal MS PSC 88 and Staatsbibliothek zu Berlin, MS Sprenger 205.

Figure 1 Ownership statements on the first page of MS Or 5880, showing the manuscript's presence in a library in Ardabil before it entered the possession of the Safavid prince Abu'l-Fath Sultan Muhammad Mirza in Lucknow in 1212/1797–8. Courtesy of the British Library Board.

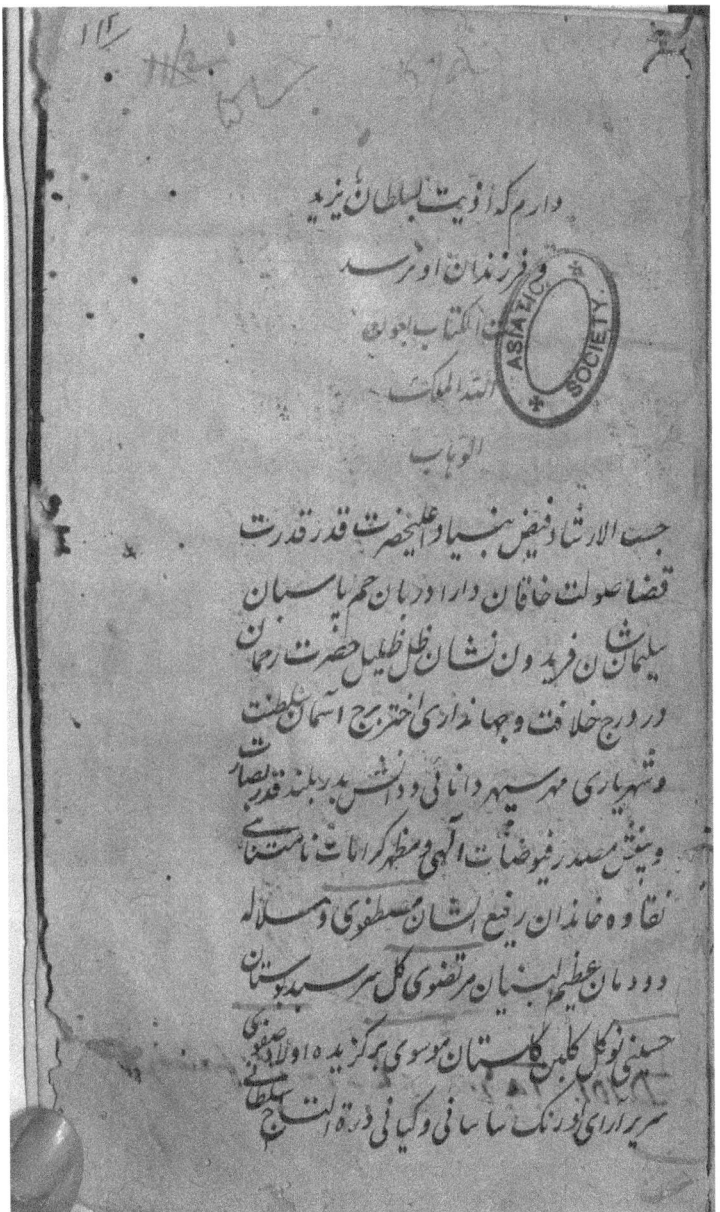

Figure 2a,b Colophon of the Calcutta manuscript made for Lumsden from Abu'l-Fath Sultan Muhammad's copy, showing the names of both. By kind permission of the Asiatic Society, Kolkata, MS PSC 87.

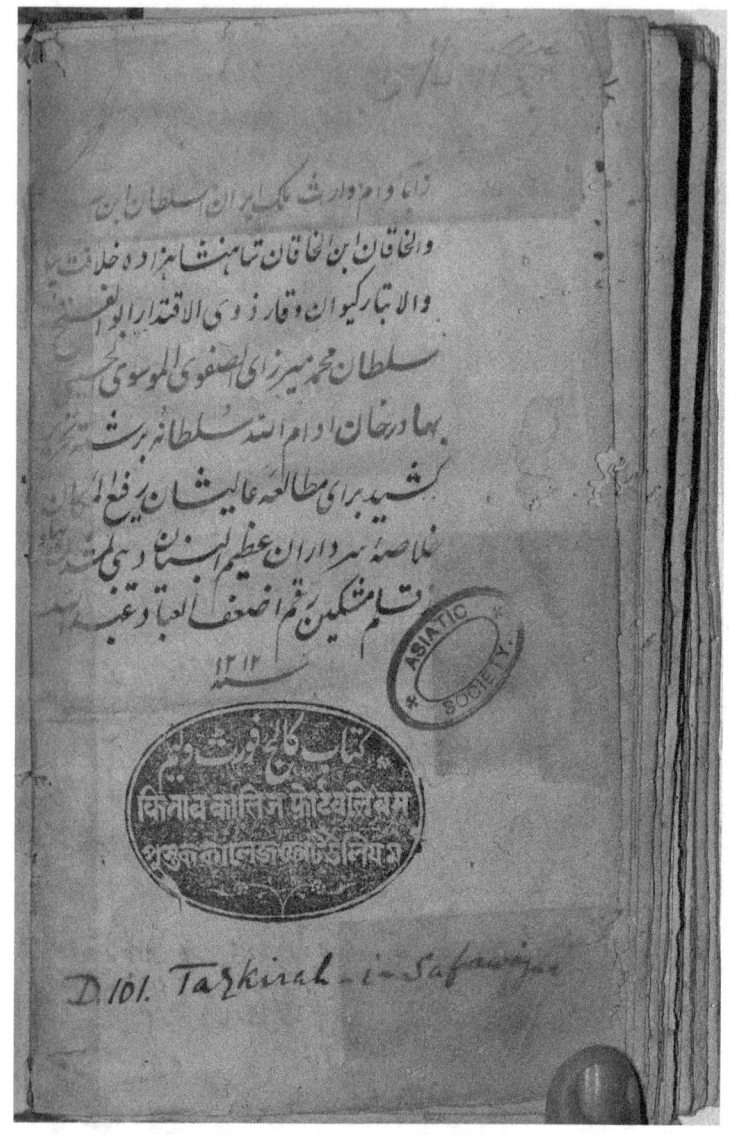

Iranian history. The earliest edition, published in Tehran in 1885,[92] was used by Paul Horn as the basis for the text he published in 1890, which he supplemented with the Berlin manuscript (Sprenger 205) and the two Calcutta ones.[93] Although Horn's edition was strongly criticized by Zhukovsky shortly after it appeared,[94] it must be said that subsequent editions have not improved its quality. In 1912, an edition by Douglas Phillott appeared in Calcutta, based on the Calcutta manuscripts (subsequently reprinted in Tehran in 1984),[95] while the Kaviani publishing house in Berlin produced a version of the text again based on the Berlin manuscript in 1924.[96] To date, then, no proper critical edition of the text has been published, and the most important early witnesses to the text have been neglected. The one exception is a handwritten transcription of St Petersburg, MS Dorn 302, accompanied by a Georgian translation and copious notes by Tabatadze, that appeared in Tbilisi in 1976, which has been, it seems, almost entirely forgotten by scholarship in the West and Iran.[97]

A proper critical edition of the text remains a desideratum, but would require collation of the numerous manuscripts in Iran presently inaccessible to me. The present translation is based on the text edited by Horn, which I have checked against the oldest witnesses available to me: British Library MS Or 5880, which provides a more accurate text than its later descendants; Gulistan MS 831, to which I have had access via a microfilm; its text is often preferable to that

---

92 Shah Tahmasp, 'Ruznama', in *Matla' al-Shams*, ed. Muhammad Hasan Khan I'timad al-Saltana, 3 Vols. (Tehran, 1301–03), II, 165–216.
93 Paul Horn, 'Die Denkwürdigkeiten des Šah Ṭahmâsp I von Persien', *Zeitschrift der Deutschen Morgenländischen Gesellschaft* 44, No. 4 (1890): 563–649; *Zeitschrift der Deutschen Morgenländischen Gesellschaft* 45, No. 2 (1891): 245–91.
94 See his review in *Zapiski Vostochnogo Otdeleniia Imperatorskogo Russkogo Arkheologicheskogo Obshestva* 6 (1891): 377–83.
95 *Tazkira-i Shah Tahmasp*, ed. D. C. Phillott (Kolkata, 1912; reprinted with additional notes, and edited by Amrallah Safari, Tehran 1984).
96 *Tazkira-i Shah Tahmasp* (Berlin, 1924).
97 K. Tabatadze (ed. and trans.), *Mukalama-i Shah Tahmasp ba Ilchiyan-i Rum/Shah-Tamazis Saubari Osmaletis Elchebtan* (Tbilisi, 1976).

of Or 5880, but it is also marred by substantial lacunae in places; and MS Dorn 302 as transcribed by Tabatadze. While the text of the latter sometimes diverges from that of the long recension that is translated here, on occasion it provides the only coherent readings. The end notes indicate where I have preferred the manuscript readings to the published text, except for minor corrections to the orthography of personal names which I have corrected without comment.

This book represents the first translation of the text into English. Previously, the text has been translated into German by Paul Horn, in a Gothic script edition that few will find convenient today; Horn's annotations are also extremely cursory.[98] A Turkish translation of the *Memoirs* also exists, without any commentary.[99] Finally, as noted earlier, Tabatadze translated the short recension into Georgian. The present translation has benefited from the work of these scholars, but does not always agree with them in its understanding of the text.

---

98 Paul Horn (trans.), *Die Denkwürdigkeiten Schah Tahmasp's des Ersten von Persien 1515–1576* (Strassburg, 1891).
99 Hicabi Kırlangıç (trans.), Şah Tahmasb-i Safevi, *Tezkire* (Istanbul, 2001).

Note on the translation

The translation aims to provide a readable version of the Persian original, but makes no attempt to render the numerous poetic quotations into verse. In any event, their purpose is more to point a moral or to exhibit the author's mastery of the classics than literary ornament. Nonetheless, readers will certainly find the plethora of personal names in the *Memoirs* a challenge. The tendency to name such a large number of now forgotten individuals, who may be attested in other chronicles, but with precious little additional detail, was a feature of historiography of the period. It may be that these individuals, or their descendants, were intended to be part of the original audience of the work, and such namings were intended to suggest who currently enjoyed royal favour or disfavour.

Another feature of the nomenclature is that the Qizilbash frequently have Turkish monikers that, if translated literally, seem to be nicknames – 'Kechel', 'scabby headed', is one; Köpek or 'dog' is the name of a very senior Qizilbash, while another is called Badinjan, 'aubergine'. It is hard to judge how such names would have sounded to a contemporary audience, and they have been left untranslated, although occasionally meanings are pointed out in the notes. While the notes identify the main contenders in the politics of the period, no attempt has been made to comment on every obscure amir. To elucidate some of the events the text describes somewhat allusively (or occasionally in downright misleading terms), some comparison is made with the accounts of other Safavid chronicles. In particular, I have found the works of Khurshah and Hasan Rumlu useful, but it should be emphasized that in no sense is the accompanying commentary meant to exhaust the analysis of the text that could be made through comparing it with a wider range of sources, which must remain a subject for future research.

Quotations and phrases in Arabic are rendered in italics in the translation. Qur'anic passages have been translated afresh, not because the efforts of previous translators such as Arberry are at all inadequate, but rather because almost all English translations reply on Sunni exegesis, and it is clear that Tahmasp frequently has a certain Shiite interpretation of the verse in mind.

Tahmasp sometimes quotes hadith, most of which can be found in major published collections of Shii hadith, such as al-Kulayni's *al-Kafi* or Ibn Babawayh's *Man la Yahduruhu al-Faqih*. Nonetheless, there is no indication of which texts exactly Tahmasp used, and it is possible that in fact he relied largely on what he had been taught orally rather than written sources. Further investigation of the influences on Tahmasp's religious education is required, and to avoid misleading the reader I have not attributed these hadith to any specific authority. For the verse quotations, I have identified the author whether this can be traced, but there are a number of unattributed verses, some of which may be Tahmasp's own compositions. References to Hafiz refer the numbers of *ghazal*s in the edition published by Muhammad Qazvini and Qasim Ghani (1941).

Modern Turkish orthography has been used for the names of Ottoman individuals and places that lie within the modern boundaries of the Republic of Turkey, except where the modern name is significantly different from the sixteenth-century form (e.g. pre-modern Vostan for modern Gevaş), in which case the original is kept in the main text and the modern name is mentioned in a footnote. As somewhat different conventions are used for transcribing Turkish words and names found in a Safavid context, there is inevitably a degree of inconsistency, but I have endeavoured to use forms that will be easily recognizable and can be cross-referenced in the relevant secondary literature.

As noted earlier, the translation is based on the text published by Horn in 1890, representing the long recension. While a full collation of the manuscript has not been attempted, major textual variants from the three main witnesses not consulted by Horn that have a bearing on the meaning of the text are listed in endnotes. Minor and obvious mistakes in the printed edition such as the misreading of names owing to the displacement or absence of diacritics have been corrected without comment in order to keep these notes to a reasonable size. The few more significant divergences between manuscripts and recensions that significantly affect the narrative are mentioned in the footnotes.

The notes refer to the manuscripts with the following sigla:

B = Horn's edition
G = Tehran, Gulistan MS 831
L = London, British Library MS Or 5800
S = St Peterburg, National Library of Russia, Dorn MS 302

AD dates are given for clarity in brackets. Minor adjustments to the text for the purposes of clarity, and the introduction of chapter headings which are only sporadically given in the original, are not signalled. While I have sought to avoid overburdening the translation with unfamiliar terms, in the interests of precision, for some offices and positions it has been thought preferable to keep the Persian word, as for example, with the military term *qūrchī*. Such terms will be found in the glossary at the end, with more detailed explanations in the notes where required.

Translation of the *Memoirs*

1

Introduction and the affair of Ulama

In the Name of God the Beneficent, the Merciful, whose aid we seek.[1]

Limitless praise is due to His Majesty the Divine King, on whose aid the fortune of victorious and conquering earthly emperors depends. Through His mercy and compassionate protection the status of the kings of this world is elevated, for He has singled them out from all mankind with His special care and exalted them, and He has distinguished them from other men by their greater dignity and pomp, and their loftier station and fortune. He has done this so that they arrange and dispose the constitution of the world's endeavours, which is the foundation of the common good.

> Verse
>
> Aspire not to the verdure of sharia's garden without the flashing sword of mighty sultans;
>
> Without the protection of strife-quelling kings no one can rest for a single moment in safety's abode.

Countless praise and blessings should be showered upon his excellency the Seal of Prophets, peace be upon him and his family, who completed the prologue *I was a Prophet while Adam was between*

---

[1] For the text of the introduction in the short recension, see introduction to this book, pp. 30–2.

*water and clay*² with the conclusion *He is God's messenger and the Seal of the Prophets.*³ He authenticated the proof of *I was sent to perfect worthy morals* through his proclamation *There is no prophet after me.* Praise and blessings also upon the True Executor⁴ and absolute, Direct Successor, that is, his excellency the Commander of the Faithful and imam of the pious, the prince of the faith, God's victorious lion, the manifestation of wonders and marvels, the eminence of whom was proclaimed *God and his prophet are your friend*, the crown-bearer of the sura of *Has there come?*⁵ and the champion of the field of *there is no hero but 'Ali b. Abi Talib*. One of the prophetic hadith that are related about him runs as follows: *Had people agreed in their love of 'Ali b. Abi Talib, God would not have created hellfire*. He is an imam even a fraction of whose qualities mere mortals cannot describe. If the sea became ink, trees became pen, and the seven heavens became paper and men and jinn wrote until the Day of Judgement, they could not write a thousandth of his description.⁶ Abu'l-Husayn 'Ali b. Abi Talib is the gate of the Prophet's city of learning,⁷ God's blessings be upon him and all the immaculate imams.

I am the poor slave of Almighty God, this wretched follower of the Last Prophet (may God's peace and blessings be upon him), and sincere slave of the 'Ali and his descendants, Tahmasp b. Isma'il b. Haydar al-Safavi, al-Musavi, al-Husayni.⁸ It occurred to my defective mind to

---

2 A hadith attributed to the Prophet, indicating the Prophet's name was pre-eternal.
3 Qur'an 33:40, indicating Muhammad is the last of Prophets.
4 *Wasi bar haqq*: 'Ali is the executor of Muhammad's will.
5 Qur'an 76:1, which starts, 'Has there come upon mankind a time when he was not yet mentioned?' Verse 8 of this sura is interpreted by Shii exegetes as praising the *ahl al-bayt*, the family of Muhammad.
6 An echo here of Qur'an 18:109, but applied to 'Ali rather than God: 'Say: were the sea ink for the words of my Lord, it would be run out before the words of my lord, even were you to bring the same amount of ink again'.
7 This alludes to the Prophetic hadith, 'I am the city of wisdom and 'Ali is its gate.'
8 Tahmasp here gives his genealogy claiming descent via Shaykh Safi to the imams Musa al-Kazim (d. 799), the seventh imam, and al-Husayn (d. 680), 'Ali b. Abi Talib's son, and thus implicitly to the Prophet, and therefore to himself being a sayyid. This genealogy is repeated elsewhere in the *Memoirs* (see p. 73). On the Safavid claim to being sayyids,

write a memoir of my life and deeds, recounting how things happened from the time of my accession till today, as a lasting memorial of me and a manual for my noble children and beloved people, so that whenever our supporters read it they will remember us with a prayer. They should not criticize it for being written without artifice and they should realize it is free of the least appearance of dissimulation, lies and hypocrisy.

In the year 930 of the hijra, on the morning of Tuesday 19 Rajab (5 May 1524), corresponding to the Turkish Year of the Monkey,[9] I ascended the royal throne at the age of ten. I was born on 26 Zu'l-Hijja 920 (11 February 1515),[10] corresponding to the Turkish Year of the Dog; the chronogram for my accession is the word 'shadow' (ẓill).[11] Div Sultan Rumlu was my tutor (lāla),[12] and alongside him I appointed as commander-in-chief (amīr al-umarā')[13] Mustafa

---

with a review of relevant scholarship, see Morimoto, 'The Earliest 'Alid Genealogy for the Safavids'.

9 The year of the monkey was the ninth year of the Turko-Mongol twelve-year cycle which was introduced to Iran by the Mongols, but which remained in common use, and frequently features in Safavid historical works. See Charles Melville, 'The Chinese-Uighur Animal Calendar in Persian Historiography of the Mongol Period', *Iran* 32 (1994): 83–98.

10 As noted in the margins of the Gulistan manuscript, the other major historical sources of the period – the *Ahsan al-Tawarikh*, the *'Alam-ara*, the *Habib al-Siyar* and *Jahan-ara*, in fact date Tahmasp's birth a full year earlier, 26 Zu'l-Hijja 919 (22 February 1514). Indeed, judging from Tahmasp's extant horoscope, the 919/1514 date must be correct. See Sergei Toukin, 'The Horoscope of Shah Tahmasp', in Jon Thompson and Sheila R. Canby (ed.), *Hunt for Paradise: Court Arts of Safavid Iran, 1501–1576* (New York, 2003), 327–31.

11 This alludes to the traditional claim that the ruler is 'God's shadow on earth' (ẓill allāh fī arḍihi). The numerical values of the letter of a word give a chronogram providing the date. In this instance ẓ = 900 l = 30, giving a total of 930; short vowels and in this instance the gemination of *lām* are disregarded. For a short introduction to the system, see G. Krotkoff, 'Abjad', *Encyclopædia Iranica*, I/2 (London, 1985–), 221–2.

12 This term is an equivalent to atabeg, and designates not only teaching, but perhaps more importantly guarding the prince. In fact, on Tahmasp's accession, Div Sultan Rumlu was the principal power in the land. However, he was opposed by the Ustajlu tribe who held Tabriz. See Savory, 'Principal Offices during the Reign of Tahmasp', 65–6.

13 The office of *amīr al-umarā'* or 'military *vakīl*' was one of the most senior in the Safavid realm in the early sixteenth century but as ever with Safavid administrative titles, it is hard to pin down its exact function, if indeed it had one. It seems to have been something like a military viceregent of the shah. See Savory, 'Principal Offices during the Reign of Tahmasp', 77–8, 79.

Sultan, known as Köpek Sultan,[14] who replaced his brother Chayan Sultan in this office.[15] As vizier and head of the bureaucracy (*ṣāḥib-dīvān*), in place of Mirza Husayn I appointed Qadi-yi Jahan Qazvini, who is one of the Sayfi sayyids[16] and has no equal in knowledge, virtue, calligraphy, epistolography, etiquette and protocol. I appointed Mir Jamal al-Din Astarabadi and Mir Qiwam al-Din naqīb-i Isfahani as *ṣadr*;[17] seeing as it is a high office they should cooperate. It is a great office, and is concerned with large sums that need to reach their intended recipients.[18] I personally used to obtain information every day about income and expenditure, lest – God forbid – the least deficit appeared, which is something that deserves punishment by me and painful chastisement by God. Jalal al-Din Muhammad[19] was punished on account of wrongdoings he committed, and in the end was burned to death. In the place where he was burned, this verse was recited:

14 Tahmasp here glosses over the reality that Köpek Sultan, leader of the Ustajlu, was Div Sultan's opponent. Although for a few months in 931/1524–5 Div Sultan, Köpek Sultan and Chuha Sultan governed as a triumvirate, it seems in practice Köpek Sultan was excluded from important decisions. Savory, 'Principal Offices during the Reign of Tahmasp', 67.
15 Chayan Sultan had been *amīr al-umarā'* for Shah Isma'il, and had died in 1523, shortly before Shah Isma'il.
16 There were repeated allegations that the Sayfi sayyids of Qazvin, who claimed descent from the Prophet's grandson Hasan, were crypto-Sunnis; see Dickson, 'Sháh Tahmásp', 192; also Membré, *Mission*, 74–5, where an account of Qadi-yi Jahan's career can be found. Qadi-yi Jahan (1483–1533) had served Isma'il as an administrator, and had been vizier to Tahmasp before his accession to the throne; he served Tahmasp after his accession for fifteen years, and was affiliated with the Ustajlu faction, although not himself a Qizilbash.
17 Jamal al-Din Astarabadi had previously served as *ṣadr* under Shah Isma'il between 1514 and 1524: Colin Mitchell, 'The Sword and the Pen: Diplomacy in Early Safavid Iran, 1501–1555', PhD dissertation, University of Toronto, 2002, 192.
18 The *ṣadr* was in charge of religious affairs, including the administration of waqfs (pious endowments) which is referred to here. See Savory, 'Principal Offices during the Reign of Tahmasp', 79–83; Willem Floor, 'The *ṣadr* or Head of the Safavid Religious Administration, Judiciary and Endowments and Other Members of the Religious Institution', *Zeitschrift der Deutschen Morgenländischen Gesellschaft*, 150 (2000): 461–500.
19 Jalal al-Din Muhammad Tabrizi was what Savory describes as the 'bureaucratic vakil', that is, the head of the civilian administration; his death was actually at the instigation of Div Sultan, who aimed to concentrate power in his own hands. Savory, 'Principal

I bought a house on calamity street, and I caught fire; he who buys a house on calamity street, such is his reward.

Mawlana Adham Khiyarji Qazvini[20] was also executed. Winter quarters were established in Tabriz and I sent Chuha Sultan Tekellu to the appanage of Isfahan which I had given him.[21] After six months, Durmish Khan Shamlu, who was *lāla* of my brother Sam Mirza, died in Herat, and I appointed in his place his brother Husayn Khan who was my cousin on my father's side.[22]

In the Year of the Cock, 931 (1524–5), we went to the summer pastures of Sahand and Ujan, where we spent several days in relaxation and pleasure. Then news came of the Uzbek attack on Khurasan, whereupon we headed in that direction. When we entered Tabriz, we established our quarters in the Garden of Halfan,[23] and, gathering the commanders round, took council. Div Sultan, who had precedence over Köpek Sultan as *amīr al-umarā'*, advocated repelling the Uzbeks, on condition that the commanders of Iraq and Fars joined him in the summer pastures of Larijan, on the border of Tabaristan. I gave orders to him to the effect that Chuha Sultan Tekellu, the governor of Isfahan, 'Ali Sultan Zulqadar, the viceroy of Shiraz, Qaraja Sultan Tekellu, the governor of Hamadan, and Burun Sultan Tekellu, the governor of Mashhad, should rendezvous with him in the said summer pasture to repel the Uzbeks from Khurasan. When that contingent assembled, after deterring the Uzbek advance, they resolved to repel the Ustajlu and returned without having gone to

---

Offices during the Reign of Tahmasp', 72. Mitchell ('Sword and the Pen', 192) suggests the removal of Jalal al-Din Muhammad was intended as a 'hostile message' to the Persian elites who dominated the Safavid bureaucracy.

20 He was the personal *vakīl* (deputy, agent) of Jalal al-Din Muhammad. See Mitchell, 'Sword and the Pen', 192.
21 Chuha was the leader of the Tekellu tribe.
22 Husayn Khan's mother was Isma'il's sister. He was eventually implicated in a plot to poison Tahmasp, and was executed. See Savory, 'Principal Offices during the Reign of Tahmasp', 272–4, 280–1; on Herat in this period, see Mitchell, 'Custodial Politics and Princely Governance', 86–93.
23 On the garden of this name, see Leyla Yıldız, *Safevi Döneminde Tebrîz: Kentsel Mekânda Dönüşüm Süreçleri (1501–1736)* (Ankara, 2021), 222, 268.

Khurasan. When this news reached us, Köpek Sultan, believing that the matter would better be settled by diplomacy, received them with honour in Turkman-Kandi. Together, they came to us when we were at Charandab, outside Tabriz. After they had done homage, the very same day, on the excuse of putting down civil unrest, they executed Qaraja Beg Ustajlu and Narin Beg Qajar, and seized Qadi-yi Jahan and sent him to the castle of Lori.[24] They gave[25] the vizierate to Mir Ja'far Savaji,[26] who was attached to Div Sultan's faction. When Köpek Sultan saw what they were up to, he headed to his own appanage,[27] and Chuha Sultan was given the title of Rukn-i Saltana.[28]

In this year, Amir Jamal al-Din Sadr and Mir Hasan Razavi departed this life for the eternal abode; the chronogram for their death is 'may they enter heaven peacefully and safely' (*udkhulūhā bi-salām āminīn*). When Durmish Khan Shamlu, Sam Mirza's tutor, died in Herat, and I appointed in his place his brother Husayn Khan b. 'Abdi Beg Shamlu, his excellency Khwaja Habiballah Savaji who had been Durmish Khan's vizier,[29] his two sons and other notables such as Mirza Qasim Miraki, totalling around seventy people, were killed by the Shamlu tribe and Ahmad Sultan Afshar.[30] Ahmad Gurgani Isfahani replaced

---

24 Lori in Armenia was the furthest frontier of the Safavid realm, and noted for its impressive fortress. See Membré, *Mission*, 17, 74. Apparently the real reason was that Qadi-yi Jahan was supported by the Ustajlu, with whom Div Sultan was fighting. Still, he was subsequently reappointed by Tahmasp in 1535–6. See Savory, 'Principal Offices during the Reign of Tahmasp', 73.

25 As noted by Parsadust, *Shah Tahmasp*, 47, this verb suggests Tahmasp was not involved in the appointment – one of the few, albeit indirect, acknowledgements of his relative powerlessness at this point.

26 On him, see Parsadust, *Shah Tahmasp*, 37, 642.

27 Other sources indicate that Köpek Sultan was essentially forced to retreat to his appanage by Div Sultan and Chuha Sultan; see Savory, 'Principal Offices during the Reign of Tahmasp', 68.

28 The title Rukn-i Saltana ('Pillar of the Sultanate') was reserved for the *qūrchī-bāshī*, the commander of the royal guard. See Vladimir Minorsky, *Tadhkirat al-Mulūk: A Manual of Safavid Administration (circa 1137/1725)* (London, 1943), 46.

29 Habiballah Savaji was member of family that had been prominent in Aqquyunlu administration. Mitchell, 'Sword and the Pen', 90.

30 The text here in all manuscripts I have seen is evidently a mess. The manuscripts read: 'Habiballah Savaji, who was Durmish Khan's vizier, seized the opportunity and killed the Khwaja Sahib along with his two sons and other notables such as Mirza

him.³¹ I was patient with these developments to see what God's will was, for at that time, 'Ali Sultan Zulqadar, the governor of Shiraz, died in Tabriz; his troops and appanage had been allocated to his nephew, Murad Sultan, but as this did not take effect, they were assigned to Hamza Sultan Chemeshlu Zulqadar.

In the Year of the Dog, 932 (1525–6), Köpek Sultan Ustajlu, whose appanage had been broken up in his absence,³² came from the direction of Khalkhal to Sultaniyya at the beginning of the month of Rajab seeking to confront the Rumlu and Tekellu tribes. He was joined by some of the Ustajlu amirs like Qilij Khan b. Muhammad Khan and Niqta Beg Temeshlu, the nephew of the former chief of the royal guard (*qūrchī-bāshī*) Saru-pira, Bedir Beg the current chief of the royal guard (*qūrchī-bāshī*)³³ and Kurdi Beg, and they made for the royal encampment. They started to fight on the morning of Sunday, 14 Sha'ban (26 May 1526), in Hashtad Juft, which the Turks call Saksanjak.³⁴ Meanwhile, Qaraja Sultan Tekellu arrived from Hamadan, and was immediately killed. Burun Sultan Tekellu was also killed, but the royal guards (*qūrchīs*) together with the Rumlu and Tekellu amirs prevailed. The Ustajlu amirs fled to Abhar, but the

Qasim Miraki, totalling around seventy people. This venture was undertaken by the Shamlu tribe and Ahmad Sultan Afshar.' Seemingly a definite object marker -*rā* has been displaced after Habiballah Savaji, making nonsense of the text. It is clear from all other sources that Habiballah was the victim rather than the perpetrator, and thus the text translated reflects what it must originally have been. On the murder of Habiballah, see Dickson, 'Sháh Tahmásp', 73–7; Szuppe, *Entre Timourides, Uzbeks et Safavides*, 93–7.

31 All manuscripts consulted give his name thus; however, he is better known as Ahmad Beg Nur Kamal, in which form he is mentioned elsewhere in the *Memoirs*.
32 As so often, Tahmasp's account casts a veil over events explained more fully by other chroniclers. Hasan Rumlu (*Ahsan al-Tawarikh*, II, 1142–3; trans. Setton, *Chronicle*, 94) tells us that Köpek Sultan had been sent to wage jihad on the Christians of Georgia, and in his absence Div Sultan confiscated his estates. Evidently, Tahmasp wishes to obscure his own impotence during the interregnum.
33 For the meaning of the term *qūrchī* in this period see Masashi Haneda, 'The Evolution of the Safavid Royal Guard', *Iranian Studies* 22, No. 2/3 (1989): 59–60, 67–8, 70. Saru-pira Ustajlu had been *qūrchī-bāshī* under Shah Isma'il in 1512; for Bedir Beg, Tahmasp's current *qūrchī-bāshī*, see ibid., 70, n. 58.
34 Other sources make it clear that Shah Tahmasp was present in person at the fighting at Saksanjak outside Sultaniyya. According to Parsadust (*Shah Tahmasp*, 37–8), Köpek Sultan's revolt represented the first time in Safavid history that a Qizilbash amir openly rebelled against the shah.

Tekellu attacked them there, so they were forced to go to Tarum, to seek the intervention of Muzaffar Sultan Gilani, ruler of Rasht.³⁵ At the same time, 'Abdallah Khan Ustajlu the son of Qara Khan, the nephew of Muhammad Khan,³⁶ released Qadi-yi Jahan from the castle of Lori and sent him to us and openly revolted against the Rumlu and Tekellu. Ahmad Sultan Sufioghli Ustajlu, the governor of Kirman, joined them. Two more great battles between these tribes and Ustajlu took place in the appanage of Kharzavil. Many of the infantry who had come from Gilan to help were killed, and the Ustajlu and Gilanis suffered a great defeat. I was in Qazvin when the news of the victory reached me. They took so many heads from the killed soldiers that they built a tower in Qazvin out of them. The survivors retreated to Rasht, and Ahmad Sultan and the rest went to Rayy and Khwar. The occasion of this victory coincided with the first time winter quarters were established in Qazvin.

In this year, there was also the affair of Mir Shahi b. 'Abd al-Karim b. 'Abdallah, one of the Qiwami, Mar'ashi sayyids who for one generation after another have been the rulers of Mazandaran.³⁷ He was the grandson of the Amir Qiwam al-Din known as Mir Buzurg al-Mar'ashi who died in Muharram 731 (October 1330) and was buried in Amol. These people are sayyids of authentic pedigree, as Mir Qiwam al-Din was the son of sayyid Sadiq b. sayyid Abi Sadduq 'Abdallah b. sayyid Hashim b. Sayyid 'Ali b. Sayyid Abu Muhammad b. Sayyid Hasan b. 'Ali Mar'ashi b. Sayyid 'Abdallah

---

35 Muzaffar Sultan was the title of Amir Dubbaj, who was in fact independent ruler of Gilan, which was only incorporated fully into the Safavid state in 1592. Muzaffar Sultan/Dubbaj had been an unreliable vassal of Shah Isma'il, and was also corresponding with the Ottomans, doubtless in the hope of maintaining his independence. Shah Tahmasp's description of him as the 'ruler of Rasht' (*ḥākim*, which also is commonly used for governor) suggests that was an attempt to play down his independent status. See Manouchehr Kasheff, 'Gīlān. v. History under the Safavids', *Encyclopaedia Iranica*, X/6, 635–42.
36 Muhammad Khan (d. 1514), brother of 'Abdallah's father Qara Khan, was a senior Qizilbash commander killed at Chaldiran.
37 This local dynasty, similar in origins to the Safavids and closely allied to them, were promoted by Tahmasp as part of his programme of Shiitization. On them, see Mitchell,

b. Sayyid Muhammad al-Akbar b. al-Husayn al-Asghar b. Imam ʻAli b. al-Husayn Zayn al-ʻAbidin, peace be upon him, and Qiwam al-Din had several sons, among them Sayyid Nasir al-Din the governor of Amol, Sayyid Fakhr al-Din, the chief of part of Rustamdar province, and Sayyid Kamal, governor of Sari, who succeeded their great ancestor in the rule of the appanage of Mazandaran. Mir Shahi sent me many presents when I was in Qazvin, and complained about Agha Muhammad Ruzafzun[38] and his own cousins, who had promised to collect whatever surplus revenue of Mazandaran there was and remit it to our court. I assigned the task of collecting it to Burun Sultan, grandson of ʻAli Khan Beg Tekellu, and ordered that Mir Shahi's cousins, Mir ʻAbdallah and Sayyid Zayn al-ʻAbidin, be brought before us, and that Agha Muhammad Ruzafzun should not be allowed to interfere in the affairs of Mazandaran. On the night of Friday 5 Shawwal 932 (15 July 1526), I awarded Mir Shahi the title of Khan and magnificent robes of honour, and sent him off to that province accompanied by ʻAli Khan Beg Tekellu. After fourteen[ii] months, they brought Mir ʻAbdallah and Sayyid Zayn al-ʻAbidin to Qazvin. I made Mir ʻAbdallah share office with Mir Murad Khan. As his performance was unsatisfactory, he was dismissed and, taking to opium,[iii] he died in Rabiʻ II 938 (November–December 1531). He was an extremely heavy drinker and bloodthirsty, but his brother, Zayn al-ʻAbidin, was a God-fearing and scholarly man, whom I appointed to administer the Noble, Honourable Imamzada of Husayn b. Sultan ʻAli b. Musa al-Riza (peace be upon him) along with making him

---

Practice of Politics, 107–10; Jean Calmard, 'Une famille des sādāt dans l'histoire d'Iran: les Marʻaši', *Oriente Moderno* 18, No. 79 (1999): 413–28.

38 The Ruzafzun family were condottieri who were related to the Marʻashi sayyids, but competed for power with them in Mazandaran. Agha Muhammad's father, Agha Rustam, had evinced pro-Shaybanid sentiments, and Agha Muhammad had been locked up by Shah Ismail. However, in 1526 Agha Muhammad Ruzafzun was released from the high security prison of Alinjaq in Nakhchivan, and seized control of his ancestral lands again. See Khurshah, *Tarikh-i Ilchi*, 90.

naqīb al-ashrāf.[39] Now I desire to send him as an ambassador to the sultan in Istanbul, as he is a scholarly and pious man.

In the Year of the Pig 933 (1526–7), news arrived of trouble with the Uzbeks and the siege of Herat. I decided to go to Khurasan in person, but news arrived in Savuj Bulagh that Akhi Sultan Tekellu and Mari Sultan Shamlu had been killed in battle with 'Ubayd the Uzbek.[40] Other reports came from Azerbaijan that the Ustajlu amirs had gone from Rasht to Ardabil. Badinjan Sultan Rumlu, who was governor there, was killed by Ahmad Aqa Chavushlu,[iv] Köpek Sultan's muster-master (*tuvāchī*).[41] From there they had headed to Chukhur-i Sa'd where Div Sultan's headquarters was located.[42] When this news reached Div Sultan and Chuha Sultan on Friday 29 Ramadan (29 June 1527) at Arpa-Chai in Nakhchivan, they fought back and landed a defeat on the Ustajlu; Köpek Sultan was killed, and Muhammadi Beg, the son of Bahram Beg Qaramanlu, was taken prisoner and executed on 26 Shawwal (26 July 1527).[43] When I heard these reports, I returned to Qazvin, and when the secret agents came, this news was confirmed. Darvish Beg and Hamza Beg Hajlu-yi Turkman, the chamberlain

---

39 The *naqīb al-ashrāf* was the chief representative of descendants of the Prophet and acted as an intermediary between them and the government. The Imamzada (shrine complex) of Husayn, son of the Eighth Imam al-Riza, was promoted by Tahmasp in Qazvin as a pilgrimage centre, and it is probably this institution which is meant. However, other Imamzadas of Husayn from the period, for example at Varamin, also exist.

40 'Ubayd allah Khan, the Shaybanid ruler. Savuj Bulagh was a staging post outside Rayy. See Dickson, 'Sháh Tahmásp', 93. There was another place of this name in Azerbaijan, the present day Mahabad, but it seems clear from the context that Tahmasp was not in Azerbaijan at this time.

41 On the office of *tuvāchī* see Willem Floor, *Safavid Government Institutions* (Costa Mesa, 2001), 242–3; he was in charge of the mobilization and review of troops.

42 The Ustajlu had realized that the absence of Tekellu and Rumlu rivals on campaign in Khurasan had left their territories in Azerbaijan and Chukur-i Sa'd (the region around modern Yerevan) undefended, so decided to attack. Shah Tahmasp was apparently abandoned as the Tekellu and Rumlu commanders hurried north to deal with the invasion, meaning the campaign against the Uzbeks had to be aborted. However, the resulting victory of the Rumlu and Tekellu marked the end of Ustajlu hegemony. See Dickson, 'Sháh Tahmásp', 93–4.

43 As so often, Tahmasp obscures the really important event that took place on 26 Shawwal, the killing of Div Sultan, see further note 45.

(*īshīk-āqāsī*)⁴⁴ who had turned against the court, quarrelled with each other and both were killed. In truth, these events were a great God-given victory.

At this time, I properly became shah in Qazvin, and I somehow got rid of all of the rebels that were everywhere.⁴⁵ On Friday 12 Zu'l-Hijja (9 September 1527), at an auspicious hour, I entered my father's Royal Precinct (*dawlatkhāna*)⁴⁶ at Qazvin, and ordered that all the amirs, cavalrymen, notables and courtiers should attend. Firstly, I dealt with the affair of Akhi Sultan Tekellu and Damri Sultan Shamlu who had been killed fighting with 'Ubayd the Uzbek, having departed on campaign without my approval.⁴⁷ They desired to be brave and glorious, not realizing that the outcome does not depend on the effort alone.

> Oh you who striven to pursue fortune, fortune and good luck is not acquired by knowledge
>
> Whoever possesses rank, wealth and retinue does so only by the support of the heavens.

---

44 The *īshīk-aqāsī* was in principle subordinate to the *īshīk-aqāsī-bāshī* (grand chamberlain), but it seems the latter office is meant.

45 Again Tahmasp is somewhat economical with the facts. According to other sources, after the victory over Köpek Sultan, Chuha Sultan persuaded Tahmasp that Div Sultan needed to be disposed of as the author of the discord among the various Qizilbash tribes. Tahmasp in person shot Div Sultan in the chest as the latter entered his tent, and he was then finished off by the royal guards. However, for the next three years, Chuha rather than Tahmasp became the dominant force. See Savory, 'Principal Offices during the Reign of Shah Tahmasp', 68; Aldous, 'Qizilbāsh and Their Shah', 751.

46 The *dawlatkhāna* refers to the entire complex of palaces, workshops, administrative buildings, kitchens, gardens and so on; the later *dawlatkhāna* at Isfahan is partially preserved, and there were in Tahmasp's time *dawlatkhāna*s at both Tabriz and Qazvin. See Sussan Babaei, *Isfahan and Its Palaces: Statecraft, Shi'ism and the Architecture of Conviviality in Early Modern Iran* (Edinburgh, 2008), 119–20. However, on occasion it seems the term *dawlatkhāna* was used to refer to an independent building adjacent to the royal palace, although exactly what its function was is unclear. See Yıldız, *Safevi Döneminde Tebriz*, 495–7, 728–30.

47 The identification of these Qizilbash amirs is complicated by confusion in the sources over the territories they governed and in some instances their tribal affiliation. Akhi Sultan was probably Tekellu governor of Qazvin although occasionally he is also described as a Zulqadar governor of Bistam. Damri Sultan was governor of Damghan. See Dickson, 'Shāh Tahmāsp', 102.

I gave Akhi Sultan Tekellu's position and appanage in Qazvin to Muhammad Beg Sharaf al-Din Oghli Tekellu,[48] and I bestowed on him the honorific Muhammad Sultan. I gave Damri Sultan's position to Muhammad Beg Rumlu, who had been one of his officers. Likewise, I appointed as governor of every province and region competent individuals. At this time the Chief Equerry's messenger[49] came and I asked him for news. He said that Zaynal Khan, the governor of Astarabad, Chekirge Sultan Shamlu, the lord of Sabzavar, and Mustafa Sultan, the fiefholder (*tiyūldār*)[50] of Sava had fought a battle at Firuzkuh[51] with Zaynash Bahadur,[52] the Uzbek, in which all three had been killed.[53] The Uzbeks prevailed completely.

I made the necessary preparations, and I headed to Khurasan with a well-equipped army at the beginning of the Year of the Rat 934 (1527–8). At Tehran, news reached me concerning Zulfiqar Beg, son of ʿAli Beg, who was known as Nukhud Sultan and at that time was

---

48 Muhammad Beg (or Khan) Sharaf Oghli (d. 1557) was the leading Tekellu amir, governor successively of Qazvin, Baghdad and Herat, and tutor (*lāla*) to prince Sultan Muhammad (the future Shah Muhammad Khudabanda). For his career, see Maria Szuppe, 'Kinship Ties between the Safavids and Qizilbash Amirs in Late Sixteenth-Century Iran: A Case Study of the Political Career of Members of the Sharaf al-Din Oghli Tekelu Family', in Charles Melville (ed.), *Safavid Persia: The History and Politics of an Islamic Society* (London, 1996), 79–104, esp. 81–2.
49 *Āqā-yi jilawdār*, lit 'the holder of the reign'; the *jilawdārs* were grooms who rode before their masters, under the command of the *amīr-ākhur-bāshī-yi jilaw*, who had overall responsibility for the royal stables. The *Āqa-yi jilaw* is presumably equivalent to the later attested *jilawdār-bāshī*, who was the senior deputy of the *amīr-ākhur-bāshī-yi jilaw* . For the office, see Minorsky, *Tadhkirat al-Muluk*, 52, 120.
50 *Tiyūldar* is translated as fiefholder here, but the position was in theory not hereditary; *tiyūls* ('fiefs') were granted only for a set period of time. However, in practice, *tiyūldārs* tried to convert their holdings into permanent and hereditary holdings, over which they enjoyed more rights than simply the collection of taxes and which had been the original purpose of the *tiyūl*. See Minorsky, *Tadhkirat al-Muluk*, 27–9.
51 Firuzkuh near Mt Damavand; the battle took place on 21 Shaʿban 934/11 May 1528. See Parsadust, *Shah Tahmasp*, 64, and Dickson, 'Sháh Tahmásp', 116–17.
52 Zaynash Bahadur was the Uzbek governor of Astarabad. ʿUbaydallah Khan had succeeded in wresting Astarabad from its Safavid governor, Zaynal Khan. See Parsadust, *Shah Tahmasp*, 64–6.
53 All three amirs were Shamlu, and it seems that in fact the court had ordered them to confront the Uzbeks. See Dickson, 'Sháh Tahmásp', 116–17.

governor of the Kalhor Kurds.[54] He had attacked his uncle Ibrahim Khan Mawsillu who had been assigned the troops of Amir Khan and appointed governor of Baghdad and Arab Iraq,[55] and at that moment was in the summer pasture of Mahi-Dasht.[56] Zulfiqar Beg executed his uncle and most of his cousins in Baghdad, killing, most remarkably, Amir Khan's son Merjumek Sultan and becoming governor of the entirety of Arab Iraq. I said, 'Now is not the time; whatever God wills shall be. This was a victory indeed, and Baghdad can be reckoned as ours.'[57] I did not allow myself to be preoccupied by other things, but instead headed off to repel the Uzbeks. Battle took place outside Jam.[58] Firstly, the Uzbeks launched an assault on the Qizilbash. Ya'qub Sultan Qajar, Ulama Sultan Tekellu and other amirs on the right flank were defeated and fled. The Uzbeks started looting. I put my trust in God and sought the intercession of the love of the inviolable imams, the blessings of God upon them all, and I advanced a few paces when, by chance, one of our *qūrchī*s reached 'Ubayd[59] and struck him with a sword. He moved on and got involved in fighting with someone else, and Qilij Bahadur[60] and his other bodyguards carried the wounded

---

54 The Kalhor were the dominant Kurdish tribe in Kermanshah.
55 Amir Khan Mawsillu was the Turkmen governor of Diyarbakir who handed that city over to Shah Isma'il without a fight. He subsequently became a close ally of Shah Isma'il and *lālā* (tutor) to Tahmasp. Ibrahim Khan Mawsillu was his younger brother, who inherited leadership of the Mawsillu tribe on his death (Parsadust, *Shah Tahmasp* 24–5, 503–4). Arab Iraq roughly corresponds to the modern state of Iraq, and was so called to distinguish it from 'Iraq-i 'Ajam 'Persian Iraq', which refers to the west of Iran, in particular the region around Isfahan.
56 Mahi-Dasht is in the region of Kermanshah.
57 In reality, Tahmasp did hesitate over whether to proceed to Khurasan, fearing – rightly – that the disturbances in Baghdad were more than simply a local intra-Qizilbash dispute, but that the Ottomans might open a second front against him there. In fact, Zulfiqar was indeed in communication with the Ottomans, as Ottoman sources reveal. See Dickson, 'Sháh Tahmásp', 119–22, 142–3.
58 The Battle of Jam on 10 Muharram 935/24 September 1528 was one of the major battles in the Shaybanid-Safavid war over Khurasan, and is described in numerous other sources. For an evaluation of the battle, see Dickson, 'Sháh Tahmásp', 127–41; Aldous, 'Qizilbāsh and Their Shah', 752–3.
59 'Ubaydallah Uzbek Khan.
60 One of 'Ubaydallah's bodyguards.

'Ubayd away. When Küchkünji Khan and Jani Khan Beg[61] found out about this they fled in defeat, not stopping till they reached Marv. The men of our army who had fled rejoined us that day. We spent the night in that desert, not knowing what had happened to 'Ubayd the Uzbek. It occurred to me it might have been a trick or feint.

That night I saw in a dream my lord and master, the Commander of the Faithful, imam of the pious, King of the faith, God's victorious lion, 'Ali b. Abi Talib, peace be upon him. He smiled at me, saying 'You will win a great victory, praise be to God.' When morning dawned, I realized that the Uzbeks had been defeated and had fled. We followed them as far as Nishapur, killing every man of their army there was left, so that Khurasan was cleansed of the foul pollution of the Uzbeks' existence and the filth of their troops. I entered Nishapur but did not halt on account of the news about Baghdad, and returned to Qazvin. I ordered my troops to take up winter quarters in Qum, and in Qazvin I made preparations to campaign in Arab Iraq. That winter, all the necessities were prepared, and I appointed suitable people to some of the positions that were currently vacant. The position of *ṣadr* was shared between Mir Ni'matallah Hilli, who claimed to be a *mujtahid*, and Mir Qiwam al-Din Husayn naqīb-i Isfahani.[62]

---

61 Whereas 'Ubaydallah was the Shaybanid ruler of Bukhara, his cousin Küchkünji Khan was ruler of Samarqand (r. 1511–33), and until his death, was the senior member of the family. Janibeg ruled Karmina and Miyankal (the area between Samarqand and Bukhara). See Dickson, 'Sháh Tahmásp', 35–6.
62 Mir Ni'matallah Hilli was a Lebanese scholar who had previously migrated to Iraq, and a pupil of the famous scholar Muhaqqiq-i Karaki, with whom he subsequently fell out (Parsadust, *Shah Tahmasp*, 623, 646). Tahmasp's comment that 'he claimed to be mujtahid' (*da'vī-yi ijtihad mīkard*) may seem somewhat strange given that Shiite clerics are generally accepted to be able to exercise ijtihad. However, it may reflect the fact that subsequently when Karaki was granted the title of Mujtahid al-Zamān (Mujtahid of the Age) by Tahmasp, Ni'matallah Hilli fell from favour and was exiled from court. Indeed, Ni'matallah's feud with his former teacher seems to have started precisely because of his claims to be a mujtahid (Parsadust, *Shah Tahmasp*, 646; Savory, 'Principal Offices during the Reign of Tahmasp', 82). It may also reflect attitudes in the Safavid court in the 1560s, when the *Memoirs* were compiled. Another influential émigré cleric, Husayn b. 'Abd al-Samad al-Harithi (d. 1576), who exerted considerable influence over Shah Tahmasp from 1548, was concerned to protect society from false mujtahids, and argued

At an auspicious hour of the Year of the Ox, 935 (1528–9), we set off for Baghdad from Qazvin. The weather was very hot, and the siege drew on and on, the conquest of the citadel being extremely difficult. By God's grace and the intercession of the immaculate imams, God's blessings be upon them, victory was achieved. As it happened, 'Ali Beg Begtashoghli, the grandson of Sufi Khalil Mawsillu,[63] and his brother Ahmad Beg, overcame Zulfiqar Beg, killed him and brought his head before me on Thursday 3 Shawwal 935 (10 June 1529).[64] In this way, Baghdad was conquered.

I bestowed on Muhammad Sultan Sharaf al-Din 'Ali Tekellu the honorific of Muhammad Khan and made him governor of Baghdad. I put in order the citadel's affairs, its garrison, arsenal and provisions. I informed myself about everything, entrusting nothing to others, and then returned to Persian Iraq. In the vicinity of Farsijin near Abhar, Mir Qiwam al-Din Husayn died. When we reached Qazvin, I gave his position to Mir Ghiyath al-Din Mansur Shirazi,[65] and made him share it with Amir Ni'matallah Hilli. After the latter's death, he became *ṣadr*.[66]

In the Year of the Tiger 936 (1529–30), the remainder of the Ustajlu amirs who were in Gilan, such as Bedir Khan, Mentesha Sultan[67]

---

that the shah was not qualified to determine who a true mujtahid was. See Abisaab, *Converting Persia*, 32–7.

63 Sufi Khalil Mawsillu (d. 1491) was one of the leading amirs of the Aqquyunlu state, and effective ruler of Arab and Persian Iraq and Fars. After his death, many of the Mawsillu joined the Safavid cause.

64 'Ali Beg and Ahmad Beg were on the staff (*mulāzim*) of Zulfiqar (see Parsadust, *Shah Tahmasp*, 505). 'Ali Beg's name Begtashoghli refers to his descent from his great-grandfather Begtash, Sufi Khalil's father.

65 Mir Ghiyath al-Din Mansur Dashtaki Shirazi (1462–1541), better known as a prominent philosopher. On him, see Andrew Newman, 'Daštaki, Ġiāṯ al-Din', *Encyclopaedia Iranica*, VII/1, 100–2.

66 Tahmasp is somewhat disingenuous. In fact, Ni'matallah Hilli was dismissed for challenging the position of Tahmasp's favoured jurist, 'Ali Karaki (d. 1533) that Friday prayer was permissible during the occultation of the imam, as well as conspiring to have Karaki removed, to the extent that he was implicated in forging a letter attributing to Karaki that contained various slurs against Shah Tahmasp. Ni'matallah Hilli was thus exiled to Baghdad, and shortly afterwards, in 938/1531–2, Ghiyath al-Din was himself dismissed after disagreeing with Karaki. See Newman, 'Daštaki'; Rula Jurdi Abisaab, 'Karaki', *Encyclopaedia Iranica*, XV/5, 544–7.

67 Mentesha Sultan (d. 1545), a senior Ustajlu amir who was variously governor of Qazvin and Mashhad. On him, see Parsadust, *Shah Tahmasp*, 38, 90, 200; Membré, *Mission*, 73.

and Hamzah Sultan, the brother of Chayan Sultan, came to Qazvin to offer obeisance.[68] I assigned each one an appanage, and told them that 'The days you previously witnessed have gone, now know how you should behave. For I have realized for sure that God grants rule, and the amirs' power, strength and might bring nothing but harm to everyone. Therefore, in this respect preserving divine favour and striving to improve the lot of the weak, the poor and the people is more conducive to peace of mind.'

In order to repel the Uzbeks who had mustered in Marv, we set off in that direction.[69] Because Sam Mirza and Husayn Khan had previously abandoned Herat and gone to Fars by way of Sistan,[70] I appointed Bahram Mirza[71] as governor of Herat, and had made Ghazi Beg, son of Cherken Hasan Tekellu, *lāla* to the prince.[72] We came to Isfahan via the desert route through Tabas and Yazd and established winter quarters there. When the Uzbeks had heard that we were coming, they had abandoned Marv[v] and fled to Transoxiana.

At that time, scholarly debates were held between the *Mujtahid al-Zamān* Shaykh 'Ali 'Abd al-'Ali (Muhaqqiq-i Karaki) and Mir Ghiyath Mansur al-Din. Although the *Mujtahid al-Zamān* emerged victorious, they did not recognize him as mujtahid and persisted in disobedience.[73] I chose the side of right, and confirmed him as supreme mujtahid.

---

68 It seems the real reason Tahmasp restored these Ustajlu amirs to favour was to counter Chuha Sultan's refusal to allow a further campaign against the Uzbeks, who had in the meantime again seized Herat. See Dickson, 'Sháh Tahmásp', 177–8.
69 In fact, while Tahmasp was distracted with the conquest of Baghdad, the Uzbeks had seized Herat. It seems that Chuha Sultan vetoed the shah from making any attempt to relieve the city, owing to his rivalry with Herat's governor, Husayn Khan, who he hoped would fall into Uzbek hands. See Dickson, 'Sháh Tahmásp', 152–5.
70 Husayn Khan Shamlu was guardian of Sam Mirza, Tahmasp's brother, and governor of Herat; he was forced to abandon it to Uzbek because of Chuha's failure to come to his aid. Savory, 'Principal Offices during the Reign of Tahmasp', 70.
71 Tahmasp's younger brother.
72 Ghazi Beg was also governor (*amīr al-umarā'*) of Khurasan; see Parsadust, *Shah Tahmasp*, 85; Dickson, 'Sháh Tahmásp', 281.
73 'Ali Karaki (d. 1533) was a leading Twelver cleric who had been influential under Shah Isma'il, and was especially favoured by Tahmasp who, a few years later in 1532, granted

In the Year of the Rabbit, 937 (1530–31), was the affair of Husayn Khan and Sam Mirza, who had wilfully abandoned Herat and gone to Shiraz.[74] The amirs interceded for them at the winter quarters of Ganduman near Isfahan, bringing them to the royal audience place with their troops and retinue. Sam Mirza touched the ground with his forehead several times before coming to offer obeisance. He was extremely ashamed. I gave him hope of forgiveness, and took him as my companion into the harem. There he saw the Begum,[75] who was like a mother to him,[76] and his sisters were delighted to see him. This enraged Husayn Khan,[77] who one morning came fully armed with his retinue and troops into the Royal Precinct (*dawlatkhāna*) and started an enormous commotion. The Zulqadar and Shamlu *qūrchī*s who were in the royal bodyguard (*keshik*) fought bravely. The survivors among Husayn Khan's men fled with him to Fars by way of Isfahan.[78]

---

him the titles of *nā'ib al-imām wa-khātam al-mujtahidīn* (deputy of the imam and seal of the Mujtahids). In addition to the role alluded to in the title he is referred to here, *mujtahid al-zamān* (Mujtahid of the Age), Karaki played a crucial role in disseminating and institutionalizing Shiism in the Safavid domains, for example by sending prayer leaders to towns and villages, but was strongly opposed by rival factions at court. The disagreements between him and Ghiyath al-Din Dashtaki ostensibly revolved around questions such as the permissibility of prostration before the ruler and the direction of the qibla, and the latter was the topic of the court debate to which Tahmasp alludes here. In fact, the toxicity of these debates was exacerbated by personal factors, especially the dismissal of Ni'matallah Hilli. See further Abisaab, 'Karaki'; Newman, 'Myth of Clerical Migration', esp. 96–104, and Arjomand, *Shadow of God*, 132–7, where this passage of the *Memoirs* is discussed.

74 In fact, Dickson argues, Husayn Khan was obliged to surrender Herat owing to the total lack of support he received from the Safavid court, as a result of Chuha's machinations against him. See Dickson, 'Sháh Tahmásp', 155.

75 Parsadust, *Shah Tahmasp*, 260, n. 164, argues that the Begum of the *Memoirs* is to be identified with Shah Tahmasp's mother Tajlu Begum (also known as Tajlu Khanum), who exerted a great influence over him. She was eventually exiled to Shiraz in 1540 for conspiring to put her other son, Bahram Mirza, on the throne, dying shortly afterwards.

76 Sam Mirza was Tahmasp's half-brother, his mother being a Georgian princess.

77 As noted by Aldous ('Qizilbāsh and Their Shah', 753), Husayn Khan's anger derived from the fact that the prince was his trump card – losing possession of Sam Mirza owing to his decision to stay in the harem severely weakened the Shamlu's already weak hand, having been kicked out of Khurasan by the invading Uzbeks.

78 It is interesting that Tahmasp specifies that Shamlu amirs in the *keshik* fought against Husayn Khan's Shamlu contingent, suggesting that loyalty to the shah as members of his personal bodyguard trumped tribal affiliation.

Afterwards, when I had given Chuha Sultan's position to his eldest son Shah Qubad, I gave the latter's former position to his younger brother 'Ali Beg, and bestowed on both of them the honorific of 'Sultan'. The Ustajlu, Zulqadar and Afshar amirs, having long endured the dominance of the Tekellu, grew angry and secretly plotted to riot. Without my approval, the two sons of Chuha Sultan had killed two or three members of the Ustajlu, Zulqadar and Afshar, so the tribe of Tekellu as a whole, ready and armed, had gathered at the gate of the Royal Precinct.[79] I was greatly perturbed at this. I decreed that the Tekellu should be massacred; distinguished amirs from that tribe such as Pervane Beg, the *qūrchī-bāshī*, and Ibrahim Khalifa, the keeper of the royal seal (*muhrdād*), were killed, and the sons of the Tekellu amirs were brought to court (*dargāh*), bound one after the other and tied up. They were given a taste of the same medicine that they had made the Shamlu warriors taste a few days previously in the episode of Husayn Khan. The chronogram for this year (938/1531–2) was 'the Tekellu calamity'.[80] The survivors fled to Muhammad Khan Sharaf Oghli, the governor of Baghdad, who killed some of those who were a source of strife and evil, such as Qubad Sultan, son of Chuha Sultan, and Qudurmush Sultan, the instigators of the revolt. Because he was on our side,[81] Muhammad Khan sent their heads to court.

I sent a decree of conciliation to Fars for Husayn Khan Shamlu. He came to court, where I showed him favour. I gave the position of *amīr*

---

79 In reality, the disturbance seems to have been caused precisely the appointment of Shah Qubad, which was seen as entrenching Tekellu privilege by the other tribes. See Aldous, 'Qizilbāsh and Their Shah', 755.
80 *Āfat-i Tekellū*; this chronogram yields 938, although the 'Tekellu calamity' in fact began in the last month of the previous year, 937. For a discussion of this chronogram, see Dickson, 'Sháh Tahmásp', 198, n. 1. The 'Tekellu calamity' was so called not merely because the vicious intra-Qizilbash fighting affected the court, but also because it distracted the Safavids from confronting a renewed Uzbek invasion of Khurasan and an Ottoman threat.
81 Muhammad Khan Sharaf Oghli was a Tekellu amir and governor of Baghdad. When the Ottoman armies advanced on Iraq in 1535, unlike the other Tekellu in the city, he had remained loyal to Tahmasp at great personal hardship, although eventually was forced to surrender Baghdad to the Ottomans. See Parsadust, *Shah Tahmasp*, 164–6.

al-umarā' to him and 'Abdallah Khan Ustajlu.⁸² Because Husayn Khan detested Mir Ja'far Savaji, he requested that he be sacked; on account of his opinion, I sacked Mir Ja'far as vizier and appointed in his place Ahmad Beg Nur-i Kamal Isfahani.⁸³

When the Tekellu revolt had died down, I appointed the sons of leading chiefs of the tribes (*uymāq*) to high positions befitting their rank. I promoted some who were not yet amirs to the rank of amir, and the world become safe and peaceful.

In the Year of the Dragon, 938 (1531–2), was the affair of Ulama Tekellu.⁸⁴ In my royal father's time he had been aide-de-camp (*yasāvul*) and later was promoted to chamberlain (*īshīk-āqāsī*). I had given him the rank of amir, and in the Year of the Tiger [936/1529–30], when we were on the successful campaign in Khurasan, I had appointed him *amīr al-umarā'* of Azerbaijan. I decreed that he should send 300 men to campaign in Khurasan while remaining in Azerbaijan. At the time that the Tekellu revolt and fighting broke out, Ulama had gone to the capital, Tabriz, with the intention of seizing the city prefect (*dārūghā*).⁸⁵ Taking possession of the royal horses that were in that province, he seized the slave girls we had left in the care of the

---

82 'Abdallah Khan Ustajlu (d. 1564) had previously served in Durmish Khan's administration of Herat, and then that of Husayn Khan. He was also a cousin of Shah Tahmasp. See Dickson, 'Sháh Tahmásp', 201, Posch, *Osmanisch-safavidische Beziehungen*. Index, s.v.
83 In fact, this event marks the beginning of the three-year supremacy of the Shamlu, with Husayn Khan not even allowing Tahmasp any say in appointees. See Savory, 'Principal Offices during the Reign of Tahmasp', 70.
84 Ulama was the Tekellu governor of Azerbaijan, and a protégé of Chuha Sultan. However, he had originally been in the service of the Ottomans, but under Beyazid II (1481–1512), he had turned Qizilbash, joining the pro-Safavid rebellion of Şahkulu in Anatolia (1511–12). Safavid sources are silent about his earlier Ottoman affiliation. See Dickson, 'Sháh Tahmásp', 266; the Ottoman historian Celalzade calls him 'one of the family of amirs of Ardabil and the ruler of Azerbaijan (silsile-i Erdebil ümerasından Azerbaycan sultānı), while mentioning his role in Şahkulu's revolt; Mustafa Çelebi Celâlzâde, *Ṭabaḳātü'l-memâlik*, ed. P. Kappert (Wiesbaden, 1981), fol. 242b. The favour he was shown by the Safavids is shown by the fact that he was married to Tahmasp's foster-mother (*dāya*), see Sharaf al-Din Khan b. Shams al-Din Bidlisi, *Sharafnama*, ed. Vladimir Véliaminof-Zernof (St Peterburg, 1862), I, 419.
85 The *dārūghā* was the official in charge of public order. On this term, of Mongol origin, see Minorsky, *Tadhkirat al-Mulūk*, 142.

goldsmiths of Tabriz who were to make gold embroidered clothes for them. He shared them with his accomplices, and also took possession of our royal embroidered tent which was in the royal textile store (*farrāshkhāna*) of Tabriz. He arrested every one of the wealthy men in that region on some pretext, confiscating their assets, and then left Tabriz, accompanied by some Sarulu tribesmen who were well known as rank heretics.[86] Outrageously, in their licentiousness they share their women with one another. They acquired much wealth and many possessions, and increased greatly in number.

My ministers presented this news to me some days after it had been ascertained. I sent a contingent of brave warriors in search of him. En route, they held a council of war at which they decided to fall upon Ulama's camp by night without warning and retrieve the property and possessions that he had acquired by oppression and extortion. However, the villain found about the plot, and, leaving his camp by night, fled to Van. On the night when our warriors fell upon his camp, there was nothing there but some baggage,[vi] slave girls and servants. As his time was not yet up, he had got away, but the property and possessions that he had abandoned were seized, and a contingent set off to capture him. Basically, he was a deceitful and fraudulent man who was able to cheat everyone except the immaculate imams – God's blessings upon them. He fled from Van to the Ottomans. It is said that he became very intimate with Ibrahim Pasha, to the extent that Ibrahim Pasha confided his acute fear of prince Mustafa to him.[87]

---

86 The Sarulu were a Turkmen grouping, apparently a sub-tribe or clan of the Tekellu; allegations of such wife-sharing practices also occur in Ottoman documents dealing with Qizilbash groups. See Sümer, *Safevi Devleti'nin Kuruluşu ve Gelişmesinde*, 62, 80–1.

87 Ibrahim Pasha (d. 1536) was Süleyman's Grand Vizier. In 1534, he was put in charge of the Ottoman campaign against Iraq. In fact, Ottoman sources indicate that Süleyman's son Mustafa, who at this point was governor of Manisa, was reputed to have very close relations with Ibrahim Pasha, to the extent that these were a factor in the Grand Vizier's fall and execution in 1536, seemingly on accusations that he might help Mustafa seize the throne. See Feridun Emecen, 'İbrahim Paşa, Makbul', *Türkiye Diyanet Vakfı İslam Ansiklopedisi* (1988–2016), vol. 23, 333–5; Şerefettin Turan, 'Mustafa Çelebi', *Türkiye*

Ulama replied that 'The eastern provinces are empty, and most of the Qizilbash amirs are my allies. If you head there, I promise that I will subdue that territory, and you will be king of Azerbaijan, Iraq and Fars, sending tribute each year to his majesty the sultan.[88] Now give me Bitlis, and will I go ahead and win over the people who are my allies, and you follow on later. As his majesty the sultan would not contradict what Ibrahim Pasha says, if he disapproves in one case, he will make up for it by agreeing in another.'

Ibrahim Pasha was deceived by Ulama's speech, and gave him Bitlis and troops to accompany him, and sent him against Sharaf Beg the Kurd.[89] Sharaf Beg was unable to resist, and he came to us. Even though Habil Beg the *mihmāndār* was with his majesty the sultan,[90] having been sent by us as ambassador, troops were given to Ulama and he was sent off. After his majesty the sultan had travelled three stages towards the Franks,[91] Habil Beg was sent on his way with a letter asking for Sharaf Beg to be arrested and sent to the Ottoman court. Our amirs said, 'If his majesty the sultan was well-disposed towards us, he would not have granted Ulama an appanage in our region and sent him to confront us. Inciting our dependents against us and making them rebel against us is a hostile act.' They advised that another ambassador should be sent to ascertain whether his majesty the sultan had friendly intentions. I sent Husayn Khan Shamlu,

---

Diyanet Vakfı İslam Ansiklopedisi (1988–2016) vol 31, 290–2; Şahin, *Peerless among Princes*, 187.
88 The Ottoman sultan Süleyman is meant.
89 Sharaf Beg, grandfather of the famous historian of the Kurds who shared his name, ruled Bitlis as an Ottoman vassal between 1514 and 1532. On him, see J. -L. Bacqué-Grammont and C. Adle, 'Quatre lettres de Šeref Beg de Bitlîs (1516–1520). Études turco-safavides XI', *Der Islam* 63 (1986): 90–118. It appears that Ulama was granted Sharaf Beg's ancestral territories of Bitlis as his appanage, precipitating Sharaf Beg's defection to the Safavids. See Fahrettin Kırzıoğlu, *Osmanlılar'ın Kafkas-Elleri'ni Fethi (1451–1590)* (Ankara, 1998), 129–30; also Khurshah, *Tarikh-i Ilchi*, 112, where Tiflis should be corrected to read Bitlis.
90 The *mihmāndār* was the Safavid official responsible for incoming embassies.
91 The reference is to Süleyman's unsuccessful campaign against Vienna in 1532. See Şahin, *Peerless among Princes*, 155–7.

Mentesha Sultan, 'Abdallah Khan, Abul Aldi Aqa[92] and Hajji Lor, who had previously been deputy of Verdik[vii] Sultan and subsequently became the guardian of Isma'il Mirza,[93] with a letter saying that

> 'Ulama has fled from us to you. Send him in exchange for Sharaf Beg. Why should Ulama and Sharaf Beg be a cause of strife between kings of Islam?'

The Ottomans did not accept this argument, replying,

> 'Ulama has taken refuge with us, he cannot be handed over. Hand over Sharaf Beg, and if anyone else subsequently comes from your court, we will send them back.'

It became clear from this news that the sultan was about to wage war, and he would either attack us in person or send an army against us. Mentesha Sultan said, 'There is no need for us to fight the Ottomans. We shall advance to the region of Erciş; when they hear, they will flee.' We set off immediately in that direction, and when we reached the environs of Qaranqu Dere near Khoy, Yadgar Rojaki[94] came from the fortress of Bitlis with a message that Fil Pasha[95] had fled, discarding his horses' saddlebags in his haste. Hearing this news, I summoned the amirs, officers (*yūzbāshī*s),[96] *qūrchī*s and wise men and asked their counsel, saying, 'What should we do now?' The group consulted and replied that

---

92 In S, this is part of 'Abdallah Khan's name: 'Abdallah Khan Il Aldi.
93 Isma'il Mirza was Tahmasp's second son, and later took the throne as Isma'il II (1576–7).
94 Rojaki is the name of the Kurdish tribal confederation from which the rulers of Bitlis came. Yadgar is also mentioned by the historian of the Kurds, Sharaf al-Din, who calls him Qara Yadgar and says he was nicknamed Duruk. However, he indicates that the shah's army was actually in Ahlat at this point. He records the news was received with great rejoicing, Yadgar was richly rewarded and adds that his grandfather, the prince of Bitlis Sharaf al-Din, held a great celebration for Tahmasp in Ahlat. Sharaf al-Din Khan, *Sharafnama*, I, 425; on Yadgar, see also ibid., I, 417.
95 Fil Ya'qub Pasha was the Ottoman governor general (*beylerbeyi*) of Diyarbakır, who had been ordered to assist Ulama. Fil Ya'qub Pasha's report to the sultan on these events is published by Jean Bacqué-Grammont, 'Un rapport de Fîl Ya'ķûb Paşa, beylerbey de Dîyâr Bekir en 1532', *Wiener Zeitschrift für die Kunde des Morgenlandes* 76 (1986): 35–41.
96 *Yūzbāshī*s were the officers of the *qūrchī*s, nominally in charge of a hundred men.

The sultan has gone to fight the Franks, so let's enter his territory. Fil Pasha has fled to Diyarbakır, so let's go to Sivas. If the people of those districts[97] join us in order to plunder and pillage, let us plunder and then halt in Mar'ash[98] to acquire aid from the locals. When the sultan returns to Istanbul, let us burn the entire region and make it a desert. Let us carry off anyone who accompanies us and resettle them, but kill and plunder anyone who doesn't join us. Let us remain in Diyarbakır until the sultan heads to the province of Çorum and Amasya; then, having burned and plundered Diyarbakır, let us go to Baghdad. After crossing the River [Tigris] at Mosul let us take up winter quarters in the region of Baghdad. If the sultan attacks us in the spring let us return via Shahrazur to Tabriz, and if the sultan advances on Tabriz, let us make for Sivas via Diyarbakır.

When they had finished speaking, I replied, 'Friends, his majesty the sultan has gone to fight holy war [*ghazā*][99] against the Franks, so if we invade his territory, it will not advance our interests. Even if he kills my brother and my son, as he has gone to fight holy war against the Franks, let us not invade his territory, nor sell religion for this world.'

Some said, 'If he attacks us, what will happen to us?' Mentesha Sultan was holding an apple which he tossed into the air, and replied, 'Anything might happen before it falls to the ground!'[viii] Our interests are best served by returning to our country and wintering there; perhaps the sultan will not come in the spring.'

We returned to Tabriz via Chukhur-i Sa'd, by God's grace.[100] Then news came that 'Ubayd Khan the Uzbek had attacked Herat

---

97 The people are presumably the local Qizilbash population.
98 Modern Kahramanmaraş.
99 This word is used by Tahmasp, but does not appear in his advisors' speech. On subsequent occasions, such as in 1541, Ottoman chronicles accuse Tahmasp of conspiring with Christian rulers against the Ottomans, and the embassy of Michele Membré to the Safavid court suggests such claims were not totally without foundation. See Boyar, 'Ottoman Expansion', 122.
100 This was actually a very substantial diversion; the shah at this point was in Khoy, roughly 80 miles north-west of Tabriz; Chukhur-i Sa'd, which refers to Yerevan and the region around it, is another 150 miles to the north of Khoy.

and besieged it. The man was an utter tyrant who saw no difference between infidels and Muslims, to the extent that one day when a learned sayyid was brought before him, he ordered him to be killed. Some people interceded, saying, 'He is a sayyid and innocent.' 'Ubayd replied, 'It is precisely because he is a sayyid and learned that I am killing him.' May God curse him; on another occasion, someone said in one of his salons, 'Anyone who does not have a barley-corn of hatred for the Commander of the Faithful 'Ali is not a Muslim.' The accursed 'Ubayd was holding an orange, and said, 'Praise be to God, I have in my heart the equivalent of an orange in hatred for him!'

At that time, Bahram Mirza was in Herat. His messenger came, explaining that the people of Herat had reached such straits that they were forced to eat the flesh of dogs and cats.[101] We perforce advanced on Khurasan, and when the accursed 'Ubayd learned that we were on the way, he fled back to his country.[102] In that year, we established winter quarters in Herat, and I sent the amirs and army to every district to winter. They reported that Ulama attacked Sharaf Beg and Achih Sultan and the amirs who were with him and Sharaf Beg himself was also killed in the fighting between them. The situation was far ideal, but we turned a blind eye and paid no attention to it. We wintered in Herat, saying, 'What God wills will be. If Ulama operates like a pickpocket and thief, that does not oblige us to move. The sultan has not instigated this and has not attacked our country.'

---

101 The Uzbek siege of Herat began in spring 938/1532, and lasted for a year and a half. Unmentioned by Tahmasp, the Uzbeks also conducted extensive raids into Iranian held Khurasan and as far west as Rayy. Dickson, 'Sháh Tahmásp', 212–24.

102 In fact the Uzbeks abandoned the siege of Herat on 14 Rabi' I 940/3 October 1533, two months before Shah Tahmasp entered the city. Dickson suggests that 'Ubaydallah's abandonment of Herat may in fact have been connected with his election as Grand Khan of the Uzbeks, following the death of Abu Sa'id around this time. His election, however, was not unopposed and he may have needed to return to Transoxiana to enforce his claim to the throne. See Dickson, 'Sháh Tahmásp', 228–37.

Introduction and the Affair of Ulama 73

In the spring of this year, I sent my brother Alqas, accompanied by some amirs, to Marv. I sent Mentesha Sultan, Husayn Khan and Amir Beg Rumlu with some *qūrchī*s to Gharchistan,[103] and I went to pay my respects to his excellency the Eighth, Guarantor Imam Abu'l-Hasan 'Ali b. Musa al-Riza, peace be upon him.[104] This coincided with their conquest of Marv and Gharchistan, after which they came to Herat. Having performed the pilgrimage, I too returned to Herat where I stayed for one month. From 11 Zu'l-Hijja (940/23 June 1534), I halted for forty days in the meadows of Ulang-i Nishin in order to muster an army to march on Balkh.[105]

The belief of this poor servant, Tahmasb al-Safavi al-Musavi al-Husayni, is that if someone sees in a dream his excellency the Commander of the Faithful, 'Ali, peace be upon him, whatever 'Ali says will come true. There is no doubt about this. On the night of 14 Zu'l-Hijja (940/ 26 June 1534) we were three stages away from Herat when I fell ill with a fever and was sick for several days. I saw in a dream his excellency the Commander of the Faithful, peace be upon him, in Zaynal Khan's house which is in Qazvin.[106] He was seated in the Royal Precinct (*dawlatkhāna*), and a youth with a black beard, about twenty-five years old, was standing behind his excellency. Presenting

---

103 The Marv and Gharchistan campaigns took place in 940/1534, and were unusual examples of offensive action on the part of Tahmasp, most of whose military campaigns were defensive. The purpose of the attack on Marv, which the Safavids held for a few months, was evidently to stop it from being used as a staging post for campaigns against Herat, but the purpose of the Gharchistan campaign is unclear, although as it was led by three of the most senior Qizilbash commanders, it was evidently regarded as significant. The local ruler fled, and a Qizilbash governor was briefly installed, but this also did not remain a lasting conquest. See Dickson, 'Sháh Tahmásp', 249–50.
104 This is the shrine of al-Riza in Mashhad. The Eighth Imam was given the title *al-ḍāmin*, 'the guarantor', owing to a story that he had saved the life of a gazelle by 'guaranteeing' to a hunter who had entrapped her that she would feed her fawns and return to him; on seeing that she did this, the hunter released the gazelle.
105 The Ulang-i Nishin pastures were a staging post and military muster point outside Herat.
106 Zaynal Khan Shamlu was the Qizilbash governor of Khurasan and Astarabad. See Parsadust, *Shah Tahmasp*, 23, 24, 64, 65.

myself to his excellency, I kissed the ground before him, and, kneeling down in reverence, I asked, 'Your excellency, may I be your sacrifice![107] If I go in that direction, will I end up in a battle with Uzbek's men or not?' His excellency the Commander of the Faithful replied, 'Tahmasp, till now which of your objectives has been achieved by war? Why do you anticipate it will this time?' Again I asked, 'May I be your sacrifice, what will be our situation on the other side?' He replied, 'On the other side of the river is nothing, everything is on this side of the river.'[108] I repeated the same question three times, and received the same reply. Then his excellency 'Ali, peace be upon him, summoned me to draw near, and said, 'I tell you three things, mark that you strive to do them: firstly, don't forget the 'Alqama river;[109] secondly after the conquest of Samarqand, you or your children must build a dome for me like the dome of the Eighth Guarantor Imam, al-Riza, peace be upon him.'[110] Thirdly, he gave me an instruction regarding Fathi Beg, who had been my father's personal secretary (*parvānachi*),[111] saying, 'Make him custodian of the sacred shrine,[112] for he is one of our own.' Waking up in the morning happy, I summoned him and my companions after morning prayers and explained the dream to them. I told them, 'Our fight with the Uzbeks will be on this side of the river.'

---

107 A set phrase denoting humility towards a superior.
108 Evidently the Oxus is meant; in other words, 'Ali says the fighting should be done on the Iranian, not the Uzbek side of the Oxus. See Dickson, 'Sháh Tahmásp', 251.
109 This is a branch of the Euphrates that flows near Karbala', site of the notorious massacre of Husayn by the Umayyad Caliph Yazid in 680. 'Ali is telling Tahmasp always to remember this event.
110 Tahmasp did indeed fulfil this obligation: the Jannatsara or 'Paradisal Palace' at the dynastic shrine in Ardabil was started by Tahmasp in 1537, intended primarily as a place for Sufi rituals. It has been suggested that it is this 'dome' (*gunbad*) referred to in the *Tazkira*, which was built in emulation of 'Ali al-Riza's shrine in Mashhad. See Kishwar Rizvi, *The Safavid Dynastic Shrine: Architecture, Religion and Power in Early Modern Iran* (London, 2011), 85–91. In fact, however, the Jannatsara seems to have commemorated Tahmasp's victories over the Ottomans in 1536, as he never captured Samarqand.
111 The *parvānachi* attended upon the shah to write down his orders. See Floor, *Safavid Government Institutions*, 60.
112 The shrine of the Eighth Imam, al-Riza, at Mashhad is meant.

After twenty-one days, Ahmad Beg the vizier arrived;[113] he was agitated and disturbed. I asked him, 'You don't drink so why do you look as if you have a hangover?' He replied, 'I wish I'd died so that I hadn't lived to see this day. Perfidious Ulama came to Tabriz and took prisoner all the families and children of the Qizilbash.' I asked whether Ibrahim Pasha was his accomplice, but Ahmad Beg replied that he wasn't. 'Was it the sultan?' I asked; 'He's in Istanbul', he replied. I said, 'May almighty God punish Ulama and Ibrahim Pasha for they accrue curses and ill wishes towards their patron; He will indeed punish them.' I compared it to the story of the Israelites. Thirty thousand of them would pray all night and fast all day, but among them were three who were wicked fornicators. When divine wrath descended on them all thirty thousand perished. The Prophet Moses interceded with the court of God on high, saying, 'God, there were men who were sinners out of this people, what crime have the rest done?' God replied, 'The rest of the people were capable of preventing these three, but did not, so the whole group were implicated in the sin.'[114] Now Ibrahim Pasha ignores God on high, and gives free rein to Ulama to cause all this bloodshed, plunder, raiding, mobilization, expenditure and provisioning. His behaviour has brought about and will bring about every type of wickedness and evil. Shortly afterwards, in outrage, the Creator decided to turn the sultan's mind against him, and he was killed and went to hell. The following verses are apposite:

Faridun had a praiseworthy vizier, who was both enlightened and farsighted.

---

113 This is Ahmed Beg Nur-i Kamil Isfahani, mentioned earlier in the text, p. 67.
114 A similar story, attributed to Joshua rather than Moses, is found in Husayn b. ʿAli al-Khuzaʿi al-Nishapuri, *Rawd al-Jinan wa Rawh al-Janan*, ed. Muhammad Jaʿfar Yahaqqi and Muhammad Mahdi Nasih (Mashhad, 1375), vol. 7, 49–50, where it occurs in the exegesis of Qurʾan 5:63. This was a well-known Persian Qurʾan commentary composed in the twelfth century, the author of which is better known as Abuʾl-Fath al-Razi.

First he made sure to make God happy, then he implemented the king's orders.

A wretched governor oppresses the people, claiming, 'It is royal policy and in the interests of profit.'

If one doesn't protect God's due, God will punish one by the king's hand.[115]

On hearing this, I said to Bahram Mirza and Ghazi Khan,[ix] 'Are you going to stay in Herat or not?' Ghazi Khan replied, 'Our men are in distress and have suffered great oppression of late, as if they were being scourged. They do not have the provisions or strength to bear another siege.' Aghzivar Khan[116] agreed to remain there, saying, 'Give Sam Mirza to me and I will protect Herat.' Mentesha Sultan, Amir Beg Rumlu, Ghazi Khan, the governor of Shiraz, having conferred privately, responded that, 'It is not advisable to hand over Sam Mirza to Aghzivar Khan and leave him in Herat.' I replied, 'Since they are not to be trusted, they should not come with us; if there is reason for concern, it would be better for us to let them to stay in Herat.' I related the story of how Darius was killed in battle with Alexander by his own men.[117]

After the news about Ulama, we remained in Herat for twenty-seven days. Then I sent Muhammad the *qūrchī-bāshī* with some *qūrchī*s and Mentesha Sultan ahead, while I myself followed later. In Isfara'in, Timur Kurd, who was Master of the Stables of the Royal Guard (*amīrākhūr-i qūrchī-bāshī*)[118] in that place, caught up

---

115 The verses are from Sa'di's *Bustan*, Chapter 7. Faridun was a legendary pre-Islamic Iranian king.
116 Aghzivar Khan, a member of the Shamlu tribe, was a relative and protegee of Husayn Khan, and son of Damri Sultan, see Dickson, 'Sháh Tahmásp', 272–3; Szuppe, *Entre Timourides, Uzbeks et Safavides*, 102–32.
117 Tahmasp's comment reflects the breakdown in relations with Husayn Khan, who was executed around this time. He seems to be suggesting that Aghzivar Khan may plan to kill him and replace him with Sam Mirza, which was perhaps a realistic threat given the poisoning plot in Mashhad in which Husayn Khan was implicated. S uses a slightly different, and more vivid metaphor, 'If a weed is in the middle of a tree, it harms it, but if it is outside it cannot damage it.'
118 On the office of *amīrākhūr*, see Minorsky, *Tadhkirat al-Mulūk*, 50, 80, 120.

with us in the vicinity of Turbat-i Jam along with some of our spies. They reported that Ibrahim Pasha had come for sure. A letter reached us which had been written by Ibrahim Pasha to Begum and sent via one of the officers of Shams al-Din Khan, son of Sharaf Khan. The letter's contents were as follows, 'Send some weapons and bejewelled accoutrements belonging to Shah Isma'il – may he rest in mercy and paradise – as a gift. I will send these to his majesty the sultan asking for a truce, to discourage him from invading these lands. Then I will persuade him to hand over this kingdom to you, and we will withdraw.' Ulama also wrote a request to this effect to Begum.

To cut a long story short, we came from Turbat-i Jam to Kabud Gunbad outside Rayy in a march of ten days.[119] Our horses and camels were all thin and weak, and many were left by the wayside. When I reached Isfara'in, Qanbaroghli[120] said in my salon, 'Send someone else for once to get reliable information about Ibrahim Pasha and Ulama.' This annoyed me and I said in anger, 'Where could I find anyone better than you to send? Only you can undertake this task.' Apparently, he set off from Isfara'in with two[x] officers in their direction. When they reached Maragha, they approached Ibrahim Pasha's camp where they encountered an Ottoman detachment. They killed three men and captured one alive before making away. By chance they bumped into another detachment. One of his officers seized the heads of the killed men[121] and the captured Ottoman soldier who was still alive and fled. Qanbaroghli and one of his officers wounded two of the enemy, but realized they could not withstand them and made a tactical retreat. One of the Ottomans swept the turban and its baton off his head with his spear, and then used it to lift them up off the

---

119 As Dickson notes ('Sháh Tahmásp', 276–8), here the shah obscures much more than he reveals. Other sources indicate he stopped at Mashhad, where he narrowly escaped an attempt on his life by poisoning.
120 This individual seems to have been governor of Isfara'in; see Parsadust, *Shah Tahmasp*, 105, 106.
121 The implication seems to be that they were carrying the heads with them as a trophy.

ground.¹²² Bareheaded, he fled from battle with the Ottomans, and the turban and its baton were brought before Ibrahim Pasha, and Ulama identified them. When we reached Qazvin, he came,[xi] and we were informed about everything that had happened from the surviving Ottoman soldier that they brought.¹²³

I then sent Shah Quli Khalifa and Muhammad Sultan Afshar to go to the tribes (*ulusāt va uymāqāt*), and to recruit anyone who wished to join us into our service and bring them along. I ordered Sevinduk Beg¹²⁴ to go to bring our family who were in Qum to Qazvin, for if Ibrahim Pasha was only accompanied by a small force, not the sultan, there was no cause for worry about them.¹²⁵

One day in Qazvin I went to the bathhouse that I had had constructed on the outskirts of the district of Ja'farabad;¹²⁶ on coming out of the bathhouse I encamped in Zaynal Khan's garden. The worthies of Qazvin cooked and brought food for us. After we had eaten, a man came from Alqas and Bahram Mirza,[xii] who were encamped by the Zanjan river, announcing that 'Ibrahim Pasha intends to withdraw.'[xiii] I immediately sent Mentesha Sultan with a hundred men to join Alqas, Bahram Mirza and another army which was at Charkhaband¹²⁷ in order to pursue Ibrahim Pasha and Ulama, hoping they would take Ulama captive. I said, 'I too will soon follow

---

122 *Jiqa-yi gandum* seems to refer to the 'baton' protruding from the top of the turban. For an illustration of such turbans see Barbara Schmitz, 'On a Special Hat Introduced during the Reign of Shāh 'Abbās the Great', *Iran* 22 (1984): 103–12.
123 It seems the captive Ottoman soldier was used to verify Qanbaroghli's account.
124 A member of the Afshar tribe, Sevinduk Beg was *qūrchī-bāshī*.
125 Evidently the family had been sent to Qum given Qazvin's relative proximity to Tabriz and the frontier.
126 Ja'farabad, named after the Sixth Imam, was the name given to the new suburb built at Tahmasp's command after Qazvin became the capital. See Ehsan Echraqi, 'Le Dār al-Salṭana de Qazvin, deuxième capitale des Safavides', in Charles Melville (ed.), *Safavid Persia: The History and Politics of an Islamic Society* (London, 1996), 111.
127 Charkhaband is a minor locality in Zanjan province, north of the city of Zanjan, coordinates 37.1195 and 48.2406 (source: https://cartographic.info/names/map.php?id=190627&f=ir). It does not seem to have been a population centre of any significance, and the army was probably encamped here to avoid the main Ottoman advance.

you.'xiv When the whole army assembled at the Nikpay caravanserai,[128] and had advanced one stage, by chance they encountered an Ottoman detachment. They killed some and took a few men alive, from whom they got intelligence that Ibrahim Pasha had made a ruse, which was that his majesty the sultan in person had entered Tabriz; on Tuesday he would leave Tabriz and advance in this direction. Zulqadaroghli arrested that contingent and brought them to me. Rumours of the sultan's advance grew with every day. I decamped from Qazvin to Abhar. Our amirs and their forces went ahead of the sultan's army, marching the local populace ahead of them and devastating the whole route until they reached Zanjan.[129] In Abhar, news arrived confirming that his majesty the sultan had entered Zanjan. I sent our troops which were in Sultaniyya and the harem via Abhar to Qum, and I myself marched from Abhar to a halting place called Qara Aghach where I rested. I sent a man to the amirs to announce that I was coming to Sultaniyya and they should remain where they were. I appointed as scouts Amir Beg, Chiragh Sultan[130] and Zulqadaroghli,[131] and I sent Khalil Agha Kengürlü to summon Husayn Khan, Mentesha Sultan and Ghazi Khan Zulqadar, governor of Shiraz, to come with two experienced men each in order to consult with us about what should be done. After Khalil Agha had brought them, Husayn Khan said, 'Our horses are thin, we cannot fight the Ottoman and his army!' I replied, 'Did I say we had resolved to fight Ottomans directly, to make you say this, and make you worry about how thin the horses are?'

---

128 S: Nik Pay; G, L, B, Nik Beg. The caravanserai is commonly known as Nikpay today. It is located north-west of Zanjan on the Tabriz road.
129 That is, a scorched earth policy to hinder the sultan's advance.
130 Chiragh Sultan Ustajlu, an important Qizilbash amir from the region of Hamadan, on whom see Posch, *Osmanisch-safavidische Beziehungen*, index, s.v.
131 Zulqadaroghli refers to Muhammad Khan Zulqadar, who had joined Shah Isma'il in his youth. After his defection to the Ottomans in 1534, described later in the text, he was appointed as governor of Erzurum and Bayburt in north-eastern Anatolia. He was subsequently posted to Rumeli and Bosnia. See Posch, *Osmanisch-safavische Beziehungen*, 72–4.

We decided to divide up the army into several sections to devastate the area around the Ottomans. I went with thirty *qūrchī*s to the top of a hill to see whether the sultan's army would leave Zanjan. I immediately observed that our army's tents had been taken down and they were heading away from Sultaniyya in another direction. I understood that the sultan had nearly reached them. Coming down from the hill, I went to my camp and sent Qanbaroghli to summon Alqas, Bahram Mirza and the amirs to me so that we did not subsequently get separated. Qanbaroghli went that very night and brought them in the morning. They said, 'Zulqadaroghli has fled with a thousand men, and joined the Ottoman camp.'

Previous to these events, when Mentesha Sultan and the army were at Charkhaband and the sultan had not yet reached Ujan, Zulqadaroghli had been sent as a scout, and had surprised a five-hundred strong Ottoman scouting party in the vicinity of Charkhaband. Sadr al-Din[132] wished to give battle and the *qūrchī*s drew up ranks. From the first that bastard Zulqadaroghli was disingenuous.[xv] He did not let them advance, claiming that 'There are many Ottomans behind that hill, they'll take us captive!' Three of Sadr al-Din Beg's men came out of the caravanserai. They did battle and the horse of one of their number stumbled over a gravestone. The Ottomans captured him, and brought him before the sultan, who gave him a robe of honour, and sent him back with a letter he had written to me. Its contents were as follows: 'Your father, Shah Isma'il, God's mercy be upon him, fought with my father. You also claim to be brave. Come on, let's fight; if you don't fight, stop going on about bravery.'

In reply to his letter, I wrote,

> The greatest of all creation is the Creator, glorious and mighty is He, who in his Holy Book has commanded, 'When you fight with

---

132 Presumably Sadr al-Din Khan Ustajlu.

the infidel, do not risk your destruction.'¹³³ For he has said, '*Do not throw yourself with your own hands into destruction*'.¹³⁴ When avoidance of self-destruction is required when fighting the infidel, how can I command battle between two Muslim armies, one of which is ten times bigger than the other, and risk the destruction of these Muslims? On the day my father did battle with your father, Durmish Khan and the rest of the amirs, indeed his whole army, were drunk. They drank wine from dusk till dawn and then prepared to do battle. This was a stupid and vile affair. From that time, whenever the story of the battle of Chaldiran is mentioned, I curse Durmish Khan, because he deceived my father Shah Isma'il and led him to battle. Also God, glorious is his name, has commanded that, 'One Muslim should not fight with two infidels', so what can we do when we are outnumbered approximately ten to one? How can we break God almighty's command, and knowingly put ourselves in mortal danger? We'd have to be mad or drunk to fight a senseless battle, and risk our destruction out of bravado and vain-glory.

Praise be to God, the army of my realm have repented from wine and debauchery, indeed every vice.¹³⁵ In my entire kingdom, all the taverns, alehouses,¹³⁶ brothels and other practices contrary to sharia have been abolished. When I departed from Herat going to Mashhad to pay my respects at the holy shrine, the angels' nest, of his excellency Imam Riza, peace be upon him, I saw in a dream Mir Sayyid Muhammad, the imam of Medina and the bearer of God's message, peace be upon him and his family, saying to me, 'Forego

---

133 This is evidently a paraphrase of Qur'an 2:190, which in fact reads, 'Fight in God's path those who fight you but do not transgress.'
134 Qur'an 2: 195.
135 This is the so-called Edict of Sincere Repentance, which in fact was reissued several times during Tahmasp's reign. For a discussion, see Matthee, *Angels Tapping at the Wine-Shop's Door*, 136–8; as Matthee notes, enforcement of the ban was erratic, especially for members of the Safavid family.
136 *Būzakhāna*: boza is a millet based mildly alcoholic drink, still consumed in Turkey; it is contrasted with *sharābkhāna*s, places that sell wine.

vices, so that you obtain victories.'¹³⁷ In the morning I explained my dream to Ahmad Beg and some other amirs who were present. Some of them said, 'Let us forego some vices, but we cannot forego others such as drinking which is a royal necessity.' Everyone had something to say about this subject. In the end I said, 'Tonight I will sleep on it, and I will act in whatever way I am shown', for his excellency the Messenger of God, peace and blessings be upon him and his family, said, *'The true believer dreams the true dream'*; he also said, *'nothing remains of prophecy but good tidings'*. That night I saw in a dream that, outside the window by the foot side of the grave of his excellency the Guarantor Imam Riza, upon him be a million greetings and praise, I was grasping the hand of his excellency Mir Hadi the *muḥtasib*.ˣᵛⁱ I repented from drinking, adultery and all vice. In the morning I related this dream to the assembled company. By the strength and grace of almighty God, just as I had seen in my dream, the aforesaid *muḥtasib* was present in exactly the same place. Grasping his hand, I repented of all vices. I was twenty years old when this auspicious event occurred, and I composed the following quatrain:

> For a while we wore ourselves out looking for emeralds,
>> For a while we were stained by wet ruby,¹³⁸
>
> Whatever they were, they were defilements,
>> But we washed ourselves with the water of repentance and were refreshed

Praise and thanks be to God that from this date when I received this happy revelation, vice and debauchery have been abolished from the entire kingdom, and day by day, by the grace of God, ever more victories have been obtained, of which it had not even occurred to me

---

137 The word used for victories (*futūḥāt*) could also imply divine revelations. Mir Sayyid Muhammad (d. 1560) is otherwise largely unknown, but apparently was an émigré from the Jabal Amil in Lebanon. See Abisaab, *Converting Persia*, 29.
138 'Wet ruby' refers to wine; 'emerald' may refer to cannabis.

that the least part was possible. All intelligent men were amazed at these events, and, however brave I am, in my whole life I could never give enough thanks for the least part of these events.

> If every hair of mine becomes a tongue,
> Each one will sing your praises
> Because I lack a tongue to thank you, I am still asleep
> I have not said even one of the hundred praises you are due.

Later, Mentesha Sultan and our *qūrchī-bāshī* rebuked the envoy who brought the letter, and tried to kill him. I stopped them. At that time 7,000 men were accompanying me, of whom no more than 3,000 were any use. Since we had advanced at speed from Herat, all the horses were tired and thin. Some of our soldiers like Husayn Khan, Ghazi Khan and Malik Beg of Khoy and their followers had hostile hearts and friendly tongues, and were constantly on the look out to take advantage of some weakness in our situation. I was very distressed at these events, and took refuge in the Lord creator, and entrusted Him to deal with those who wished ill to religion and state. I kept praying, repeating the Qur'anic verse *God suffices for us, for he is the best disposer of affairs*,[139] *the best lord and the best helper*.[140] Then the story of the Prophet Abraham, peace be upon him, came to mind: when they put him in a mangonel to throw him into the fire, Gabriel, peace be upon him, came and said, 'Abraham, are you asking for help?' He replied, 'I am, but not from you.' Then the sea of the mercy of God – glorious is his name – swelled up, and He ordered, '*Fire! Be cold and safe for Abraham.*'[141] I thought of these verses by Shaykh Nizami,[142] and read them repeatedly,

---

139 Qur'an 3:173. This verse is commonly used as a prayer by those in distress. It was originally said by the Prophet Ibrahim/Abraham when threatened with being thrown in the fire.
140 Qur'an 8: 40.
141 Qur'an 21:69.
142 From Nizami's *Makhzan al-Asrar*.

> O You from whom all of existence came, frail human dust became strong through You
>
> All beings are below Your banner; we exist through You, just as You exist through the Essence
>
> Your being is not face and body; You do not resemble anyone, and no one resembles You
>
> You are that which is not susceptible to change; You are that which has not died and will not die
>
> We are all transient, You alone have permanent existence; You possess the kingdom of heaven and holiness
>
> The caravan has set off, look on us who are left behind; Friend,[143] look on our friendlessness!
>
> Help us! For we have no helper. If You banish us, to whom can we turn?

The sultan swiftly took advantage, for as soon as we had returned from the campaign in Herat and the war with the Uzbeks, he invaded our lands, all thanks due to wretched traitors,[xvii] may the Creator aid us. I extemporized the following verse in Turkish:

> In this world God alone helps; on an evil day He shares His slave's woes

By chance, we were constantly able to stay one stage ahead of them, and we only reached the outskirts of Qazvin thanks to divine aid and the grace of the infallible imams, God's blessings be upon them all. As Hafiz said:

> If you entrust your affairs to God, Hafiz, oft will you enjoy divine favour.[144]

---

143 The Prophet is meant.
144 Hafiz, *Divan*, ed. Muhammad Qazvini and Qasim Ghani (Tehran, 1941), Ghazal 481.

At the beginning of the onset of Scorpio, on the night of Tuesday, 13 Safar (941/24 August 1534),[145] it snowed so heavily that the sultan's army got stuck. A week later, having suffered a hundred thousand trials, they set off in the direction of Darguzin. Meanwhile, the governor of Kuhgiluya came with 1,000 men bringing many herds of fresh horses. In the night, I summoned Qara Mahmud, the hunt master (*avjībāshī*), and I sent him with horses and fifty *qūrchī*s to spy on the enemy. On the outskirts of Qaraqan,[146] they clashed with a contingent of Sarilu Tekellu Turkmen, with whom they did battle. Husayn Beg Qilijoghlu lost a hand in the fighting and five Ottomans were captured along with seventy dead. We asked one of the Ottomans, who was talkative, about their plans, which he explained in their entirety with total accuracy. He said, 'The sultan has conferred with his senior ministers, and they have decided to head to Baghdad. Ulama and Zulqadaroghli and their troops and a group of the *müteferrika* unit[147] have been detached from their army and ordered to go to Tabriz.'

When I understood the situation and found out about their intentions, I sent Rajab Abdal and Hamzah Beg Ghazal oghli to Muhammad Khan, son of Sharaf al-Din,[148] instructing him to throw all the supplies in that region into the river, to cross the river himself and to come via the Jazira[xviii] route with his troops. The Qizilbash

---

145 It is evident this hijri date, though supported by most manuscript witnesses, is wrong, as Scorpio would fall 23 October to 22 November, and snow in August is most improbable. S does not give the hijri date, and indeed gives a different version in events in which it is Tahmasp's army that gets stuck. 'On the same night, which was the fifth of Scorpio, it started to snow so heavily that our army got stuck in the snow. Then we marched from there to Darguzin.' For an account of the campaign based on Ottoman sources, see Feridun M. Emecen, *Kanuni Sultan Süleymân ve Zamanı* (Ankara, 2022), 238–57; see also Parsadust, *Shah Tahmasp*, 161–2. After entering Tabriz, the Ottoman army advanced through Azerbaijan to Sultaniyya, where it appears the snowfall happened; their objective, though, was Baghdad, which is why they headed towards Darguzin, near Hamadan.
146 An alternative spelling for Kharraqan, near Qazvin.
147 This seems to reflect Ottoman usage. *Müteferrika* are guardsmen attached to the sultan, also used for diplomatic missions.
148 Muhammad Khan Sharaf al-Din Oghli Tekellu, the governor of Baghdad: this was in fact Tahmasp's instruction for him to surrender the city to the Ottomans. See Parsadust, *Shah Tahmasp*, 164–6.

gathered around me, saying, 'Let's go after the sultan and win a victory.' I replied, 'We have no business with the sultan; my business is with Ulama. All this strife and turmoil that has happened is his fault, and we must take revenge on him, for he has injured both us and the sultan greatly.' Qaraqanbar[xix] and Mentesha Sultan said, 'Now that we are less worried about the Ottomans, Ghazi Khan – who by tongue professes Shiism and in his heart is like Marwan[149] – should be killed.' Since we had sworn oaths in Herat that I would not kill him as long as there were no reports that he was involved in a rebel army that was attacking us, I did not permit him to be killed on this basis. Two or three days later, one night Ghazi Khan and a few of his long-serving men fled. If we had gone after him, we could have captured him. People said that he would go to the sultan. We let him go, and attacked Ulama.[150] As it happened, Ghazi Khan was also going to him, and entered Tabriz on 8 Rabi' II (941/ 17 October 1534). He informed Ulama that we would come after him. Because the road was muddy and our camels were thin and weak, we only entered Tabriz one day later, on the Monday. That night, Ulama and Ghazi Khan fled. We halted for twenty days in Tabriz, and then marched off towards Van, accompanied by 5,400 soldiers, of whom 1,600 were *qūrchī*s and the rest were the amirs' troops.[151] We besieged the fortress of Van and had almost conquered it when Qaya Agha, one of the officers of Husayn Beg Yuzbashi, the prefect (*dārūghā*) of Tabriz, arrived. I was having a bath when Mentesha Sultan and Amir Beg Mirza brought him in, and I asked him about the situation. He said, 'Sam Mirza has revolted, and the sultan is calling him his own son. The kingdom is in tumult.'

---

149 The fourth Umayyad caliph, Marwan (r. 684–5), was demonized by Shiite tradition, both for opposing 'Ali b. Abi Talib at the battles of the Camel and Siffin, but particularly for opposing the burial of Imam Husayn next to his grandfather the Prophet.
150 Ulama had been appointed governor of Azerbaijan by Süleyman, and was based in Tabriz. See Parsadust, *Shah Tahmasp*, 164; Emecen, *Sultan Süleyman ve Zamanı*, 251–2.
151 The amirs' troops were thus Qizilbash tribesmen.

I replied, 'I also called Zulqadaroghli my own son, and look how he treated me. What is Sam Mirza up to with the sultan? I have always treated him well, never badly, but he is treating me badly by cutting the ties of kinship. I will entrust dealing with him to my master, his majesty the king, the refuge of sovereignty, the Commander of the Faithful, 'Ali.' When the garrison of Van fortress learned of these dealings, their willingness to surrender the fortress turned to wariness and they had misgivings. As the situation turned out like this, there was no choice but to decamp from the foot of the fortress rock and march off.

2

A brief account of the affair of Ghazi Khan

Ghazi Khan was a fellow who was full of cunning, a cheat and a liar, possessing satanic attributes. This verse is apposite:

> As sly and cunning as a fox, he even cheats the heavens.

Escaping from Tabriz with Ulama, he made for Baghdad, telling Ibrahim Pasha that, 'Sam Mirza has rebelled. The best course is for you to head to the Qizilbash province[1] and announce that the sultan has adopted Sam Mirza as his own son, and given his majesty Shah Isma'il's kingdom to him. I will bring him to the presence of the sultan.' He deceived Ibrahim Pasha, giving him to believe that although the sultan had conquered Baghdad and left our territory, he had instilled in him a desire to return there and, in short, the sultan was marching in this direction having set his sights on conquering our lands.

> I heard that in the days of yore, in the hands of saints, stone turned to silver.
>
> Don't imagine this is impossible; when you're content, stone and silver are the same.
>
> A beggar is satisfied by a single dirham, but Faridun is only half satisfied with the kingdom of Persia.[2]

---

1 This refers to Safavid Iran as a whole.
2 Sa'di, *Bustan*, Chapter 6.

When news came from Tabriz that the sultan was returning,[3] I put my trust in the Inscrutable Being, His Divine Majesty, glorious is He, and decided to send Sayyid ʻAbdallah the *lāla*, a descendant of the Prophet, on behalf of the Begum,[4] and Mir Shahsuvar Kurd, on behalf of Mentesha Sultan, as ambassadors to Ibrahim Pasha. Perhaps a truce could be arranged, averting strife and discord, in order to protect the weak and the poor, who are entrusted to us by God. They reached Ibrahim Pasha and gave him the letter. Ibrahim Pasha, who was an opium addict, would say when he was under the influence, 'The sultan's behaviour is under my control; I command him as I wish.'[5] However, when he was not under the influence, he would say, 'What can I do? I am but a poor humble slave, what can I do? It is the absolute command of his majesty the sultan.' In the end that vile wretch would not agree to a truce. He sent a letter full of threats which reached me when I was in Ujan.[6] People said, 'Sam Mirza has rebelled, and on the other hand the sultan has come. What will happen next?' In reply, I recited these verses by Shaykh Saʻdi:

> God did not forget you when you were an unconscious embryo
>
> He arranged the ten fingers on your hands and two arms on your shoulders
>
> He gave you a soul, understanding, sense and intelligence, along with perfect intellect, bodily form and mind
>
> Now, do you think that he will ever forget you, lowly though you are?[7]

---

3 Süleyman advanced from Iraq in the spring of 1535, occupying Tabriz for a second time in June 1535; see Parsadust, *Shah Tahmasp*, 170–1; Emecen, *Sultan Süleyman ve Zamanı*, 252–3.
4 Again the reference is evidently to Tajlu Begum, Tahmasp's mother.
5 Literally, 'If I wish I open, if I wish on the contrary I bind.' The reference is to the *ḥall wa-ʻaqd* 'loosing and binding' which denotes a sovereign's absolute authority.
6 Ujan, about 50 km from Tabriz, had been a favoured royal encampment since Mongol times owing to its extensive pastures. See Membré, *Mission*, 43, and for its use by the Mongols, see Ralph Pinder-Wilson, 'The Persian Garden: Bagh and Chahar-Bagh', in *The Islamic Garden*, ed. E. B. Macdougall and R. Ettinghausen (Washington, DC, 1976).
7 Saʻdi, *Gulistan*, Book 7, ch. 2.

Whoever seeks the help of anyone but God, is lost.[8] Trusting in the Divine Being, glorious is He, we marched from Ujan towards Sultaniyya. When we reached Zanjan, I renewed my favour towards Kechel Pir 'Ali Hajjilar[9] and sent him as an ambassador to the sultan bearing presents, gifts and tribute (*pīshkash*),[10] with a message that a conflict should be averted, for *a truce is better.*

Ulama and Zulqadaroghli again incited the sultan's anger and so he advanced on Iraq.[11] We reached Darguzin, and stayed there for two or three days, when Pir 'Ali came and said, 'This is the situation at the moment: the sultan has come, fighting is averted, there is a truce.' I replied, 'If it's a truce, why is the sultan marching in our direction?' Burning all the crops in the district of Darguzin, we sent the royal household back to Isfahan, and we ourselves headed towards Hamadan. When the sultan reached Darguzin, he saw the situation was different from what he expected, and his army would become weak from lack of water, food and fodder for its animals. He retreated, while we advanced on Tabriz from behind the Alvand Mountains.

In the previous year, when we marched on Tabriz after Ulama and Ghazi Khan had fled, one night I saw the Commander of the Faithful, 'Ali, peace be upon him, in a dream. He said, 'Child, come to circumambulate the shrine.[12] Circumambulate around your holy ancestors, and bring twelve candles as an offering. Then go wherever you wish.' At that time, we were not favoured by the opportunity

---

8   A well-known hadith.
9   The nickname Kechel indicates that his scalp was affected by skin disease, possibly ringworm. For another example of such a nickname see Membré, *Mission*, 79.
10 The term *pīshkash*, rendered here as tribute, properly means a present given from an inferior to a superior, at least in usage from the fifteenth century onwards. It is likely that Tahmasp's intention is to show that he did everything possible to placate the sultan, rather than that he literally entered a tributary relationship to him. On the term see A.K.S. Lambton, '*Pīshkash*: Present or Tribute?' *Bulletin of the School of Oriental and African Studies* 57 (1994): 145–58.
11 It seems Süleyman's objective was in fact to capture Tahmasp, who was in the Hamadan region. Here Iraq probably means 'Iraq-i 'Ajam, that is, western Iran. See Emecen, *Sultan Süleyman ve Zamanı*, 253–4.
12 Literally the 'Threshold.' The dynastic shrine at Ardabil is meant.

to do this, so without doubt our affairs therefore did not prosper, victories eluded us and the perfidious Ulama was not taken captive. Now, when the sultan entered Tabriz, we went to Ardabil via the Abbasi caravanserai route. We brought an offering of twelve candles as we had been instructed, along with other offerings, and after circumambulating the holy ancestors and praying in the shrine precincts, I slept next to the door of his majesty sultan Haydar's tomb,[13] God's mercy be upon him. I saw in a dream shaykh Safi, God's mercy be upon him, saying 'After twenty days you will make an appearance' (I don't remember whether he said 'appearance' (*zuhūr*) or 'emergence' (*khurūj*), he used one of these two words). When I woke up, I said to myself, '"Appearance" is the prerogative of the Mahdi Imam, God's Proof upon his earth, the awaited one, the champion of the family of the Prophet, peace and blessings be upon him. But what does "emergence" mean?'[14]

Leaving Ardabil, we marched to Sarab where we caught up with the army. When his majesty the sultan left Tabriz,[15] we went from Sarab to Maragha. News came that the sultan had reached Ahlat, so we headed to Qaranquy Dere near Khoy. We were fishing,[16] when two spies came and reported that his majesty the sultan had left his artillery, wagons and baggage[xx] in Ahlat and had retreated towards Istanbul, and now Ulama was occupying Van.[17] I was standing naked

---

13 Haydar (d. 1488), Tahmasp's grandfather and spiritual guide of the Safavid order, who had been reburied at Ardabil by Shah Isma'il. See Rivzi, *Safavd Dynastic Shrine*, 62.
14 Both the terms *zuhūr* and *khurūj* are associated with the appearance of the Mahdi at the end of time; however, *khurūj* may imply more an armed insurrection or revolt. Tahmasp seems to be suggesting that it was ambiguous whether his success was to be down to military might or not.
15 Süleyman withdrew from Tabriz at the end of August 1535. Emecen, *Sultan Süleyman ve Zamanı*, 255; Şahin, *Peerless among Princes*, 184.
16 Tahmasp's enthusiasm for fishing is also mentioned by Membré, *Mission*, 25, 27, who describes how the shah would take the court on fishing expeditions in the mountains around Maragha; apparently, Tahmasp disliked the more conventional forms of courtly hunting such as with dogs or birds of prey.
17 Having been obliged to abandon Tabriz, it seems Süleyman's objective was to fortify the Lake Van region to prevent any Safavid advances in that area. See Emecen, *Sultan Süleyman ve Zamanı*, 255.

and muddy in the river catching fish. I washed myself in the cold water, and we immediately rode off in great haste till we arrived at the zawiya of Mulla Hasan. When we reached the zawiya, I had a fever. We dismounted, the tents were put up and I slept. Mulla Muhammad the storyteller[18] and some of the amirs were sitting around telling stories, but although I had fever and needed rest I could not because I was so unsettled. I decided that Qaya Beg Shukroghli and Shir Hasan the *qūrchī-bāshī* should go with a contingent to attack Van. The next day, in the afternoon, two *qūrchī*s came bringing intelligence that Ulama had fled from Van. We marched off and reached Van, where we stayed for two days. I ordered Ghazi Khan, the governor of Shiraz, and Ya'qub Sultan Qajar to be accompanied by a large contingent of *qūrchī*s, and Köpek-Qiran[19] to accompany Hasan Beg Yuzbashi. I gave them 5,000 of the amirs' men to raid the appanage of Sayyid Muhammad.[20] From Khoy, I ordered the Bahram Mirza, Mentesha Sultan, Amir Beg Rumlu, Shah Quli Khalifa, Budaq Khan, Sadr al-Din Khan the *sufrajī*,[21] the aide-de-camps (*yasāvul*), palace gatekeepers (*qapūchī*)[22] and court tailors (*qaychajī*)[23] and all the people in the workshops to go after the Ottomans. Budaq Khan and Sadr al-Din Khan were sent as scouts; they clashed with Hajji Beg,[24] whom they fought and defeated.

---

18 The storyteller (*qiṣṣakhwān*) would typically relate heroic romances on Islamic or ancient Iranian themes, such as the *Hamzanama* and parts of Firdawsi's *Shahnama*. See Kumiko Yamamoto, 'Naqqāli', in *Encyclopaedia Iranica* Online, © Trustees of Columbia University in the City of New York. Consulted online on 2 September 2023, http://dx.doi.org/10.1163/2330-4804_EIRO_COM_363720.
19 His Turkish nickname means 'dog-slayer'; his real name was Husayn 'Ali Beg Qajar; see also Membré, *Mission*, 21, 35, 72.
20 Sayyid Muhammad was the lord of the Shanbo' Kurds, a frontier principality in the region to the south of Lake Van. See Posch, *Osmanisch-safavidische Beziehungen*, 49.
21 *Sufrajī* was a court office, responsible for serving meals.
22 *Qapūchī*s (gatekeepers) were responsible for the security of the harem; see Minorsky, *Tadhkirat al-Mulūk*, 63–4.
23 There were tailors for both royal and amirs' clothes; for the organization of this department of the court, see Minorsky, *Tadhkirat al-Mulūk*, 65–6.
24 Probably Hajji Beg is identical with the Kurdish chief Hajji Shaykh, against whom Tahmasp is known from other sources to have sent another expedition in 1540; it is not entirely clear where his territories were located; although some have identified him as a

He escaped with a small band, but 250 of his men were captured alive and 1,000 were killed. The severed heads were sent to us with the live Ottoman captives and loot.

The next day, Sulayman Sultan Rumlu[25] went to the shore of Lake Van to do his prayers. When he had finished, it was afternoon, and he came before me and said, 'By the lake shore is a meadow, its air is fresh. Why don't you come for a stroll?' His motive was to show me a cloud of dust that he had seen between Khoy and Erciş. He said, 'The dust cloud you see is most assuredly the sultan's army, which Ibrahim Pasha and Ulama have brought to attack Bahram Mirza.' I immediately sent Shah Verdi Khalifa Süglenoghli – who is presently standard-bearer (*ʿālamdār*) but at that time was a *qūrchī* – to the amirs and Bahram Mirza, to tell them, 'This dust cloud is a sign, watch out lest they attack you from the side and catch you unaware. Everyone who saw the dust cloud estimated that it comprised no less than 30,000 men. Send news; if need be, we will come to your aid.'

That day and night, no news came. In the morning I wanted to decamp and march in the direction of Sultaniyya. I was perturbed because of the dust cloud, and hesitated and delayed. We were sitting around at noon, when Halhal Bahadur Arapgirlu and Kureshji Chemishkezeklü,[26] who had gone to stroll by the lakeside, came bringing an Ottoman they had captured, along with the heads of two of Ulama's men, who had clashed with our forces while they were fleeing from him back to their own country. I asked the Ottoman for intelligence. He replied, 'I accompanied Ulama and Ahmad Pasha; when they came to Vostan,[27] they wanted to continue to Van,

---

Baban Kurd of Shahrazur, this involves chronological difficulties. See Membré, *Mission*, 46, 71; Posch, *Osmanisch-safavidische Beziehungen*, 58, 98–9.

25 This is presumably the Qizilbash chief mentioned in other sources as Sulayman Sultan Çepni, see Posch, *Osmanisch-safavidische Beziehungen*, 313–15.

26 'Arabgirlu and Chemishkezeklü, according to some accounts, were subdivisions of the Ustajlu Qizilbash tribe. Others consider the Chemishkezeklü to be Kurds. See Posch, *Osmanisch-safavidische Beziehungen*, 189; Sümer, *Safevi Devletinin Kuruluşu*, 53–6.

27 Modern Gevaş, on the southeastern shore of Lake Van.

accompanied by their provisions and troops. As they heard that the shah was in Van, they didn't come, and went off in the direction of Diyarbakır.' I regretted this deeply, saying, 'It's a pity we didn't ride out and clash with Ulama that day.' Then I ordered seventy *qūrchī*s to go to Vostan. A few days later the amirs who had gone on this mission returned. I said to them, 'It's a pity Ulama was so close but has escaped us.' Sulayman Sultan said, 'Come, let's check what they have done.' We sent a man to summon the Turkmen *qūrchī*s from Vostan, in order to muster the troops and head to Erciş to help Bahram Mirza. Meanwhile, Qara Ismail Qurchi and Kur Shah Suvar came, bringing one dead and one live Ottoman.

I asked the Ottoman for intelligence, and he replied, 'I am the sultan's slave; in Ahlat, I was entrusted with charge of the governance of Van, which was then given to Ulama. Yesterday I received reports that Ulama was in the region of Vostan, waiting for you to decamp from Van; he will then attack Van.' Hearing Ulama's name, I became impatient and ordered that the army mount its horses. I donned arms and armour. That very night we lit bright torches and departed. I sent ahead 300 *qūrchī*s – Turkmen, Zulqadar and Ustajlu – as the vanguard (*charkhjī*),[28] while we advanced. Some men crossed by the bridge, some went through the river. When 'Abdallah Khan, Gökche Sultan, Yadgar Muhammad Sultan, Ya'qub Sultan and Hasan Beg[29] who had returned from raiding Sayyid Muhammad's territories, reached the bridge, they saw a fire from afar. Imagining it was our royal headquarters (*ordu*) and that we had dismounted, they too dismounted and fell asleep in the same place, thinking they would catch up with us in the morning. By chance, it was in fact Ulama and Ahmad Pasha who had encamped there. In short, by the time we

---

28 *Charkhjī*s were the advance patrols of an army, who led the attack. On the position, see Floor, *Safavid Government Institutions*, 265–6.
29 Qizilbash amirs. 'Abdallah Khan and Hasan Beg were Ustajlu, while Ya'qub Sultan and Gökche Sultan were Qajar. See Parsadust, *Shah Tahmasp*, index s.v.

reached the place where we had traced Ulama, he had been alerted, and fled. The *qūrchīs* and some of the amirs went after him, and we too pursued him with 2,000 men for two stages. A large number of his men who were left behind were taken captive or killed. They took captive his secretary (*parvāna*), whom I asked for intelligence. He replied, 'Ibrahim Pasha has raised a large army and desires to attack Bahram Mirza.'

As soon as we heard this news, a fine victory was obtained. Accompanied by the amirs, we went to the aid of Bahram Mirza. When we reached the river Gevaş[30] we slept there and in the morning entered Vostan. A man came from Bahram Mirza and the amirs came with him. Our spies brought reports. We laid an ambush[xxi] and took the enemy unawares; we killed a great many men, and took the others captive. Ibrahim Pasha headed off towards Diyarbakır. When this victory happened, it was the twentieth day since the dream I had in Ardabil. Erciş entered our possession without any opposition.

Verses

When by your endeavours your affairs prosper, remember that is due to divine support not your own efforts.

Ibrahim Pasha remained in Diyarbakır until an officer came from the sultan and executed him. Civil strife and revolt ended entirely, and the fire of fighting was extinguished.[31] Even if friendship was not in evidence, there was no disturbance or fighting. Muslims lived in ease and safety until the time that Alqas Mirza, in his foolishness, revolted against us.

---

30 Presumably the modern Engli Çayı.
31 Ibrahim Pasha was executed on Süleyman's orders in 1536, but in Istanbul according to all other sources. Ottoman accounts in fact attribute his execution to his lacklustre prosecution of the war against Tahmasp. See Celalzade, *Tabakat,* fol. 277a–278a. As so often, Tahmasp tells rather less than the full story. In fact, Ghazi Khan regained his favour and was appointed as *lāla* to Tahmasp's brother Alqas in Shirvan, where he also received substantial appanages. See Posch, *Osmanisch-safavidische Beziehungen,* 278–80.

3

The affair of Alqas Mirza

Whenever I read the history of Timur, and reached the following lines,

Verses

Shahrukh became his companion in fighting, like two swords in a single scabbard,

I would say that Alqas Mirza and I were in the same situation.[1] I loved him more than any of my brothers and sons, to the extent that I ordered that the 250 tomans that had been loaned to the sayyids and the virtuous and pious dependents of the holy shrine of the Imam al-Riza – peace be upon him – should not be repaid as long as Alqas Mirza was alive, so that in that holy shrine they would constantly pray for his life to be lengthened. The stupid man rebelled for no reason.[2] Two explanations alone occurred to me for his rebellion. The first is that he had a reprehensible affair with a fellow named Ughurlu,[xxii] who today is in the Ottoman lands, and he feared lest I hear about it and harm or punish him.[xxiii] Some members of his wretched retinue

---

1 Shahrukh (1377–1477) was the son of Timur (1335?–1405). Most likely the 'history of Timur' mentioned is Sharaf al-Din Yazdi's *Zafarnama*, composed in 1421–5 for Timur's grandson Ibrahim Mirza, although I have not been able to identify these lines in a published edition. The *Zafarnama* was a highly popular work of Persian historical writing and circulated widely.

2 Alqas was Tahmasp's brother and in 1538 has been appointed governor of Shirvan, after its conquest by the Shirvanshahs. Rumours of his insubordination evidently reached Tahmasp before he started to revolt openly in 1546–7. A contemporary Kurdish source suggests Alqas's revolt was incited by the followers of Ghazi Khan Tekellu, who had been executed by Alqas; Ghazi Khan's followers then entered Alqas's service. See Parmaksızoğlu, 'Kuzey Irak'ta Osmanlı Hakimiyetinin Kuruluşu', 209.

apparently used to drink wine with him,³ and, fearing that I would hear about it and punish them, taught him evil ways and turned him into an infamous rebel. The second is that before his rebellion spread and became public knowledge, I had sent the venerable 'Ali Aqa to him to advise him to forsake revolt rather than ties of kinship, explaining that this venture would not have a good outcome, resulting in both earthly and eternal harm, and that he should ask for forgiveness and turn back from this foolishness. I would also swear an oath that I was not angry at his behaviour and I would not seek to harm him or to get revenge on him. If he accepted, well and good, and I would entrust this affair to His Divine Majesty, mighty is He. 'Ali Aqa gave him advice to this effect, but he did not give any reply at all. Next, I sent a few of the more eminent amirs with a message saying, 'I've never done you wrong; you bring shame on your ancestors for this deed, for an evil from either side is repellent; your ill repute will last till the resurrection. If you do not desist from this enterprise which is a vain figment of your imagination, my lord 'Ali, who ripped down the gate of Khaybar,⁴ will cut your head from your body *by God's hand which is above your hands*.'⁵ I thought of the following verse:

Whoever does good or ill will find good and ill, whatever he does.

His good judgement was such that he swore an oath in the presence of the amirs, the military judge (*qāzī-ʿaskar*) and Mir Ibrahim Isfahani, who at that time was administrator of the Safavid shrine at Ardabil, that he would desist from this enterprise and come to his senses, and with the passage of time, would attempt to repair the evil he had done. Yet after the amirs left, he had the sermon said and coins minted in

---

3 This may refer to the retinue (*nöker*) of Ghazi Khan, who became attached to Alqas after his execution of the latter.
4 Among Shiites, one of 'Ali's famous exploits is destroying the gate of Khaybar and erecting the banner of Islam thereupon.
5 Qur'an 48:10.

his own name.⁶ When I was heading to campaign in Georgia,⁷ the fool committed some wrongful acts, for which I desired to chastise him. However, when we reached Qarabagh, he fled to Circassia by way of Darband accompanied by a few men. The Circassians wanted to seize him on some pretext and send him to us. Alqas was alerted and fled to Darband from where he sent me a letter saying, 'I'm going over to the sultan, see what I'm going to have done to you!' I replied, 'Have you not considered that there is one greater than the sultan, God *who knows all secrets*. He knows well the concealed secrets of all his servants, and gives everyone his desserts according to their intentions and deeds. Before his might, what are you or I or the sultan, and what importance do we have?'

Verses:

A gnat came and sat for a moment on the summit of Mount Kaf, drunk with pride

Then he flew off and disappeared into void; what did he add to or detract from that mountain?

Beside His might thus are we all, whether in the heavens or on earth. ⁸

Happiness depends on God's will, not the use of violence.⁹

However, when he set out from Kaffa to Istanbul,¹⁰ Rüstem Pasha,¹¹ who resembled Ibrahim Pasha in his evil essence, explained his

---

6 Having the *khuṭba* (sermon at Friday prayers) said in one's own name, along with the minting of coins (*sikka*) were the two main means by which pre-modern Islamic rulers asserted claims to independent, sovereign rule.
7 While Georgia was a regular target of Safavid campaigns, as a rich source of booty and slaves and a crucial frontier with the Ottomans, on this occasion Tahmasp's campaign seems to have been a feint; the real target was Alqas (see John R. Walsh, 'The Revolt of Alqās Mīrzā', *Wiener Zeitschrift für die Kunde des Morgenlandes* 68 (1976): 76).
8 Farid al-Din 'Attar, *Khusrawnama*, ed. Farshid Iqbal (Tehran, 1382).
9 Sa'di, *Bustan*, Book 5.
10 After a Safavid army under Bahram Mirza captured Alqas's last stronghold of the fortress of Darband, he fled via the Crimean port of Kaffa to Istanbul.
11 Rüstem Pasha (1505–1561), became Grand Vizier eight years after Ibrahim Pasha's execution; he served as Grand Vizier between 1544 and 1561; Alqas arrived in Istanbul in 1547.

situation rather differently to the sultan, and had him received with full honours and respect in Istanbul. He told a number of lies while he was there, claiming that all the Qizilbash were on his side and were his enthusiastic partisans. In truth, even if the Qizilbash's heads were cut off, they would not be separated from their 'crown',[12] and if Alqas had had himself crowned not one of them would have recognized him, for in the path of Sufism they only acknowledge a single guide (*murshid*). Even if there were a 100,000 princes, they would pay no attention to them. When the Qizilbash threw the crown from his head, it became clear how much they esteemed him.[13] His majesty the sultan should have first probed his understanding and intelligence, and only then acted as he suggests and had designs on our lands. In addition, his majesty the sultan should have first sent an ambassador to me and asked for his pardon. If I did not agree and give him an appanage, then the burden of proof would have been against us and any subsequent fighting would have been justified. If they violently attacked us then, they would have been in the right. In addition, they should have kept Alqas in Istanbul lest he should one day prove useful to them. However, Rüstem Pasha wronged us, but we are not angry with him. Having eaten the sultan's bread, he should have first said, 'Let us first talk to the Qizilbash about this matter, and find out what we don't know. When the truth of what he says is established, let's attack them, for otherwise, should his claims be baseless, we will be embarrassed.'

Verse

It would be a shame if someone on whose advice the king acts should say anything but good.[14]

---

12 The *tāj* (literally 'crown') refers to the distinctive Qizilbash headgear.
13 This seems to allude to very limited support for Alqas's attempt to declare independence among the Qizilbash of Shirvan, most of whom swiftly deserted. This is a point made elsewhere in Safavid propaganda. See Walsh, 'Revolt', 69.
14 Sa'di, *Gulistan*, Chapter 1, Story 1.

Yet without probing his intelligence and understanding or his truthfulness or lying, the Ottomans have launched a campaign against us. Showing themselves to be simpletons, the respect and awe in which they were held by the people of every province has been rendered vain and futile; seemingly they never heard these verses and do not read biographies of the Prophet,[15] histories and stories.

> Poem[16]
>
> The king said to himself, 'I am entrusting the kingdom of Iran to one whose
>
> Intelligence must be tested first; according to his skill will his rank be increased
>
> One who acts without testing will impose the burdens of oppression's woe upon his heart
>
> Even someone as righteous and discriminating as Joseph took forty years to become vizier.
>
> Until many days have passed, one cannot fathom someone's depths.
>
> Watch out while you have the notch in the thumbstall, not after you've loosed the arrow
>
> It would be a pity if reaching for a sword in haste ended up in regret.

After the death of Ibrahim Pasha, the strife that had been dormant for years was reawakened. Alqas first accompanied Ulama to Sivas. They wrote a long letter to Shah 'Ali Sultan Chepni[17] the governor of Van, saying 'Seize the castle key and bring it to me, and I will give

---

15 The term *siyar* refers particularly to biographies of the Prophet Muhammad. Tahmasp's point is that the Ottomans' ignorance means they fail to emulate the ideals of kingship acquired by reading exemplary literature.
16 Sa'di, *Bustan*, Book 1.
17 On him, see Posch, *Osmanisch-safavidische Beziehungen*, 48, 94, 284 and index s.v. Here Tahmasp calls him *ḥākim*, 'governor', but other sources describe him more precisely as the *kutvāl* (castle chatelain). A few years earlier, Shah 'Ali Sultan Chepni acted as Membré's principal host in the royal camp, and the Venetian mentions him frequently, describing him at that time as a 'rather stout man, 60 years old, with his beard half and more white'. See Membré, *Mission*, 18, 21, 23.

you an appanage worth ten times Van in Khurasan.' He also wrote, 'I am the son of the sultan; his majesty the sultan has adopted me as his son, and granted me all of my father Tahmasp's kingdom.' When this letter reached me, the insanity and stupidity of the Ottomans became completely clear as they were following the words and deeds of such a person. I replied that 'Kingship comes not from me, or you, or his majesty the sultan, but from Him who grants kingship to whomever He wants, according to His divine speech, *kingship is given to him whom he desires*.'[18]

Verse

Who is there on this ancient globe who can say '*to whom does kingship belong?*'[19] except God?[20]

In another letter, he claimed that the sultan was advancing with seven years' supplies of weapons and provisions and thousands of brave, well-equipped and armed soldiers. There were 10,000 mules who were burdened with carrying water, so that if they crossed a desert, they could send 100,000 men in their wake and they would be assured of the availability of water. I said, 'I know that his majesty the sultan possesses complete dignity and greatness and can come by whichever road he likes. I desire the help of God, the Lord of both worlds and of the Day of Judgement, glorious and all-generous is He.

Though my master who drinks to the dregs has neither money nor might left, he has a generous, beneficent God who covers his faults.[21]

---

18 Qur'an 3:26.
19 Qur'an 40:16.
20 Nizami, *Makhzan al-Asrar* in Nizami-yi Ganjavi, *Kulliyat*, ed. Hasan Vahid Dastgirdi (Tehran, 2013).
21 Hafiz, *Divan*, Ghazal 123.

In another letter, he wrote that he would give me 300,000 *ashrafi* gold coins[22] in addition to horses, bejewelled equipment, textiles, mules and camels. I wrote in reply,

> 'Horses and cash will do you no good for you have sold the faith for these things. There is a hadith that *The world is carrion, its seekers are dogs*. Wise men have said on this subject:
>
> Verse:
>
> Heart, pass over the two days' worth of cash, for two days' worth is no use to you.
>
> Choose that type of cash with which on the Day of Reckoning you will acquire a place in the Eternal Abode
>
> As for the luxury items that you wrote about, you know that each one of my amirs possesses more than this. I would be as stupid as you if I were to boast of worldly cash, possessions and belongings. The cash which I always have praised and always will, to which I have given a place inside my heart and soul, which I hold a hundred thousand times dearer and more precious than my soul and all the world *and everything in it* is that which will be of use in both this world and the next, the cash of love and devotion to my lord and that of all the Muslims, 'Ali. I imagine that I have neither army, nor treasury, nor possessions, nor help from anyone in this world. You will see what use to you will be your helpers, your cash, and your possessions that you were given, and what use my cash, which is the devotion and love of my Lord and helper, 'Ali.[23]

---

22 *Ashrafis* were a type of gold coin originating in Egypt that was also widely used from the fifteenth century in eastern Anatolia and the Safavid empire. See Bert Fragner, 'Ashrafi', *Encyclopaedia Iranica* II/8, 797–8.

23 The following verses in the text, hadith and Qur'anic quotations all support a Shiite interpretation of political authority, transmitted via 'Ali, and thus underline that by taking refuge with the Ottomans and converting to Sunnism, Alqas has relinquished any legitimacy. For Shiite interpretations of the Qur'an and their political context, with reference to Shiite exegesis, see Joseph Elias, 'The Ithnā'asharī-Shī'ī Juristic Theory of Political and Legal Authority', *Studia Islamica* 29 (1969): 17–30; Hamid Manavi, 'Doctrine of Imamate in Twelver Shi'ism Traditional, Theological, Philosophical and

Verse

There is a coin in my heart which resembles red sulphur

It is a coin without which Adam's prayers would not have effect

It is a coin which when Abraham read it, not a single hair of his was burned in the fire

It is a coin without which even Moses' piety and asceticism would not have bought half a grain of silver.

It is a coin which the Prophet Muhammad made equal to himself

It is a coin that is precious and very valuable, do you know what it is? The protection of 'Ali.

My lord 'Ali is dearer to the Creator than your lord the sultan, and my sincere attachment to him is apparent. His qualities, relationship, station and reputation at the court of Almighty God is such that if for a hundred thousand years men and jinn were to become scribes, and forests became pens, and the seven heavens became paper, and the oceans became ink, they would be unable to write a fraction of his virtues.[24]

Verse:

All the water in the sea would be insufficient to wet your finger to turn the pages of the book of your virtues.[25]

Repeated evidence for the truth of what I say comes from the verses of the Noble Qur'an which we included in the letter.

Firstly, *[Abraham] said, 'And will my offspring [become leader]? God replied, 'Tyrants will not receive my covenant'* [Qur'an 2:124].[26]

Mystical Perspectives', PhD thesis, McGill University, 2005. In general on the theory of the Imamate in a Shiite Iranian context. see Arjomand, *Shadow of God*.
24 An echo of Qur'an 18:109.
25 A famous line from a qasida in praise of 'Ali by the early Safavid poet Umidi.
26 In this verse, God promises to make Abraham a 'leader to mankind' (lil-nās imāman). This verse played a crucial part in Shiite theology, for it was understood to affirm that imams were both divinely appointed and infallible.

Also: *'And none know its explanation except God and those firmly rooted in knowledge'* [Qur'an 3:7].[27]

Also: *'[God chose ...] the House of 'Imran above all beings* [Qur'an 3:33].[28]

Also the verse for the day of al-Mubahala [Qur'an 3:61]: *'Say, 'Come, let us call our sons and your sons, our women and your women, our souls and your souls.'*[29]

Also: *'Obey God, obey the Prophet and those who have authority among you'* [Qur'an 4:59].[30]

Also: *'Today I have perfected your religion, and completed my blessing towards you, and have approved Islam as your religion* [Qur'an 5:3].[31]

Also: *'Indeed your protector* [walī] *is God, his messenger and those who perform the prayer and pay alms while they are bowing down'* [Qur'an 5:55].[32]

---

27 'Those firmly rooted in knowledge' (*al-rāsikhūn fī'l-'ilm*) are understood by Shiites to be the imams. In other words, only the imams are able to undertake the exegesis of the Qur'an.
28 In the Qur'an, the full verse reads 'God chose Adam and Noah and the House of Abraham and the House of 'Imran above all beings.' Shiites sometimes identified 'Imran with 'Ali b. Abi Talib. In the abridged form of the verse that Shah Tahmasp gives, it therefore functions to justify God's choice of the family of 'Ali to be his Imams, and thus ultimately Tahmasp himself with his claim to 'Alid descent.
29 This verse, known as 'al-Mubāhala' or 'the cursing' is said to relate to dispute between the Prophet and the Christians of Najran, when both sides agreed to ask God to curse whichever of them was lying about their religious differences. The verse is understood by Shiite and some Sunni exegetes to refer to Hasan and Husayn, Fatima, and 'Ali b. Abi Talib, who were all allegedly present on the occasion and, in Shiite interpretations, played a leading role in the Mubahala. For Shiites, the Mubahala episode ultimately came to signify the divine affirmation of the 'Alids' authority over the Muslim community. See further W. Schmucker, 'Mubāhala', *Encyclopaedia of Islam*, 2nd edition (Leiden, 1966–2005).
30 In the Shiite interpretation of this verse, 'those who have authority' (*ūlū al-amr*) are understood to be the imams, and the verse is interpreted as supporting their infallibility.
31 In the Shiite interpretation, this verse was revealed after the Prophet's sermon at Ghadir Khumm shortly before his death in 632, and refers to his appointment of 'Ali as his successor to lead the Muslim community.
32 Again, this so-called verse of *wilāya* is of fundamental importance to Shiites in supporting 'Ali's claim to authority, with 'those who perform the prayer and pay zakat while they are bowing down' being interpreted as 'Ali b. Abi Talib, making him third in authority after God and the Prophet. The Shiite interpretation hinges on their understanding of the word *walī*, which Sunni authorities deny means anything more than 'friend' in this context.

Also the noble verse: *'Those who believe and do good works, they shall enjoy blessedness and a fair everlasting abode'* [Qur'an 13:29].[33]

Also the noble verse that was revealed at Ghadir Khumm: *'O Messenger, Proclaim what has been revealed to you from God, and if you do not you have not proclaimed his message. God will protect you from people'* [Qur'an 5:67].[34]

Also: *'Say: God is a sufficient witness between me and you, and whoever has knowledge of the Book'* [Qur'an 13:43].[35]

Also *'We shall call together all people with their imam'* [Qur'an 17:71].[36]

Also: *'Say: were the sea ink for the words of my lord, it would run out before the words of my lord, even were you to bring the same amount of ink again'*[Qur'an 18:109].

Also: *'God desires to remove impurity from you, People of the Household, and to purify you completely'* [Qur'an 33:33].[37]

Also: *'God is his protector, and Gabriel, and the righteous believers'* [Qur'an 66:4].[38]

Also *'Say: I do not ask for any recompense except love of kinsfolk'* [Qur'an 42:23].[39]

---

33 The word translated here as 'blessedness', *ṭūbā*, has a particular significance for Shiites. *Ṭūbā* is considered to be the name of a tree in paradise, whose roots stretched into 'Ali b. 'Abi Talib's house. Alternatively, the *ṭūbā* tree was closely associated with Fatima, 'Ali's wife and the Prophet's daughter, for in Shiite stories of 'Ali's heavenly wedding to Fatima, the marriage was celebrated beneath the tree. See David Waines, 'Tree(s)', in *Encyclopaedia of the Qur'an* (Leiden, 2005); Denise L. Soufi, 'The Image of Fāṭima in Classical Muslim Though', PhD dissertation, Princeton University, 1997, 39–40. Whatever the interpretation, Qur'an 13:29 to a Shiite audience would have recalled God's special favour to the 'Alids.
34 In the Shiite understanding, this verse refers to Muhammad's proclamation of 'Ali as his successor at Ghadir Khumm shortly before his death.
35 Shiite exegetes would understand 'whoever has knowledge of the Book' as referring to 'Ali b. Abi Talib.
36 For Shiites, a crucial verse in justifying the existence of the imamate.
37 According to Shiite exegetes, this so-called Purification verse confirms the infallibility of the 'People of [the Prophet's] Household' (*ahl al-bayt*), that is, Muhammad, 'Ali, Fatima, and their sons Hasan and Husayn, and thus ultimately the 'Alid imams.
38 Exegetes understand this as referring to God protecting Muhammad from his wives Hafsa and 'A'isha.
39 In the Shiite interpretation, this is an injunction to believers to love the imams, who are Muhmmad's kinsfolk.

And the noble verse: *'Oh you who believe, when you consult with the Prophet, present a charitable offering before your consultation'* [Qur'an 58:12].[40]

They say that the water-bearer of the pool of Kawthar in paradise was the Commander of the Faithful 'Ali b. Abi Talib, blessings upon him and his family, in accordance with the noble verse *Indeed the pious will drink from a cup containing a mixture of camphor* [Qur'an 76:5], and the verse *They perform the vow and fear a day of which the evil is widespread, and feed the poor, the orphan and the prisoner for love of Him* [Qur'an 76: 7–8], *And He has rewarded them with Paradise and silk for what they endured* [Qur'an 76: 12], and the noble verse *Of what do they ask each other? Is it of the great news? No, but they will know* [Qur'an 78: 1–3], and the noble verse *Indeed we have given you Abundance*[41] [Qur'an 108: 1].

Verse

The third of the discourse is praise of the imam, without doubt, whoever doubts this denies God.[42]

There are also the hadith of his excellency the Messenger of God, Muhammad, peace and blessings be upon him and his family. *The Messenger of God said, 'Oh 'Ali, your flesh is my flesh, your blood is my blood, your body is my body, and your spirit is my spirit.'* Another hadith is *'You are in relation to me as Aaron was to Moses, except that there is no prophet after me.'* Another hadith: is *'Whoever I am his lord, 'Ali is his lord.'* The Prophet prayed for him, *'God, be a friend*

---

40 This verse was subsequently abrogated; only 'Ali b. Abi Talib obeyed it and paid to consult with the Prophet. The function of the verse here is thus to underline 'Ali's unique obedience and special status within the community.
41 Abundance (*al-kawthar*) is interpreted by Shiites as referring to Fatima, 'Ali's wife and Muhammad's daughter.
42 'The third of the discourse' (thalāth al-kalām) seems to refer to Qur'an 4:49 cited earlier in the text, *'Obey God, obey the Prophet and those who have authority among you'* in which, according to Shiites, the third being to whom obedience is enjoined, 'those who have authority among you' refers to the imam.

to their friends, an enemy to their enemies, help those who help them, denigrate those who denigrate them and curse those who oppress them.' Another hadith is related from Ibn Malik. '*God, send me the most beloved of your creation to me to eat this bird.*'[43] Another is '*You are the sun and 'Ali is the moon*.' There is a divine hadith[44] '*There is no hero but 'Ali and no sword but Zu'l-Fiqar*'[45] and another is '*I am the city of knowledge and 'Ali is its gate*.' Another: '*Oh 'Ali, no one loves you but the pious believer and no one hates you but the wretched hypocrite.*' Another: '*'Ali and I come from a single light.*' Another: '*'Ali and I are God's proof to his servants*.' A divine hadith: '*If the people had agreed to love 'Ali b. Abi Talib, God would not have created the hell-fire*.'

In short, on 24 Jumada al-Awwal 955 (1 July 1548), spies came bringing intelligence that his majesty the sultan had reached Sivas, where he was staying for three weeks so they could rub the camels with oil.[46] We were in Qazvin, and I summoned the nobles, the chief inhabitants and the ordinary people of each quarter and said, 'I have appointed a unit of our troops to go ahead of the Ottoman army and burn all the crops and produce, and consume what they could. Be reassured, and do not curse us for being the cause of this strife and conflict, whatever losses you incur I will compensate in cash and kind. We have had the crops of that area consumed or burned,

---

43 This alludes to the 'hadith of the roast bird' (*ḥadīth al-ṭā'ir al-mashwī*) which records the virtues of 'Ali b. Abi Talib. The Prophet was presented with a roast bird, and he asked God to send him his most beloved creature to share the meal with him. Companions like Abu Bakr and 'Umar attempted to gain entry to the Prophet's house, but he rejected them, admitting only 'Ali b. Abi Talib, thus proving that 'Ali was the most beloved of God's creation.
44 Hadith qudsi, that is, one incorporating divine speech.
45 Zu'l-fiqar ('The splitter') was the name of 'Ali's sword; this hadith was commonly used on talismans.
46 Camels were covered in tar to prevent their skin being attacked by flies, especially in spring when their fur fell off. See Jean-Baptiste Tavernier, *The Six Voyages of John Baptista Tavernier, Baron of Aubonne through Turky, into Persia and the East-Indies, for the space of forty years* (London, 1678), Chapter XI.

and the irrigation channels filled in. The nature of war is clear to the intelligent and wise: it is a game in which one must act however is possible and expedient to overcome the enemy. The Commander of the Faithful, 'Ali, peace be upon him, said, '*War is betrayal.*' In war, one must resort to flight or to deceit so as to not give an opportunity to the enemy. Now we have heard the truth from this informant, it has been verified that approximately 300,000 cavalry in addition to the Janissaries (*qulluqchi*) are accompanying his majesty the sultan. If each one of them is accompanied by a servant, that will make 600,000 mounted men. Each man and mount will require two *mann*[47] of food each day, which makes 15,000 assloads each weighing 100 *mann*. Assuming they have brought 500,000 or 600,000 camels with them to carry the provisions, this will not last them more than a month. We have eaten up and burned down everything so as not to go face to face with them in battle. How will things turn out for them? If they advance for one month, what choice will they have but retreat? Where will they find additional provisions? I have said time and again in the presence of the amirs that the Ottoman army is like syphilis, if you try to cure it at the onset of its attack, it will kill the patient. If you do not monitor it, it will be bad; one must monitor the disease and let it do as it wishes; then it can easily be cured.[48] Other than through lack of provisions, how else can the Ottomans be weakened?

---

47 *Mann* was the principal weight used in Iran; in this period, it was equivalent to roughly 3–6 kg, although its value could fluctuate to under 1 kg. Here it seems the Tabrizi *mann* is meant, approximately 3 kg, as below an 'assload' (*kharvar*) is described as equalling 100 *mann*, and an assload weighed 300 kg. See Ulrich Rebstock, 'Weights and Measures in Islam', in Helaine Selin (ed.): *Encyclopaedia of the History of Science, Technology, and Medicine in Non-Western Cultures* (Berlin: Springer, 2008), 2261.

48 Medical theory of the period suggests that the best way to treat syphilis was to stimulate it, in order to bring the disease to the surface and then expel it. See C. Elgood (trans.), 'A Persian Monograph on Syphilis', *Annals of Medical History* 3 (1931): 465–87, esp. 471–4.

> If you have all the highest quality gold, a man with nothing to his name will not move a single step
>
> In the desert cooked turnip is better to a thirsty stranger than raw silver.[49]

Shaykh Muslih al-Din Sa'di has also said in this connection:[50]

> The ear may not hear the drum, the lute or the reed pipe its life long
>
> The eye can forego the sight of a garden; the brain can survive without roses and the eglantine.
>
> Someone who doesn't have a pillow stuffed with feathers would sleep soundly with a stone beneath his head
>
> If he doesn't have a beloved to share his bed, he can put his arms round himself
>
> But this useless, wiggling stomach doesn't have the patience to adapt itself to lack.

As for treating the problem of the Ottoman army, there is no other remedy than this. If they occupy our country, our treatment is to block provisions from reaching them by every route. Our war with them is conducted in the same way. Otherwise it is madness and nonsense to shed the blood of Muslims for no reward and risking our own destruction is contrary to what the Creator has ordered us, glorious is He.

When his majesty the sultan came to Khoy, we sent a man to 'Abdallah Khan,[51] and to a group of amirs we had sent as scouts. I sent instructions to them, saying 'Make their surroundings into a desert, do not let yourselves be seen at all, and return on the same day to rendezvous with us in the summer pasture of Eshkenber.[52] When his

---

49 Sa'di, *Gulistan*, Chapter 3, story 17.
50 Sa'di, *Gulistan*, Chapter 3, story 29.
51 'Abdallah Khan Ustajlu.
52 The summer pasture of Eshkenber lies in the Karaja Dagh, the mountains between Tabriz and Ardabil. See Posch, *Osmanisch-safavidische Beziehungen*, 431, 432, 445, 452.

majesty the sultan enters Tabriz, we will send ten thousand men to march to the foot of the fortress of Van to attack Ulama,[53] and perhaps we will capture the wretch.'

When our messenger reached the amirs, he halted there for a day. They burned some of the areas that had been allocated for their own provisions, and the sultan's vanguard caught up with them, so they returned to us. When his majesty the sultan reached Tabriz, the following groups of amirs were at a distance of five farsakhs from the city. First there was Bahram Mirza with 1,800 men, then Chiragh Sultan with 1,500 men, 'Ali-Quli Beg Turkman with 2,000 men, Allah-Quli Beg, the governor of Darabjird, with 500 men, Charandab Sultan, the governor of Ij and Shabankara,[54] with 500 men, Amir Khan, the governor of Shiraz with 3,500 men, Shah Quli, the governor of Kirman, with 2,000 men, Köpek Sultan, the governor of Kazarun, with 800 men, Mahmud Khan, the governor of Kuhgiluya, with 3,000 men from the Afshar tribe, the irregulars and *qūrchīs* of Qavzin who were 1,600 men, and men of Süglen and Ardabil, who were 450 strong and fully armed.[55] We held a council of war with the amirs and troops, and suggested that we go to Ahar and wait there until the aforementioned forces could join us, so that we would all be gathered in a single place. When we had marched the first stage, Chiragh Sultan, Charandab Sultan and 'Ali-Quli Beg arrived, and

---

53 Ulama by this point had been appointed as governor of Erzurum by the Ottomans, in which capacity he was prosecuting operations against the Safavids, principally by besieging the crucial fortress of Van. He served as governor between March and September 1548. On his tenure, see Dündar Aydın, *Erzurum Beylerbeyliği ve Teşkilatı: Kuruluş ve Genişleme Devri (1535–1566)* (Ankara, 1998), 102–4.
54 Ij is located in Fars, southeast of Shiraz; although now a small village, in earlier times, it was a town and political centre (Ibnu'l-Balkhī, *Fārsnāma*, ed. G. Le Strange and R. A. Nicholson (London, 1962), 131, 162). Shabankara refers both to a Kurdish tribe and the region they dominated in Southern Iran.
55 For the rather different figures given in other sources, see Posch, *Osmanisch-safavidische Beziehungen*, 208. Tahmasp's estimates of the strength of Safavid forces are consistently higher than those found in other Safavid chronicles.

at the second stage Bahram Mirza, Ibrahim Khan, the governor of Shiraz,[56] and Allah Quli Beg did. His majesty the sultan was in Tabriz and we were in Ahar. We undertook a pilgrimage to Shaykh Shihab al-Din Ahari,[57] and cursed Alqas for the great trouble he had caused us. I supplicated profoundly to the court of the Creator, Glorious is He, saying, 'Creator, you have said, "I love broken hearts and can be found in broken hearts."[58] Now I am broken-hearted because of the tumult and distress that afflicts the weak and the ordinary people. Have mercy! For nothing other than your mercy can help us.' I lamented greatly, and that very night I saw in a dream Shaykh Shihab al-Din. He said, 'All us shaykhs were praying for you today, assuredly this will be answered.' His majesty the sultan remained in Tabriz for four days after this dream. The worry and fear in his heart gathered strength and returned.

Verse

If you entrust your affairs to God, Hafiz, oft will you enjoy divine favour.[59]

Hafiz, peace be upon him, also said:

Verse

Entrust your case to God and be of good heart, for if the plaintiff does not have mercy, God will.[60]

---

56 Ibrahim Khan Zulqadar (not to be confused with Ibrahim Khan Mawsillu), who held the appanage of Shiraz at this time; subsequently he was assigned Rudan (Iraq), then Astarabad. On him, see Posch, *Osmanich-safavidische Beziehungen*, index, s.v. Parsadust, *Shah Tahmasp*, 197, 204, 519, 520, 680.

57 Shihab al-Din Mahmud Ahari (also known as Tabrizi) lived during the thirteenth century, and was reputed to be a son of the famous Sufi Shihab al-Din Suhrawardi (d. 1191). Rizvi notes that he was 'considered a spiritual ancestor to the Safavids', and his name was included in Shaykh Safi's spiritual genealogy, inscribed in the dynastic shine at Ardabil. Safavid rulers included the tomb of Shihab al-Din at Ahar (some seventy miles northwest of Ardabil) on their pilgrimage itineraries, and both Tahmasp and 'Abbas I made generous gifts to the shrine. See Rizvi, *Safavid Dynastic Shrine*, 167–73.

58 An allusion to the hadith qudsi 'I am with those whose hearts are broken for my sake' (*ana 'inda al-munkasirat qulūbuhum min ajlī*).

59 Hafiz, *Divan*, Ghazal 481.

60 Hafiz, *Divan*, Ghazal 187.

Before the sultan retreated, I was in Ahar, and said to the amirs, 'Appoint three thousand men to raise the camp and go by way of Jushin-Darbar to Ordubad. You should march with two thousand men to attack Ulama in Van. Five thousand men should go to Kars. I will follow directly after you. Try to capture Ulama; burn the vicinity of Van and everywhere where the sultan will later come where there are crops. We will go from there towards Chukhur-i Saʻd, and the army contingent that is heading towards Kars should kill the Ottoman troops who are sent to repair the damage.' The amirs replied, 'Until Bahram Mirza and his amirs come and join us, there is no point in us going anywhere.' Therefore, we decided to stay in Ahar and sent Ibrahim Khan with 3,000 men as scouts. Meanwhile, the Arab camels arrived. An arsenal of 250 assloads of munitions were left there. If we were to march, we had decided that we would halt one stage further on and divide these munitions among the troops and then return. We had gone four farsakhs, and we halted for a day, and busied ourselves with distributing the munitions, when our spies came bringing intelligence that the sultan was withdrawing. Ibrahim Khan was eight farsakhs away from Tabriz, and pursued the Ottomans as far as Tasuj.[61] We also went in pursuit, but when we reached Chaldiran, we were informed that the sultan had gone to besiege the fort of Van.

Shah Quli Sultan and Mahmud Khan, the governor of Kuhgiluyah, reached our camp [*ordu*] the same day. Some people said, 'Let's ambush the Ottomans at night.' I replied, 'Let us go from here to Erzurum, for when the sultan hears that we have entered his territories he will certainly abandon his attempt to take Van.' We agreed on this with the amirs and sent Ismaʻil Mirza with 7,000 men to attack the fort of Kars; when he had killed and pillaged the people of Kars, he would head from there to Erzurum. We went in person to Erciş two days later, and I learned that the sound of the Ottomans' guns and artillery had fallen

---

61 Tasuj is on the northern shore of Lake Urmiya.

silent. I was informed that Shah ʿAli Sultan Chepni[xxiv] had surrendered the fort,[62] on account of which I was sorely distressed and grieved, for the shadow of the Yellow Rock[63] sheltered all of Azerbaijan, and with it a pillar that upheld Azerbaijan had fallen. There was no choice but to head to Hınıs and Pasinler. When the sultan first came there, I had decided to sack the fortress of Van and not leave a single fort intact in all of Azerbaijan before they reached them. At that point there were some people standing in our way who did not allow us to do this. However, now that the story of the capture of Van and Alqas had unfolded, my zeal was renewed. I reflected that as long as Alqas was in their hands, strife and fighting would continue. I have no choice other than this: wherever we can reach in the sultan's territories, I will sack it, burn its crops and raid, without staying for a single day in any place. I will make the entire frontier a deserted wasteland, completely uninhabitable for a distance of ten days' journey, so that there will be nowhere they can go.

Everyone approved this plan and praised it. In short, we burned Hınıs and Pasinler, and were waiting in Pasinler wondering what the sultan would decide to do, when intelligence came that the sultan had come to the ruined city of Hınıs. Nonetheless we waited in Pasinler for we knew that their mounts were completely emaciated and weak, and famine had struck their camp. They retreated and we marched from there to attack Muş. Intelligence arrived that the sultan was passing via Bitlis, so we advanced from the place where we were. The Chemishkezeklü *qūrchī*s who had gone to find intelligence came back bringing two spies they had seized. I asked them for information about the situation, and they replied that 'The sultan has written a

---

62 Van fell to the besieging Ottomans, led by Ulama, Rüstem Pasha and joined by Sultan Süleyman himself on 24 August 1548. See Emecen, *Sultan Süleyman*, 403.
63 Tahmasp calls the Rock of Van by a Turkish name, 'Saru Kaya', or 'Yellow Rock'. I have not seen this term attested elsewhere, but it is clear that the great Rock of Van on which the fortress was situated is meant.

order for Ulama and Rüstem Pasha, saying that he had gone to Kara Amid,⁶⁴ and they should remain in Tercan until the first snow falls. Then they should make winter quarters in Azerbaijan.'

When I heard the report, I sent 'Ali Sultan Taqioghli with 2,000 men to burn Ahlat and Muş. People said, 'Ulama is in Tercan, we should go and attack him.' What they said concurred with my thoughts, so we marched the same day. It happened that two days before we arrived Ulama and Rüstem Pasha had set off for Bayburt, and Ulama was in Azerbaijan. We ordered that the whole of the province of Bayburt and Tercan should be burned and sacked. I decided that wherever there was a mosque, I would establish a senior army officer so that no one would threaten mosques. Apart from that, all buildings were burned down except for mosques. Every time they invaded our lands they saw our property as licit for them, but we never saw their property and subjects as licit to us, but we did bear off those things that were licit – chickens, sheep, oil, provisions and other things. On this occasion too we had taken licit items according to custom and we had decided that every day, thirty trays of food would be prepared for me in the morning and fifty trays at night. At this time, one day during the blessed month of Ramadan, we were riding by the banks of the lake⁶⁵ to catch fish to eat which we considered licit, when twenty men on foot approached. They said, 'We are from Hınıs, we have been raided and if we stayed there we would die of hunger. We have come to go to Diyarbakır.' From horseback, I cursed Alqas, and I wept at their condition. We marched on and halted at Ab-i Tutun.⁶⁶ Two of our Chemishkezeklü spies came and reported that it was confirmed

---

64 Kara Amid (also written Kara Hamid) refers to Amid/Diyarbakır. This was evidently intended to be winter quarters for the bulk of the Ottoman army.
65 Āb, literally 'water'; most probably Lake Van is meant, but it could also be another lake or river, conceivably the Euphrates which rises in this region.
66 All manuscripts have here Ab-i Tutun 'Tobacco Juice', a non-existent place. Posch argues this must be a copying mistake for Kötür near Tercan, where other sources attest that the shah stopped. See Posch, *Osmanisch-safavidische Beziehungen*, 501, 768, n. 348.

that Alqas had been sent to Hamadan. Our troops and our amirs were in Bayburt and Azerbaijan, and other than the *qūrchī*s there was no one with me. The spies further reported that the sultan himself had withdrawn to Harput, and had sent Ahmed Pasha[67] with 2,000 musketeers (*tüfenkçi*s) to Kiği,[xxv] which they had reached.

After that I consulted my *qūrchī*s about what should be done. Ibrahim Aqa-yi Burbur[68] said, 'Let's march on Mama Hatun[69] and send a messenger to summon the amirs in Bayburt and some of the amirs who are in Azerbaijan; and the amirs who burned down Erzincan should also come. Let's send two thousand men. If Ahmed Pasha reaches Kiği,[xxvi] they can show him our might.' Jilawdar Muhammad Yuzbashi and Maqsud Beg Inan Oghli said, 'This is strange behaviour for the Ottomans to let Alqas go to Iraq. They must have taken him to the Pasha of Baghdad, in order to go to Derteng, Khaniqin and Qizil Ribat,[xxvii][70] thinking that if we heard that Alqas had gone to Iraq, we would retreat. After our retreat, they would send someone to bring Alqas back.' Muhammad Aqa and Inanoghli added, 'We are ten farsakhs from Erzincan, why do we not march on Erzincan and completely burn it down. Why should we pass up the opportunity simply because Ahmed Pasha has advanced? If the sultan himself comes, we'll escape via Bayburt.' I thought their suggestion was sensible. We marched on Erzincan, and when Osman Pasha[71]

---

67 Kara Ahmed Pasha (d. 1555), subsequently (1553–5) grand vizier of the Ottoman Empire, and at this point third vizier. On him, see Posch, *Osmanisch-safavidische Beziehungen*, 486–9; M. Cavid Baysun, 'Aḥmad Pas̲h̲a, Ḳara', *Encyclopaedia of Islam*, 2nd edition (Leiden, 1966–2005).
68 Ibrahim Aqa-yi Burbur and the subsequently mentioned Jilawdar Muhammad Yuzbashi and Maqsud Beg Inanoghli are all Shah Tahmasp's *qūrchī*s. See Posch, *Osmanich-safavidische Beziehungen*, 501.
69 This refers to Tercan near Erzincan, the burial place of the twelfth-century Saltukid princess Mama Hatun.
70 Derteng, Khaniqin, and Qizil Ribat are all settlements on the Iran-Iraq border; Derteng lies in modern Iran but at the time was under Ottoman control, as were the other settlements. Evidently the fear was that Alqas was being sent to lead a cross-border attack on the Safavids from Baghdad.
71 Osman Pasha was the Ottoman governor (*sancakbey*) of Malatya. See Posch, *Osmanisch-safavidische Beziehungen*, 504–8; Emecen, *Sultan Süleyman*, 404, 406.

clashed with the Zulqadar and Ustajlu *qūrchī*s whom we had sent as scouts, he was defeated, sent packing and a huge number of Ottomans were killed.

Then we marched from Erzincan to Bayburt where the Qizilbash took captive many Armenian children.[72] We gathered them up, put them in baskets[73] and we left. We ordered 'Abdallah Khan to bring them to the foot of the citadel and leave them, and come to us. Then we went to Erzurum. Oghlan Qasim Pazuki,[74] who was a member of the large contingent who came out of the citadel, was taken captive by the *qūrchī*s. He also reported that Alqas had gone to Hamadan. I said, 'I find it very strange for the Ottomans to let Alqas go his separate way on his own.' This verse occurred to me:

Verse

Much good fortune may befall you on the road, but if you are not alert you will lose the way.[75]

The troops also took some children captive there. We treated them in the same way, sending them to the foot of the citadel. Then we ourselves headed to Chukhur-i Sa'd. I still did not believe that the Ottomans had let Alqas go. I sent Isma'il Mirza to Shirvan as governor (*mutaṣṣarif*) there.[76] I sent the *qūrchī-bāshī* with 2,500 men to take Shakki.[77] I gave permission to Bahram Mirza and

---

72 According to Ottoman sources, the shah departed from Erzincan on 17 October 1548. See Posch, *Osmanisch-safavidische Beziehungen*, 508.
73 It seems they were put in baskets that were to be carried by camels for ease of transport.
74 The Pazukis were Kurds, a subdivision of the Rojaki who dominated Bitlis, who had alliances with both the Safavids and the Ottomans. It is possible that the name is a copyist error for Aslan, for a certain Aslan Beg Pazuki is mentioned by Sharaf al-Din as one of Tahmasp's *qūrchī*s. See Posch, *Osmanisch-safavidische Beziehungen*, 86–7; Sharaf al-Din Khan, *Sharafnama*, I, 330.
75 Nizami, *Khusraw u Shirin*.
76 What Tahmasp does not mention is that a member of the former ruling Shirvanshah dynasty, Burhan 'Ali Sultan, who was also Alqas's nephew, was asserting himself as ruler of Shirvan with Ottoman support. The appointment of Tahmasp's son, Isma'il Mirza, with Gökche Sultan Qajar as his *lāla*, was intended to shore up faltering Safavid authority in this critical border region. See Posch, *Osmanisch-safavidische Beziehungen*, 653–8.
77 A strategically important town in Shirvan.

Ibrahim Khan and the amirs of Iraq, Fars and Kirman to return to their own appanages, and I went to Qarabagh to establish winter quarters. Meanwhile, recurrent reports arrived that Alqas had reached Iraq, and had raided the households of Bahram Mirza and Chiragh Sultan, and had divided up the slavegirls he had taken as booty, and carried off Bahram Mirza's son. A man came from Alqas reporting that he had said to his entourage, 'If I take Bahram Mirza's son to the sultan, he will order me to kill him, and after I do that, Bahram Mirza will kill my own sons in recompense. So it is better not to go to the sultan.'

In the end, news that we were coming reached him in Qum. He fled towards Shiraz, taking Bahram Mirza's son along with the money and effects he had plundered, but did not stop there in his frenzy, instead heading to Baghdad via Shushtar. En route to Shushtar, he sent a letter asking for peace terms. I replied to his request by writing a formal letter of conciliation, but my entourage were saying, 'If tomorrow Alqas comes from one direction and the sultan from the other, who knows how things will turn out for us?' They thought it advisable to grant him Shirvan and avoid conflict by sending him there. I was so sorely wounded and distressed at this that I wept. While I was weeping, the following verses from the Seven-strophe poem (*haft-band*) of the late Mawlana Hasan Kashi came to mind, and I read them out weeping all the while:

> O great Ka'ba of Union that Muhammad described, qibla of the earth and faith, soul of Muhammad's world.[78]
>
> Your mouth was filled with the pearls of wisdom since your lips kissed Muhammad's.
>
> No one since Muhammad has been worthy until you stepped into Muhammad's mighty shoes.

---

78 The Shiite poet Hasan Kashi (*c.* 1281 – after 1337) was the author of the famous *Haft-band* ('Seven Strophes'), a poem devoted to praise of 'Ali b. Abi Talib.

Your sword is a cloud, bountiful as the sea; its water of victory refreshes the garden of Muhammad.

Since the firmament of the Law is full of his light, there has never shone in Muhammad's sky a moon brighter than you.

Wayfarers of the world of verification (i.e. Sufis) have no way to Muhammad's sky save by kissing the floor before your door.

Mere mortals' tongues cannot express the attributes of your Being; the only one who could would be Muhammad.

I cannot sing a panegyrist's praises in this court, O you whose encomiast is God through Muhammad's tongue.

There is no need to plead for my needs with you, for you know what they are; you know that my salvation is in the family of Muhammad.

Obligation to people has driven me to despair; have mercy on me! By Muhammad's life save me from the people's obligations.

Do not turn mercy's face away from me, oh my heart's desire; by the revered face of the Prophet, cast a glance towards me.

In the end, Rüstem Pasha wrote a letter to Mehmed Pasha, the governor of Baghdad, to the effect that it was not advisable to kill Alqas in this region lest civil strife ensued. Instead, someone should be appointed to make sure he left Ottoman territory, and if he did not agree he should be executed or expelled so he did not return to these parts. When Alqas understood his situation, he fled alone to Ardalan. He got Badi' al-Zaman, son of Bahram Mirza, to intercede for him and seek peace terms. A few days later, Badi' al-Zaman and Mirza Baqir, who was a long-standing companion of Alqas, came to me and explained the situation. I did not give a response. Three days later, reports arrived that Mehmed Pasha, the governor of Baghdad, had sent an army against him, and he had also fled from that place to Surkhab Sultan.[79] When Bahram Mirza and the amirs were informed,

---

79 Surkhab Sultan was a member of the Kurdish dynasty that ruled Ardalan and Shahrizor, but a rival of his Safavid-inclined brother Bege Beg. Alqas thus tried to manipulate

they set off to attack him. Surkhab Sultan seized Alqas and took him to the castle of Shibla.[80] He sent a messenger saying, 'Send the holy sayyid Shah Ni'matallah[81] to come and swear that you will not kill him, and I will hand him over.' The aforementioned holy sayyid was brought by the amirs. Meanwhile I prostrated myself in thanking God that, having entrusted the affair of Alqas to my lord the Commander of the Faithful and Imam of the pious, the Lion of God the victorious Commander of the Faithful 'Ali b. Abi Talib, peace be upon him, he has delivered Alqas into my hands.[82] When he was captured and brought before me, I said, 'You see that my lord is more powerful than your protector, and how he sent you before me *again*.' I said nothing else.

Verse

Whoever blows out the candle which God has lit will have his beard burned.[83]

I found the following verses by the Shaykh Sa'di apposite:

Those who know the truth and are possessed of certain faith relate

That a pious man mounted a tiger, and rode it with a snake in his hand.[84]

In short, they didn't bring him before me again for a few days. One day, I was in the *tawḥīd-khāna*,[85] and he came to me. I said, 'When

---

the rivalries among the Kurdish frontier principalities, but his Ottoman patrons had already turned against him, frustrated at his lack of success and the absence of the promised Qizilbash support; see Posch, *Osmanisch-safavidische Beziehungen*, 100–2, 104, 570–2.

80 Ottoman sources indicate that Surkhab Sultan's brother, Bege Beg, attacked and besieged him and Alqas; the castle's name is also given as Mash'ala. See Posch, *Osmanisch-safavidische Beziehungen*, 571–2.

81 Shah Nur al-Din Ni'matallah Baqi Yazdi (d. 1564), a direct descendant of the famous Sufi saint Shah Ni'matallah Wali (d. 1431), who was also married to a daughter of Shah Isma'il's. See Posch, *Osmanisch-safavidische Beziehungen*, 573–4.

82 Alqas's surrender took place on 1 October 1549, see Walsh, 'Revolt', 73.

83 Verses attributed to the Sufi Abu Sa 'id b. Abi'l-Khayr (d. 1049), which have become proverbial.

84 Sa'di, *Bustan*, Part 6.

85 The *tawḥīd-khāna* was a building in which Sufis gathered for prayer; unlike a zawiya it was closely connected to the dynasty, and ceremonies were presided over by the chief

you were on good terms with me, you did not drink wine, and did not do wrongful and licentious deeds. When you rebelled, you embraced wrongfulness and licentiousness; it seems you also rebelled against the Lord Creator, glorious is He.

Verses

Whoever strives on God's behalf, through God will all his affairs prosper.

No affair is settled but by God, I swear to God no mortal can do so.[86]

After a few days I realized that he did not trust me and was constantly calculating, so I sent him with Ibrahim Khan and Hasan Beg Yuzbashi to the fortress. He was brought to the fortress of Alamut where he was imprisoned. Six days later, when the guards were not looking, two or three men whose fathers had been killed by Alqas avenged their fathers by throwing him from the fortress to the ground. After his death, the world became calm. I decided to attack the Circassians and Georgians, fighting only infidel, not Muslims, until suddenly İskender Pasha appeared. The contents of these verses express what happened:

Verses

If a pious man desires for a moment to live without troubles,

Fate will produce a fly that'll land in mercy's ointment.[87]

---

of the Safavid order, the *khalīfat al-khulafā'*; perhaps significantly in the context here, it was also a place where criminals could seek refuge. See Babaei, *Isfahan and Its Palaces*, 119, 134–5 for further discussion of this building, of which an example survives in Isfahan to this day.

86 Sana'i, *Hadiqat al-Haqiqa*, ed. Mudarris Rizavi (Tehran, n.d.), 108; only the second verse appears (with the minor variant of *kār-i tū* in place of *kārhā*) in the *Hadiqat al-Haqiqa*; however, both verses are cited in Sharaf, *Sharafnama*, I, 229.

87 Adapted from a *muqaṭṭaʿ* by Anvari (d. 1189).

4

The account of İskender Pasha

At that time İskender was pasha of Erzurum.[1] He got the idea in his head to provoke strife and evil, and however much the amirs wrote to him offering advice, he did not accept it and replied with threats. On one occasion he sent a letter to Husayn-jan Sultan[xxviii] saying, 'I have besieged the fortress of Ardanuç in Georgia.[2] If you attack me I will do battle. If I defeat you I will have defeated the king of the east and if I am defeated myself, then it is merely that a slave has been defeated.' I sent a message to Husayn-jan Sultan telling him to reply that this was a stupid thing to say which sprang from ignorance and a lack of intelligence, for a clever man knows his limitations and should not always be going after battle and death. Once Shah Quli, the governor of Chukhur-i Sa'd, wrote down these verses and sent them to him:

---

1 İskender Pasha (1490–1571), known to contemporaries as Çerkes İskender Pasha owing to his Circassian origins, had played an important role in Süleyman's 1548 campaign against Iran, and in 1551 was appointed governor of Erzurum, serving that position till 1553. He subsequently held positions as governor of Diyarbakır, Baghdad and Egypt (see Abdülkadir Özcan, 'İskender Paşa', *Türkiye Diyanet Vakfı İslam Ansiklopedisi* (1988–2016), vol. 22, 565–6; Aydın, *Erzurum Beylerbeyliği*, 122–34).
2 Ardanuç, located in modern north-eastern Turkey, fell to İskender Pasha after a siege of thirty-three days on 13 June 1551. Özcan, 'İskender Paşa', 565; Aydın, *Erzurum Beylerbeyliği*, 122–4. Husayn-jan Sultan Rumlu was one of Tahmasp's leading Qizilbash commanders in Caucasia, having played an important role in securing Shirvan and in campaigns against the Ottomans; shortly before these events, he had been governor of Chukhur-i Sa'd, although Tahmasp makes it clear that this position was now held by Shah-Quli. The *Tarikh-i Ilchi* (177) refers to Husayn-jan at this juncture as the 'governor of the frontier' (*ḥākim-i sarḥadd*), suggesting he had general responsibility for frontier provinces in the region. On Husayn-jan, see Posch, *Osmanisch-safavidische Beziehungen*, index, s.v.

Verse

'There should not be hatred and conflict between two intelligent men, and only an ignorant man would fight with a stupid one.[3]

You are an intelligent man, and it does not befit you to mistreat the descendants of the Lord of Messengers,[4] Muhammad the Chosen one, peace and blessings be upon him and his family. Everyone who is hostile to this family will be punished, and you will see with which misfortunes you will be afflicted. Have you not read the histories that relate how when the accursed Umayyads fought with the imam Husayn, his children and companions at Karbala', no one was spared but the imam Zayn al-'Abidin, peace be upon him? In those days there were a thousand Umayyad babies in cradles with golden cupolas, and now, by the might of God, you do not see a single trace of any of them; yet how many thousand sayyids are there from the former lineage!'[5]

However often the amirs sent messengers to the gate of the sultan's vizier, they were obstructed and not allowed to proceed. Ambassadors, merchants and travellers were obstructed and plundered. He had reached such a height of arrogance and boasting that he even denied we were sayyids and he wrote in a letter to Shah Quli Khan the Qur'anic verses *'He is not one of your people, for he is a wrongdoer.'*[6] He said many lies, and Shah Quli Sultan replied with a long letter in which he quoted the hadith of imam Ja'far al-Sadiq,[7] peace be upon him. He took no notice of these words, and did not desist from his wickedness. I saw that our affairs were in no way prospering, and that it was necessary to chastise him.

---

3 Sa'di, *Gulistan*, Chapter 4, Story 5.
4 The Safavids are meant, referring to their claim to sayyid status.
5 Tahmasp refers to the killing of 'Ali b. Talib's son Husayn by the Umayyads at Karbala' in 680. Zayn al-'Abidin (d. 713), the fourth Shiite imam, was Husayn's son, and one of the few survivors of the massacre. After the fall of the Umayyads in 750, their successors the Abbasids tried to extirpate all surviving members of the dynasty.
6 Qur'an 11:46.
7 Ja'far al-Sadiq (*c*. 702–765), the sixth Shiite imam, but also regarded by Sunnis as an authoritative source of hadith.

Verse

A task that does not conform to intelligence requires madness.⁸

In the end there was no choice but to equip an army to attack Erciş and Ahlat to send a warning to him, for it would be unbecoming to attack him directly. In fearsome Rajab,⁹ we set off in that direction, and by the blessed month of Ramadan¹⁰ we were in Ahlat. We purchased the garden of Shams al-Din Khan where we kept the fast. Then İskender Pasha learned of the 500 men from Khachin[xxix] in Qarabagh and Georgia who had gone to Dav İli,¹¹ and attacked them with 10,000 of his men.¹² Although the men who faced him in the battle were from Khachin, it is evident that 500 men are ill equipped to fight with 10,000. They fled, but some of them were killed, and their heads sent in great pomp to Istanbul. He branded this a great victory, and permitted himself to feel a quite inexplicable amazement and pride at these events. It thus occurred to me that if I attacked him, he would not leave his fortress and thus it would be impossible to capture the fortress of Erzurum at this point.

I sent Isma'il Mirza with a contingent of amirs to attack him. He left the fortress to face them in battle; when in confusion he saw them, he immediately fled back to the fortress. The amirs plundered the environs of Erzurum, then came to us, and we headed to Nakhchivan. I explained all of this in a letter which I sent with Mahmud Beg, the governor of Biga, who had been captured in the battle of Erzurum

---

8 A verse popularly attributed to Nizami, but absent from scholarly editions of his works.
9 Rajab is often branded *al-murajjab*, 'the fearsome' or 'respected'. For Shiites it is a month of particular significance as 'Ali b. Abi Talib was born then. Rajab 959 = June 1552. Khurshah, however, gives the year as 961, which must be a mistake (*Tarikh-i Ilchi*, 178). For the chronology of these campaigns, see Kırzıoğlu, *Osmanlılar'ın Kafkas-Elleri'ni Fethi*, 207–14; Parsadust, *Shah Tahmasp*, 203–6.
10 Ramadan 959 started on 21 August 1552.
11 Sometimes also written Dad-İli, this refers to the mountainous area north of Erzurum, deriving from its Georgian name of Tao. See *Mukalama-yi Shah Tahmasp*, ed. and tr. Tabatadze, n. 196; Kırzıoğlu, *Osmanlılar'ın Kafkas-Elleri'ni Fethi*, 171–3, 211–13.
12 The figures are different in S: the men from Khachin and Georgia are 900 strong while İskender Pasha attacks with 7,000 men.

and for a period was imprisoned by us. I released him, granted him a robe of honour[13] and sent him to his majesty the sultan. After a while, letters arrived from Haseki Sultan[14] and Sultan Selim,[15] and from the sultan's daughter addressed to my sister,[16] and from Rüstem Pasha addressed to the amirs. The contents, to summarize, were as follows: 'Send an ambassador to arrange a peace treaty and let us resolve that from today, the weak and destitute should not be downtrodden.'

In response to their letter and initiative, we appointed the noble sayyid Amir Shams al-Din as envoy.[17] After he had departed for Istanbul, Rüstem Pasha and his damnable cohort started saying unpleasant things. They exerted great efforts to thwart him, and they prevented the affair from being resolved happily. They sent a long letter by the hand of the said noble sayyid, saying that 'All the ulama and senior scholars of the Ottoman Empire have issued a legal ruling [fatwa] saying that the blood, property, kinsmen and children of all the people of the east, both soldiers and civilians, Muslims, Armenians and Jews alike is licit to be shed and plundered, and war with them is holy war [*ghazā*].'

I said, 'This is a very fine fatwa! They call us infidels when we are the ones who recognize prayers, fasting, hajj, alms giving and all the other obligations of the faith and put them into practice. The lord

---

13 A symbol of vassalage. Mahmud Bey was *sancakbey* of Biga, near Çanakkale in western Anatolia, and was among several *sancakbey*s to be captured by Tahmasp in the battle. See Kırzıoğlu, *Osmanlılar'ın Kafkas-Elleri'ni Fethi*, 217; Emecen, *Sultan Süleyman*, 470.
14 The Ottoman sultan Süleyman's wife, Hürrem Sultan (d. 1558), whose title was Haseki Sultan.
15 Süleyman's son, the future Selim II (r. 1566–74).
16 Khurshah, *Tarikh-i Ilchi*, 179, specifies that the sultan's daughter's letter was addressed to Shahzada Sultanum. Royal women frequently participated in diplomacy. For further discussion see Maria Szuppe, 'La participation des femmes de la famille royale. à l'exercice du pouvoir en Iran safavide au XVIesiècle (deuxième partie)', *Studia Iranica* 24 (1995): 61–2.
17 The envoy's name is recorded in the Safavid sources as Shams al-Din Dilijani, indicating an origin from Dilijan near Ganja in modern Azerbaijan. See Parsadust, *Shah Tahmasp*, 280, n. 356; Kırzıoğlu, *Osmanlılar'ın Kafkas-Elleri'ni Fethi*, 217, n. 284.

God will judge between us and them.' At that very time, on Friday 27th of fearsome Rajab in the year 957 (11 August 1550),[18] I dreamed that a great moon was stationed in the middle of the heavens, with another appearing to the east and another to the west. The moon that emerged from the west was very big, while that in the east was small, A figure of light stood beside me and said, 'The moon in the west is the sultan, and the moon in the east is 'Ubayd the Uzbek, and the moon in between is yours.' I saw that when the first moon in the east approached the moon in the middle, it became detached, sank to the earth and disappeared. Next the moon in the west in the same way sank to earth. The middle moon slowly emerged on a path like a strip of paper in the sky until it settled over our royal throne in Qazvin and the place where I was sitting which had been covered with textiles.

The next occurrence was on 18 Safar 961 (23 January 1554) in Nakhchivan. I dreamed that writing appeared in the sky in the direction of the qibla, in the place where the sun is in the afternoon. The page of the heavens was inscribed in Arabic script[xxx] which was the same colour as the heavens, except that the script was more translucent. It was like a stamp on European paper, a *sīr* and a half in weight,[19] as big as the large mihrab which is two and a half cubits in breadth and three and a half cubits in height. I read that in this script was written the following verse, '*And God will suffice you against them, for He is the all-hearing, all-knowing.*'[20] On seeing this script I trembled and

---

18 Although Tahmasp says that he had this dream 'at that very time' (*dar hamān ayyām*), this is not possible, as the negotiations with the Ottomans took place in autumn 1553; see Kırzıoğlu, *Osmanlılar'ın Kafkas-Elleri'ni Fethi*, 216–17. Reading 959 rather than 957 (as per S) gives a date of July 1552, which does not solve the problem. At any rate, 'Ubayallah was long dead by this point, having died in 1540.
19 According to Steingass, *Persian-English Dictionary* 1 sīr = 15 mithqals, or approximately 0.65 kg.
20 Qur'an 2: 37. The phrase '*And God will suffice you against them*', *fasayakfikahum Allāh* is the longest word in the Qur'an, and was commonly invoked and inscribed for its talismanic and protective properties. See Sheila Blair, 'Invoking God's Protection: The Iconography of the Qur'anic Phrase fasayakfikahum allāh', in Shahin Aryamanesh (ed.), *Farr-e Firouz, vol. 5 of Distinguished Scholars of the Cultural Heritage of Iran, Special Edition in Honour of Dr Firouz Bagherzadeh* (Tehran, 2019), 191–206.

was greatly agitated. I saw that the script billowed like the waves, and a part of the furthest heavens which was on the western side of the script was trembling as if it was about to break off from the heavens. Then I saw this script and mihrab come forth trembling, and out of that a door opened in the heavens. In my agitation I dreamed that I had awakened and that I was in the summer quarters at Khoy. A great hurricane blew up from the direction of Van, and people were saying that 'The Ottomans have attacked you!' It was feared that if the hurricane reached our camp,[xxxi] it would destroy all our tents. In my dream, I was saying to the harem *qūrchī*s and Ya'qub Agha[xxxii] the Yuzbashi of the harem, 'Find Parikhan Khanum and Sultan Ibrahim Mirza,[21] take them and flee! We will go ahead on horseback.' I was dreaming that the hurricane was gradually advancing to the meadow and campsite where we were staying, but before it reached the edge of the royal camp, it vanished and not a single piece of dust or dirt landed on us. It was completely obliterated, and from behind the dust and dirt appeared many cows and rams, all fat-tailed like sheep. I was saying to my amirs, 'Anyone of the troops who wants to hunt and go after them, may do so.' They went after them. I was carrying a mountain cow and a wounded ram[xxxiii] and was saying, 'My horse has been too long in the stable, I can't go forward.' I was saying to Sultan Ibrahim Mirza and the children, 'Roast these while we wait for the amirs to come and I will sit in the tent.' After that they came, each of them bringing thirty or forty that they had captured. Then I dreamed that I woke up but I was still asleep, and I dreamed that my sister had spread carpets and textiles in each of the four corners of the house. In each corner were sat beautiful women who were sublime and fair, and wore no jewellery or adornments at all. Their features were of such a beauty that is rare among the human

---

21 Tahmasp's children.

race. I asked him, 'Who are these women?' He replied, 'They have been brought from Georgia for you. One is the vizier's sister who was in our house, the others have just been brought.' I said, 'The vizier's sister looked nothing like this, how has she turned out looking like this?' He replied, 'Now this is what she looks like.' Then I half awoke, and saw myself reading the verse, *'And God will suffice you against them.'* I fell back into the same sleep as before, and again I dreamed I was reciting the verse *'And God will suffice you against them.'*[22] Then I realized in confusion that this verse is used to repel enemies, and wondered why it created such distress. I realized that when the ray of light of the Divine presence, brilliant are His names, revealed itself, its appearance would be a cause for quaking and commotion. I dreamed that I was saying, 'This is the light that stories and reports relate was revealed to Moses, God's interlocutor, peace be upon him. Muhammad the Seal of the Prophets, on the night of his ascension to heaven,[23] spoke with the Lord Creator, and it is certain that God's divine awesomeness and fearfulness made a great impression on him. It is certain that when I see such wondrous signs, my tongue will recite a Qur'anic verse.' And I reckoned that the sultan was advancing in our direction.

That is how it was. When the sultan reached Pasinler he halted so that their provisions could catch up with them. They sent one of Ulama's staff to ask for peace term, but I absolutely refused. For why should peace be contingent on Ulama's favour, when he was one of our aides-de-camp (*yasāvul*)? Why should he now act as ambassador between us and the sultan? If at least it was one of the sultan's pashas, he would have a sufficient status that we could arrange peace terms in the interests of the security of all Muslims.

---

22 Qur'an 2: 37.
23 According to Muslim tradition, in his *mi'rāj* (ascension) the Prophet Muhammad ascended to heaven and was given instructions by God, before returning to earth.

Verses

It's better to forego the master's charity than to suffer the oppression of his doormen

It's better to die hoping for meat than to suffer the evil of the butchers' exactions.[24]

On the 17th of the month of Zu'l-qi'da (960/25 October 1553) we marched off and encamped at Bazarchay.[25] News had reached Levend Khan the Georgian[26] that the sultan was coming and had already defeated and weakened the shah's army, and his son, who was serving our forces, had lost a hand in battle. As a result, he was in a state of turmoil. He sent a letter to his son by an emissary reporting this news, asking for an accurate account of the situation. The scouts brought in this individual and his letter. In response I wrote,

Poem

You say, 'How will the work of time turn out how out in the end?' That which is the desire of lovers will be realized.

A wise plan of such a sort will appear from the Inscrutable, at which eyes of the sagacious will wonder.

These signs and hints that we see: everything that was said at the beginning will be realized.

Power belongs to the family of the Prophet, that which they desire will be realized.

In the end, the sultan came to Nakhchivan.[27] A letter arrived from Saru Qaplan, son of Delü Sayyid Hasan Abdallu, according to which they had captured one of the royal cup-bearers (*mulāzim-i jāmī*). It said, 'Come so that we can do battle!' Then Hasan Beg Yuzbashi

---

24 Sa'di, *Gulistan*, Chapter 3.
25 For the chronology, see Kırzıoğlu, *Osmanlılar'ın Kafkas-Elleri'ni Fethi*, 218–19.
26 Levan, King of Kakheti (r. 1520–74).
27 Süleyman's advance on Nakhchivan took place in summer 1554. For the Ottoman perspective, see Şahin, *Peerless among Princes*, 237–40.

said to me, 'Let's send all the camels and luggage along with the royal camp [*ordu*] to the hills and mountains of Ganja and the surrounding region, so that we keep only the tents. We can observe the road from the top of a mountain. If the sultan gets separated from the main body of his army and comes to attack us, we will make for his royal camp via a different route. They can take whatever they find in our camp, and we will plunder and kill in their camp, and take off whatever we can Whatever can't be removed we'll burn and destroy.'

I did not agree, and said, 'There is nothing they loathe more than if we avoid fighting with them; if we aren't complicit in shedding their blood, they will go to hell on their own! It is clear that with a small army they will not dare invade our territory. A large army is at the mercy of supplies of fodder for animals and food. I understand from the fact they sent a letter inviting us to fight that they have resolved to retreat. For they have no choice but to say, "We invited them to fight more than once, but the enemy did not come and fled, so we withdrew."'

Three days later, the sultan withdrew. Then Shah Verdi Sultan said, 'If we order an advance and seize the provisions that are stored in Aras, by the time the sultan reaches Erzurum, we will have burned and plundered Pasinler and Erzurum.' I agreed to this, and gave him 500 men of Aq Minqan[28] to head to Pasinler. We remained for one day more, and then marched in the direction of Chukhur-i Sa'd. The day we reached Qarabagh, the first of the blessed month of Ramadan (961/31 July 1554), a story came to mind that is in the hadith collections. One day the Prophet – peace and blessings be upon him – was ascending the pulpit. When he put his blessed foot on the first step, he said, 'Amen', and he did the same when he

---

28 Also spelt Akmangan; apparently this was a summer pasture west of Gökçegöl, see Kırzıoğlu, *Osmanlılar'ın Kafkas-Elleri'ni Fethi*, 212–13.

placed his blessed foot on the second step. On account of this story, I said, 'When it is the blessed month of Ramadan, we will not attack Muslims' territories.' We decided to go towards Georgia to raid the territories of Şavşat,[xxxiv] who are infidel that must be fought, and to halt in the territory of Qvaqvare[29] to pasture our horses. The army of Kuhgiluya arrived on the same day, and we started out for Georgia. We spent a month in the territory of Şavşat, and those of Qadant the Georgian[30] and Qvaqvare. After the festival at the end of Ramadan, we sent Arzbar, one of the staff of the Georgian 'Isa Khan,[31] to Besbat the Georgian.[32] Besbat told him that Ayas[xxxv] Pasha[33] was on his own in the fortress of Oltu, while the sultan was in Erzurum. We also sent from Pereken[34] fortress some amirs, along with Shah Quli Khalifa the seal-bearer (*muhrdār*), Muhammad Beg Mawsillu, Adham Beg Rumlu, Ulughkhan Beg Sa'adlu and Tarkhan Beg. Their vanguard (*charkhjīs*) comprised Iotam and Varaze, who were sons of Qvarqvare the Georgian,[xxxvi] and Arzbar the Georgian, so that a total of 5,000 men marched to attack Ayas. At night Amir Khan, son of Shahgeldi Beg, was acting as lookout (*qarāvul*) on the left flank with 200 men, so that if someone came from the fortress of Khamkhis and Penek[35] bringing news, they would know.[xxxvii] There was a clash with Sinan

---

29 This refers to the ruler of the Turkicised Georgian frontier principality, Samtskhe-Saatabago. In fact, the ruler at this time was Kaikhosro II (1545–1573), but the rulers are often referred to in Islamic sources as 'Qvarqvare', a common name among the dynasty, irrespective of their actual names.
30 Tabatadze failed to identify this name. It seems possible that it is identical with a certain Qandurali mentioned in Ottoman documents of the period, who was evidently a Christian lord in Erzurum province allied with the Ottomans. See Kırzıoğlu, *Osmanlılar'ın Kafkas-Elleri'ni Fethi*, 233, n. 326.
31 Iesse, son of Levan, King of Kakheti.
32 Again Tabatadze does not identify this name, but suggests it may be a corruption of 'atabeg', after the title of the rulers of Saatabago.
33 Ayas Pasha had become Ottoman governor (beylerbeği) of Erzurum in May 1553, and served in this position until his execution in 1559. On him, see Dündar, *Erzurum Beylerbeyliği*, 134–43.
34 MSS پرکن or پروکن. For this fortress, see Dündar, *Erzurum Beylerbeyliği*, 119.
35 Both fortresses are in the Oltu region; the modern name of Khamkhis is Yanıkkaval; see Kırzıoğlu, *Osmanlılar'ın Kafkas-Elleri'ni Fethi*, 195, 201–4; Aydın, *Erzurum Beylerbeyliği*, 265, n. 337.

Beg,[36] who was defeated and was brought captive before me. I asked Sinan Beg for information about the situation. He told me that all of the army, apart from the sultan, had come to Oltu, and the sultan was following on in person.

Together with our amirs, we pulled back from the Oltu road and went to Kanlu Çimen[37] and caught up with our royal camp, thinking that if the army came we would fight them at the top of the pass. Meanwhile, Delü Efendi's son and the son of Bisharat Kelle,[38] both accomplices of Alqas, had fled, and it was reported that the captive pashas had fled too. I gathered the amirs for a conference. Muhammadi Beg said, 'While the sultan is resting in Erzurum, let's go to Van and raid Kurdistan. We can stop there and pasture our horses, and as long as the sultan is in Erzurum, we can stay there. If the sultan attacks us, we can head to Baghdad, and if he comes after us there, we can return to Diyarbakır. Should they come to Diyarbakır, we'll go to Azerbaijan, and devastate that whole province by burning and plundering. After we have devastated all those provinces, when the sultan attacks us in the spring, what will he be able to do? Without doubt he will retreat impotently.'

I consulted divinatory omens for war and they were ominous, then I consulted them for peace and they were auspicious. I told the amirs that if the sultan treats us badly on the account of the influence of ignorant men, let us requite his ill-treatment with good. I recited the following verses:

---

36 Sinan Beg was the Ottoman *sancakbeyi* of Oltu; see Kırzıoğlu, *Osmanlılar'ın Kafkas-Elleri'ni Fethi*, 230, 232, 239; Emecen, *Sultan Süleyman*, 498; Aydın, *Erzurum Beylerbeyliği*, 274–5.
37 According to Kırzıoğlu, *Osmanlılar'ın Kafkas-Elleri'ni Fethi*, 175, 232, Kanlu Çimen (literally 'Bloody Meadow') lies off the Sarıkamış-Pasinler road, in the Soğanlı mountains. Tahmasp's Georgian allies had suffered a decisive defeat by the Ottomans here in 1545; see Posch, *Osmanisch-safavidische Beziehungen*, 76.
38 This is presumably Delü Qaytmaz, a Circassian lord defeated by Alqas, but who subsequently joined his entourage. See Posch, *Osmanisch-safavidische Beziehungen*, 305, 313, 342.

> God created you from dust, now abase yourself slave! Why do you hold back?
>
> Do not be greedy, tyrannous or rebellious; He created you from dust, don't be like fire
>
> When terrifying fire burns inside you, clay, your entity, humbly submits to it
>
> The former shows itself to be arrogant, the latter deficient.
>
> From the former come demons, from the latter mankind
>
> A single drop of rain fell from a cloud and was ashamed when it saw the extent of the sea.[39]

I sent Ahmad Sultan to bring Sinan Beg who was imprisoned in Kurtkale.[40] I made Shah Quli accompany Sinan Beg, and sent them with a letter I had written to the sultan that said, 'You have mistreated us because of the influence of the ignorant, but we will requite your ill treatment with good, and, acting according to the hadith, we will knock on the door of peace.' I quoted the following verses:

> Young man, learn chivalry, learn manliness from men of the world!
>
> Protect yourself from the hatred of hatred-mongers, protect your tongue from the calumny of slanderers,
>
> Do good to him who did ill to you, because with that evil he damaged his own fortune
>
> When you make your work the practice of goodness, you will find only goodness redounds.[41]
>
> If you entrust your affairs to God, Hafiz, oft will you enjoy divine favour.[42]

---

39 Sa'di, *Bustan*, Chapter 4.
40 Qal'a-yi Kurt. Kurtkale was located in the Çıldır region; see Kırzıoğlu, *Osmanlılar'ın Kafkas-Elleri'ni Fethi*, 288, 295, 364; Aydın, *Erzurum Beylerbeyliği*, 72.
41 Jami, *Baharistan*, Rawza-yi chaharum in 'Abd al-Rahman Jami, *Baharistan va Rasa'il-i Jami*, ed. A 'la Afsahzad et al. (Tehran, 2000).
42 Hafiz, *Divan*, Ghazal 481.

I sent Shah Quli Aqa and Sinan Beg off to the sultan,[43] and we headed to Georgia. We conquered most of the forts and hideouts there, and took around 30,000 prisoners, and then came to Qarabagh. After Shah Quli Agha, we sent Farrukhzad, the chamberlain (*īshīk-āqāsī*), as ambassador with gifts from Georgia, and after him Vays Aqa. Praise be to God, a peace treaty was agreed and the Muslims spent several years at ease.[44]

---

43 The embassy reached Süleyman at Eleşgirt on 26 September 1554; see Emecen, *Sultan Süleyman*, 499.
44 Farrukhzad reached Amasya on 18 May 1555 and peace terms were finally agreed on 1 June 1555. The Treaty of Amasya established relatively stable borders between the Safavid and Ottoman states, with Iraq and much of Caucasia being ceded to the Ottomans, Safavid pilgrims were permitted to visit the holy cities of the Hijaz, and the two powers recognized the legitimacy of each other. Ottoman incursions into Safavid territory were also ceased. For a study of the treat and its background, see Zahit Atçıl, 'Warfare as a Tool of Diplomacy: Background of the First Ottoman-Safavid Treaty in 1555', *Turkish Historical Review* 10 (2019): 3–24.

5

The affair of Beyazid

It was reported that Sultan Beyazid was established in Amasya and was assembling an army from travellers to the province of Rum, merchants and every wayfarer who came in his direction in order to fight with his brother Selim.[1] I remarked, 'What cheek they have to wage war on each other while their father is still safe and sound on the throne.' I sent a messenger to Yadgar Beg Pazuki[2] asking him to send someone to the frontiers to get intelligence. His spies and henchmen came, bringing two henchmen of Alqas's who were with Sultan Beyazid. They immediately admitted that Sultan Beyazid had rebelled and was about to fight with his brother. They had gone to Konya to fight one another. Sultan Beyazid had sent a message to the effect that 'You should go disguised as merchants to the Shah and tell him to send one thousand five hundred tomans of gold as a loan for me. After I take my father's place, I will return them tenfold.'

I was amazed at these words, and said, 'He is even stupider than Alqas! Firstly, seeing that we have made peace with the sultan, why

---

1 Süleyman's son Beyazid (1526–1562) was widely regarded as the heir apparent, but with the death of his mother Hürrem Sultan in April 1558, he lost his most influential supporter, and the party of his brother Selim sought to advance the latter's claims. In an attempt to avoid conflict between his two sons, Süleyman appointed them to new positions, with Beyazid becoming governor of Amaya and Selim of Konya. However, the conflict descended into open fighting, with Beyazid being defeated by Selim at the Battle of Konya in April 1559. The most detailed study of these events remains Şerafettin Turan, *Kanuni'nin Oğlu Şehzade Beyazid Vak'ası* (Ankara, 1961) which draws on copious Ottoman and a number of Persian sources, but curiously does not include Tahmasp's account of the affair. See also Şahin, *Peerless among Princes*, 250–9.
2 Yadgar Beg ibn Mansur was chief of the Pazuki Kurdish principality, based around Eleşkirt. See Sharaf al-Din Khan, *Sharafnama*, I, 331–2.

should we lend you gold? And secondly, how are you going to wage war on the sultan with one thousand five hundred tomans?' I entrusted the envoys to Hasan Beg Yuzbashi to see what news would come next. After thirty or forty days, reports arrived that Sultan Beyazid had reached Pasinler. Then Shah Quli's messenger came with Çavuşbaşı Ali Ağa whom Sultan Beyazid had sent, bringing news that Sultan Beyazid had arrived in Pasinler. He sent a message to me asking, 'If I come to the Shah, will he protect me or not?' Two days later reports came that Nuh Pasha had attacked Sultan Beyazid, and he had been defeated and fled to Shah Quli Sultan in Chukhur-i Sa'd. I told the amirs, 'He has entered our territory, and he can't be allowed to go anywhere else, otherwise the sultan will think ill of us in the future.' I sent the Mulla Vazir Qazvini, Mulla Shams Ilchi and Allah Verdi Aqa the *mihmāndār* with gold and provisions to bring him to Tabriz. As Shah Quli Sultan had written to say that Sultan Beyazid was afraid of us, I told them to send a messenger to reassure him in every way possible. I sent Mir Hasan Beg Yuzbashi who had sworn an oath that he would reassure him that I would not hand him and his children over to the sultan. I also swore an oath to the same effect in front of Çavuşbaşı Ali Ağa and I sent him off accompanied by Hasan Beg Yuzbashi. Hasan Beg went to reassure him and brought him to me in Qazvin. Sultan Beyazid halted for a few days in Tabriz, and sent me a letter saying, 'Come to Tabriz, and let's advance on Baghdad with two units and on Van with one unit. Sultan Selim will confront one unit, but no-one will confront the other. The whole of the sultan's army is on my side and want me. By the time the sultan in Istanbul hears about it, they will all have come over to me.'

I wrote in reply, 'Do us the honour of coming to Qazvin,[3] and we will hold counsel, and we will do whatever seems right.' After Sultan Beyazid reached Kars,[xxxviii] Sinan Beg came as an ambassador from the

---

3   Qazvin had become the capital in place of Tabriz in 1557.

sultan, and Durak Ağa came from Sultan Selim bringing a letter which contained accusations against Sultan Beyazid. I told them to be patient until Sultan Beyazid came, then we would implement everything in their interests. Sinan Beg brought a message that I should watch out lest Durak deceive me before the official ambassadors arrived. I replied, 'There is no need to say that. Our envoys have gone to the sultan three times, and not once have our humble gifts found favour. Alqas has gone from us to them, and then started an insurrection and came back here. I restrained myself from taking action, for why should kings be moved by such words? I have never been moved by his words, and I have maintained courteous behaviour towards the sultan. Although we can't do much, I can do this: we can enter their territory, and destroy and devastate the whole border area, in order to avert them crossing it subsequently. While the sultan was in Istanbul, I wanted to go and destroy every last trace of civilization in Diyarbakır, Erzurum and Van; but when Alqas came before us, we made peace, and refrained from doing harm.'

When Sultan Beyazid came to Qazvin,[4] he bragged, 'When Alqas went to the other side, the sultan, under his influence, mustered an army to invade your territory. Why do you deliberate and not give us assistance? My two sons will accompany you to Erzurum, and I'll head towards Baghdad.'

I replied, 'The sultan was foolish to attack us on account of what Alqas said. I always say that Rüstem Pasha deceived his majesty the sultan and tricked him, so why should I act in this way, breaking the peace treaty and agreement, on someone else's say so? We thought

---

4 Beyazid arrived in Qazvin in October 1559, and was initially greeted with full honours and public ceremonies of welcome, a fact which Tahmasp avoids mentioning. However, within a few months of arrival, Tahmasp had given orders for Beyazid's accompanying troops to be dispersed. By the beginning of 1560, he had started negotiations with Süleyman over the fugitive prince. See Mitchell, *Practice of Politics*, 125–6; Emecen, *Sultan Süleyman*, 555–7; Turan, *Kanuni'nin Oğlu*, 135–6; Şahin, *Peerless among Princes*, 250–9.

it appropriate to send an ambassador to ask for him to be forgiven. If the order is given, we will take his men captive or send another messenger to ask for his wrongdoing to be overlooked. We will do everything to ensure his wrongdoing is forgiven.'

I said to myself, 'What kind of gratitude is this towards his father, when he has rebelled and failed to observe his duties and the faith which it is incumbent to uphold according to the verses of the Qur'an and the hadith? Having made peace with the sultan should I then treat him badly by assisting a rebel?' Another stupid thing he did was addressing me in writing as 'Shah Tahmasp' even though he had become one of my vassals.[5] I realized then that he was a stupid idiot.

Verses [in Turkish]

A rash fellow cannot succeed at being ruler, indeed, he can't even be a shepherd.

But Sultan Selim is wise and intelligent.

Verses [Persian]

Seek advice from a wise man; it has been said, 'don't consort with a stupid man

For then even if you're the wisest man of your age you'll become a donkey, and if you are not you'll become even stupider'.[6]

He is so stupid and ignorant that how could it be appropriate for me to ally myself with someone like that? Therefore I appointed 'Ali Aqa-yi Aqchasaqal the Yuzbashi as ambassador to his majesty the sultan, and I sent Irishdi Aqa to Sultan Selim. I kept Sultan Beyazid at my pleasure. He desired to send presents to the amirs of the

---

[5] Tahmasp's point is that the letters Beyazid addressed to him did not conform to the elaborate protocols that a vassal's should contain. Matters were probably not helped by the fact that Beyazid, an accomplished poet, himself used the penname Shahi, and wrote some distinctly discourteous verses about Tahmasp in them. See Parsadust, *Shah Tahmasp*, 314; Turan, *Kanuni'nin Oğlu*, 140.

[6] Sa'di, *Gulistan*, Chapter 8.

frontier regions, such as Gilan, Mazandaran, Herat, Qandahar, Sistan, Mashhad, Shiraz, Kirman and Azerbaijan. He sent Ferruh Beg[7] to Gilan on the pretext that he wanted to go there, and gave gifts to each of his senior commanders, sending them throughout our God-protected domains. Ferruh Beg went to Gilan, and there he agreed with Ahmad Khan to bring Sultan Beyazid from Qazvin towards Gilan on the pretence of going on a hunting expedition. From there, he would hide himself among the Turkmen, in the midst of 6,000 men. Then he would board a boat and go to Aqricha,[8] and go via Hajji Tarkhan and Kazan.[9] Sultan Beyazid used to say, 'The Russian king is my friend.[10] If I send a messenger to him saying that we are both enemies of the sultan, with his help, I'll take the Circassians into my service, and raise a great army from Crimea, the Nogai,[11] the Russians and Circassia, and we'll plunder the sultan's territory wherever we are. If the sultan sends an army to attack us, we'll retreat to the steppe, and what will he be able to do about it?'

Kara Uğurlu, Mustafa Yasakçı and Mehmed the Circassian[12] heard and marked this entire speech about this venture. They told Hasan Beg, 'We have something to say which we want to tell the Shah.'

---

7 Ferruh Beg was one of Beyazid's officers, and had held the position of Anadolu kethüdası, responsible for fiscal affairs and tax collection in Anatolia. Turan, *Kanuni'nin Oğlu*, 87, 139. In S the trip to Gilan is related as Ferruh Beg's suggestion to Beyazid.
8 Aqricha (Ogrucha) was located at the mouth of the Uzboy tributary of the Amu Darya (Oxus) river where it flowed into the Caspian. This tributary dried up in the seventeenth century. It was thus probably located roughly in the vicinity of the town of Hazar in modern Turkmenistan. See V. V. Bart'old, 'K istorii orosheniya Turkestana', in V. Bart'old, *Sochineniya*, vol. 3 (Moscow, 1965), 173, 175.
9 Hajji Tarkhan is the historic name for Astrakhan, conquered by Russia in 1556. Kazan' had also only recently, in 1552, been incorporated into the Russian Empire, having previously been an independent Khanate.
10 The Russians represented a significant threat to Ottoman interests in the Black Sea at this juncture, threatening the strategic fortresses of Akkerman and Azov in summer 1559. See Turan, *Kanuni'nin Oğlu*, 172–3. However, it seems Ottoman sources are entirely unaware of Beyazid's proposed Russian alliance.
11 The Nogai Horde were a Turkic steppe polity based on the northern shores of the Caspian and Black Seas.
12 Three of Beyazid's staff. The reason for their treachery is unknown, although they may have been concerned about the practicality of Beyazid's audacious plan.

Hasan Beg agreed to bring them before me so they could say what they wanted, but Sultan Beyazid became aware of the situation. That very night he invited them to a feast and killed them. A few days later, Hasan Beg learned of their killing and exposed these goings on to me. I feigned lack of interest, saying, 'Don't reveal this to anyone.' A few days later Arab Mehmed[13] came from Mazandaran, and one day we held a feast in the Bagh-i Jannat in Qazvin. Arab Mehmed came to see me in private, saying, 'I have a story I want to tell you.' I replied, 'After I go to the Audience Chamber (*dīvānkhāna*),[14] come and tell me.' He said,[15] 'I'm afraid of trickery later; what good will it do?' He summoned the confectioner[16] whom Sultan Beyazid had brought with him from the Ottoman lands, and in private he explained the truth to me, that they had put something in the halva to be fed to me and the all amirs. I agreed to give the confectioner a reward, and went into the gathering. I composed myself, and diverted the attention of my companions by getting up and asking for a ewer,[xxxix] saying, 'I want to throw up,' I got up and took myself to the harem, on the excuse that I was shivering. I secretly sent someone to the amirs warning them to avoid the gathering, which was abandoned that day. I also sent someone to seize some of that halva, which I kept. Sultan Beyazid became aware that Arab Mehmed had learned of his plot and had exposed it to me. That night he summoned him secretly and had him killed. Ali Ağa the *sekban-başı*[17] was Arab Mehmed's companion and grasped what had happened. Sultan Beyazid was deeply worried

---

13 In Persian Muhammad-i 'Arab. Arab Mehmed was Beyazid's *kapıcıbaşı* (chief of the palace guards, also responsible for transmitting and executing orders), see Turan, *Kanuni'nin Oğlu*, 140–1.
14 See Membré, *Mission*, 19 for a description of 'the palace where [the shah] gives audience, which they call the *divankhana*'.
15 The following five sentences, from 'He said', to 'that halva, which I kept', are absent from S.
16 *ḥalwā'ī*, a specialist in making halva, a type of confection.
17 *sekban-başı* is an Ottoman rank, the commander of the *sekban*, a unit of irregulars affiliated with the Janissaries.

and was planning to escape that night. They informed me that their plan and plot was that the following night they would leave. Kuduz Ferhad[18] came and reported that the next evening, if they prevailed, they wanted to escape to Gilan and then go to Astarabad. I investigated all these goings-on, and became certain of their truth, and realized that they had been reported by intelligent men.

Verse

Doing good to evil men is just like doing evil to good people[19]

The same day,[20] I summoned the amirs and told that a brave contingent from each tribe (*qawm*) should wait in hiding in the garden, wearing chain mail under their clothes and be ready. On the same day, on the pretext that I wanted to contract a marriage agreement with the sons of Bahram Mirza, I summoned Sultan Beyazid and his officers to an audience and arrested them. As for the group who had abetted him in these deeds, I related their crimes in his presence and had them killed. I made some of those who had arranged for the halva to be given to us to be fed it themselves; some died of tumours the same day and night, some a day later.

I said, 'Good God! What evil have I done to you? My only crime was that I did not allow strife and discord to rear their heads, and I begged to bring about peace and reconciliation, or to give you a territory in the frontier province of Qandahar, with the agreement of the sultan. I treated you the same way that I treated Padishah Humayun. And your plan was to do this to us?!' I imprisoned him but I let some of his company go free, but unarmed.[21]

---

18 Kuduz Ferhad was Beyazid's *sipahiler ağası* (commander of the household cavalry); according to Ottoman sources, the assassination attempt on Tahmasp was his idea. See Turan, *Kanuni'nin Oğlu*, 87, 136–7.
19 Sa'di, *Gulistan*, Chapter 1, Story 4. The verses are absent from S.
20 This and the following paragraph are absent from S.
21 This paragraph is absent in S, which reads instead 'I summoned him [Beyazid] to the mosque, and killed everyone who had been complicit in this plot; some I had disarmed and allowed to go wherever they wanted.'

Then, misfortune befell me when Ali Ağa came from the sultan, and told us that the presents sent by every amir were reciprocated with gifts, apart from our tribute and gifts which on this occasion were not found acceptable and they had written a letter to me full of insinuations and complaints. I said, 'So this is the situation, I have seized Sultan Beyazid and his four sons and kept them, out of regard for the sultan and Selim Khan. When I said that I would not hand Sultan Beyazid over to the sultan, the same stipulation means that when, on the sultan's instructions, Sultan Selim's envoys arrive, and I hand them over to Sultan Selim's envoys I will not be breaking my oath.' Then when the sultan's envoys arrived, I said, 'Your excellency the Pasha and Hasan Ağa, welcome, you bring peace! I will do whatever the sultan orders, and I will not contravene his instructions. I am ready to undertake whatever service he requires. However, I desire a suitable reward and gift for rendering such complete service to his majesty the sultan and Selim Khan. Out of friendship for the sultan, I hope that he will not harm Sultan Beyazid and his sons.'[22]

End of the book, by the aid of God the all-generous king.

---

22 In fact, Beyazid and his sons were strangled by Ali Ağa on Selim's orders on 25 July 1562. Tahmasp received substantial cash presents from both Süleyman and Selim in return for handing Beyazid over. Turan *Kanuni'nin Oğlu*, 156–7.

Glossary

Amīr	Commander; often also used for tribal chiefs
Amīr al-umarā'	Commander-in-chief
Beg	Title in both Ottoman and Safavid Empires usually held by military figures
Çavuşbaşı (Ott)	Assistant to the grand vizier, with particular responsibility for dealing with embassies
charkhjī	Advance patrols; an army responsible for launching the attack
dārūghā	City prefect, with powers varying between those of a police chief, governor and tax collector
dawlatkhāna	Royal precinct of various palaces, functional and administrative buildings; sometimes used for a single palace building
dīwānkhāna	Royal audience chamber
farsakh	Unit of distance equivalent to approximately 4 miles
hadith qudsi	Hadith including divine speech
ijtihād	Exercise of independent reasoning by a jurist
Imamzada	Tomb of the descendant of an imam
ishīk-āqāsī	Chamberlain
ishīk-āqāsī-bāshī	Grand chamberlain
kapıcıbaşı (Ott)	Chief of palace guards responsible for transmitting and executing orders
keshik	Royal bodyguard
lāla	Tutor, guardian
mann	Unit of weight
mihmāndār	Official responsible for dealing with embassies

muḥtasib	Official responsible for regulating markets, and more generally for upholding moral behaviour in public
mujtahid	One who exercises ijtihad, a privilege reserved for the most senior of the religious hierarchy
naqīb (al-ashrāf)	Representative of the descendants of the Prophet (*ashrāf*) in a town
ordu	The camp or headquarters, especially of the shah
pasha (Ott.)	Title of senior Ottoman commanders and governors
qūrchī	Royal bodyguard, usually a member of a Qizilbash tribe
qūrchī bāshī	Commander of the royal bodyguard
ṣadr	Official responsible for religious endowments and the judiciary, at some points essentially the head of the civilian bureaucracy
sayyid	Descendant of the Prophet
uymāq	Tribe
vakīl	'Agent' or 'deputy'; in much of the early Safavid period this was the title given to the most senior bureaucrat or commander, who was the effective head of government
yasāvul	Aide-de-camp, in particular responsible for admitting people into shah's presence
yūzbāshī	Centurion, commander of a unit of 100 *qūrchī*s
Zawiya	Sufi lodge

Textual notes

i All manuscripts read ghalqān; recte Halfān.
ii B: fourteen (chahārdah); G: four (chahār).
iii Reading with G *tiryāk khwurda* against B's *tark khwurda*.
iv While the printed text here reads *va Bādinjān Sulṭān Rūmlū ḥākim-i ānjā būda-ast Aḥmad Āqā-yi Chāvushlū-yi ṭuvāji va Kupak Sulṭān kushta shudand*, the texts of G and L agree in having: *va Bādinjān Sulṭān Rūmlū ḥākim-i ānjā būda-ast Aḥmad Āqā-yi Chāvushlū-yi ṭuvāji-yi Kupak Sulṭān kushta shud*. However, this still does not make sense, so I propose amending to *va Bādinjān Sulṭān Rūmlū ḥākim-i ānjā bi-dast-i Aḥmad Āqā-yi Chāvushlū-yi ṭuvāji-yi Kupak Sulṭān kushta shud*. Badinjan Sultan, one of the commanders of Shah Ismaʻil, was some ninety years old at this point. This amendment brings the text into conformity with the evidence of Hasan Rumlu (*Ahsan al-Tawarikh*, II, 1155–6; trans. Setton, *Chronicle*, 98), who states that Ahmad Aqa killed Badinjan Sultan in the battle, rather than, as the faulty manuscripts of Tahmasp's text suggest, Ahmad Aqa being killed.
v B has Herat in place of Marv; however, G and L confirm reading of Marv.
vi Read with L آغر و اغور.
vii S: Duruk Sultan.
viii Read *hazār charkh* in the place of the printed text's *hazār farj*. This is a proverb, expressing that in a short time many wonderful things may happen: *sīb tā farūd āmadan hazār charkh mīzanad*. 'The apple before coming to the ground turns a thousand summersaults.' See Steingass, *Persian-English dictionary*, sub *sēb*.
ix L spells his name Qadi Khan, which would have been pronounced the same as Ghazi Khan; as the latter is more common in the secondary sources, I maintain it here.
x G and S: du (two): L and B: dah (ten).
xi Reading with G: Chūn bih-Qazvīn rasīdīm ū āmada.
xii S adds: and Husayn Khan, Sulayman Sultan and Amir Sultan Rumlu.
xiii S: Ibrahim Pasha has marched from Ujan and retreated.

xiv S: I sent Qanbaroghli to Alqas and Bahram Mirza who were by the Zanjan river, saying that if Ibrahim Pasha has departed, Mentesha Sultan and the other amirs who were there should gather in Charkhaband and go in pursuit of Ibrahim Pasha when I arrived.

xv Disingenuous: Turkish *alja*, which in Azerbaijani Turkish can mean 'multicoloured', and thus allegorically 'insincere, not honest'. I am grateful to Ali Shapouran for alerting me to this meaning.

xvi Read with L Mīr Hādī-yi muḥtasib, not mīrhā-yi muḥtasib of B.

xvii Read with G and L mamnūn-i nākisān.

xviii S: Huwazah (near Basra in Southern Iraq).

xix S: Qaraqaymaz.

xx L: اغرقور

xxi The Turkish word *pusu* is used.

xxii This name appears in different forms in the manuscripts. S اغوارلو seems the best option to be read as Ughurlu, as at least this provides a name that exists in Turkish. Variants in other manuscripts produce non-existent names: B: اماغورلوL: باغورلو G: n/a. A certain Ughurlu Beg is mentioned by Ottoman chroniclers as a member of Alqas's retinue in Istanbul. See Posch, *Osmanisch-safavidische Beziehungen*, 281, 342.

xxiii S offers the most coherent text: bā aghvārlū nām pisarī kih ḥālā dar Rūm ast 'amal-i badī dāshta tarsīda kih mabādā man shinavam.

xxiv Only G has the correct reading, Shah 'Ali Sultan Chepni. The printed text has Shahquli Sultan Husayni. Other manuscripts consulted, including L, have Shah-Quli Sultan Chepni; however, Shah-Quli was a different amir, and Shah 'Ali Sultan Chepni is known from other sources to have been commander of Van fortress. See on him p. 110, n. 17.

xxv Horn's printed text and all manuscripts except S have Kaffa (كفه) in the Crimea. Tabatadze's Georgian translation (note 180) understands this as Hasankeyf in the Jazira, while the text of S reads Kīfī. However, it is clear from other sources that the text must be emended to read Kiği (كغي), for which Tabatadze's reading is evidently a simple transcription error, mistaking the graphically similar *ghayn* for *fā*'. See Posch, *Osmanich-safavidische Beziehungen*, 486–9, 501.

xxvi As in note xxv, read Kiği against the manuscript's impossible Kaffa.

xxvii Best text in S: tā Dartang va Khāniqī va Qizil Ribāṭ biravad. See also Posch, *Osmanich-safavidische Beziehungen*, 527.
xxviii Husayn-jan Sultan Rumlu. The name appears wrongly as Husayn-Khan Sultan in Horn's text; however, Husayn Khan was already dead, having being executed after the 'Tekellu calamity'. The diacritics are omitted in L, but G has Husayn-jan which is correct.
xxix Although the Persian text contains an addition *rā'* (reading Kharjin/Khurjin), this must be identical with the region of Khachen/Khachen, sometimes used as a synonym for Qarabagh as a whole.
xxx G, L, S: bi-khaṭṭ-i 'ibrī; B has bi-'khaṭṭ-i 'arabī. Despite the prevalence of 'ibrī in the manuscript witnesses, it seems necessary to accept the emendation to 'arabī, given that it is a Qur'anic quotation that was written. However, it should be noted that the Hebrew script was renowned by Muslims for its magical properties.
xxxi Only S has a sensible reading here: bi-urdū-yi mā birisad. B, G, L, bi-dunyā birisad.
xxxii S: Ya'qub Aqa; L, G, B: Iqut Aqa.
xxxiii Read with S yak qūch-rā zahm-zada miāvaram.
xxxiv Correct reading in G and S: ulkā-yi Shawshād; L, B: ulkā-yi Shīrvānshāh.
xxxv B, L, G: Abāza; S: Ayāz.
xxxvi I rely on the reading of G ولد قرقر سوبار و ورزا For the reconstruction of these names I rely on K. Tabatadze (ed. and trans.), *Mukalama-i Shah Tahmasp ba Ilchiyan-i Rum/Shah-Tamazis Saubari Osmaletis Elchebtan* (Tbilisi, 1976), n. 225.
xxxvii Following the reading of G: kih agar kas az qal'a-yi Khamkhiz va Palank kas bīrūn āmad khabardār shavand.
xxxviii L and S: Qārs; B and G: Fārs, which is clearly impossible.
xxxix Read with L salabja.

Bibliography

Manuscripts, editions and translations of the *Memoirs* consulted

Manuscripts: Berlin, Staatsbibliothek zu Berlin, MS Sprenger 205; Calcutta, Asiatic Society of Bengal, MSS PSC 87 and 88; London, British Library MS Or 5880; Tehran, Gulistan MS 831.

Horn, Paul (ed.), 'Die Denkwürdigkeiten des Šah Ṭahmâsp I von Persien', *Zeitschrift der Deutschen Morgenländischen Gesellschaft* 44, No. 4 (1890): 563–649.

Horn, Paul (ed.), 'Die Denkwürdigkeiten des Šah Ṭahmâsp I von Persien', *Zeitschrift der Deutschen Morgenländischen Gesellschaft* 45, No. 2 (1891): 245–91.

Horn, Paul (trans.), *Die Denkwürdigkeiten Schah Tahmasp's des Ersten von Persien 1515–1576* (Strassburg, 1891).

I'timad al-Saltana, Muhammad Hasan Khan (ed.), 'Ruznama', In *Matlaʿ al-Shams* 3 Vols (Tehran, 1301–3), II, 165–216.

Kırlangıç, Hicabi (trans.), Şah Tahmasb-i Safevi, *Tezkire* (Istanbul, 2001).

Phillott, D. C. (ed.), *Tazkira-i Shah Tahmasp* (Calcutta, 1912; reprinted with additional notes, and edited by Amrallah Safari; Tehran, 1984).

Tabatadze, K. (ed. and trans.), *Mukalama-i Shah Tahmasp ba Ilchiyan-i Rum/Shah-Tamazıs Saubarı Osmaletis Elchebtan* (Tbilisi, 1976).

Tazkira-i Shah Tahmasp (Berlin, 1924).

Primary sources

Babur, *The Babur-nama in English (Memoirs of Babur)*, trans. Annette Beveridge (London, 1922).

Babur, *The Baburnama: Memoirs of Babur, Prince and Emperor*, trans. Wheeler Thackston (New York, 1996).

Celâlzâde, Mustafa Çelebi, *Ṭabaḳātü'l-memâlik*, ed. P. Kappert (Wiesbaden, 1981).

Elgood, C. (trans.), 'A Persian Monograph on Syphilis', *Annals of Medical History*, N.S. 3 (1931): 465–87.
Felek, Özgen (ed.), *Kitābü'l-Menāmāt: Sultan III. Murad'ın Rüya Mektupları* (Istanbul, 2014).
Hafiz, *Divan*, ed. Muhammad Qazvini and Qasim Ghani (Tehran, 1941).
Hasan Rumlu, *Ahsan al-Tawarikh*, ed. ʿAbd al-Husayn Navaʾi (Tehran, 1384); abridged translation by C. N. Setton as *A Chronicle Of The Early Safawis Being The Ahsanu't-Tawārīkh of Ḥasan-i-Rūmlū* (Baroda, 1934), vol. II.
Ibnu'l-Balkhī, *Fārsnāma*, ed. G. Le Strange and R. A. Nicholson (London, 1962).
Jahangir, *Jahangirnama: Memoirs of Jahangir, Emperor of India*, trans. W. M. Thackston (New York, 1999).
Khurshah b. Qubad, *Tarikh-i Ilchi-yi Nizamshah: Tarikh-i Safaviyya az Aghaz ta 972 hijri qamari*, ed. Muhammad Riza Hasani and Koichi Haneda (Tehran, 1379).
Khurshah b. Qubad, *Tarikh-i-Qutbi (Also Known as Tarikh-i Elchi-i-Nizam Shah) of Khwurshah bin Qubad al-Husayni: A Work on the History of the Timurids. Chapter Five*, ed. Mujahid Husain Zaidi (New Delhi, 1965).
Membré, Michele, *Mission to the Lord Sophy of Persia (1539–1542)*, trans. A. H. Morton (Warminster, 1999).
Minorsky, Vladimir (ed. and trans.), *Tadhkirat al-Mulūk: A Manual of Safavid Administration (circa 1137/1725)* (London, 1943).
Nasir al-Din, Qajar Shah, *The Diary of H. M. the Shah of Persia, during His Tour through Europe in A. D. 1873*, trans. J. Redhouse (London, 1874, reprinted 1995, with a new introduction by Carole Hillenbrand).
Parmaksızoğlu, İsmet (ed.), 'Kuzey Irak'ta Osmanlı Hakimiyetinin Kuruluşu ve Memun Bey'in Hatıraları', *Belleten* 37, No. 146 (1973): 191–230.
Saʿdi, *Bustan*, in *Kulliyyat*, ed. Muhammad ʿAli Furughi (Tehran, n.d.); trans. G. M. Wickens, *Morals Pointed and Tales Adorned: The Bustan of Saʿdi* (Toronto, 1974).
Saʿdi, *Gulistan*, in *Kulliyyat*, ed. Muhammad ʿAli Furughi (Tehran, n.d.); ed. and trans. W. M. Thackston, *The Gulistan of Saʿdi* (Bethesda, MD, 2008).

Sana'i, *Hadiqat al-Haqiqa*, ed. Mudarris Rizavi (Tehran, n.d.).
Sharaf al-Din Khan b. Shams al-Din Bidlisi, *Sharafnama*, ed. Vladimir Véliaminof-Zernof (St Peterburg, 1862).
Tavernier, Jean-Baptiste, *The Six Voyages of John Baptista Tavernier, Baron of Aubonne through Turky, into Persia and the East-Indies, for the Space of Forty Years* (London, 1678).

Secondary literature

Abisaab, Rula Jurdi, *Converting Persia: Religion and Power in the Safavid Empire* (London, 2004).
Abisaab, Rula Jurdi, 'Karaki', *Encyclopaedia Iranica*, XV/5, 544–7.
Alam, Muzaffar, and Sanjay Subrahmanyam, 'Iran and the Doors to the Deccan, *c.* 1400–1650: Some Aspects', in *Iran and the Deccan: Persianate Art, Culture, and Talent in Circulation, 1400–1700*, ed. Keelan Overton (Bloomington, 2020), 77–103.
Aldous, Gregory, 'The Qizilbāsh and Their Shah: The Preservation of Royal Prerogative during the Early Reign of Shah Ṭahmāsp', *Journal of the Royal Asiatic Society* 31 (2021): 743–58.
Allouche, Adel, *Origins and Development of the Ottoman-Safavid Conflict (906–962/1500–1555)* (Berlin, 1983).
Arjomand, Said Amir, *The Shadow of God and the Hidden Imam: Religion, Political Order, and Social Change in Shi'ite Iran from the Beginning to 1890* (Chicago, 1984).
Atçıl, Zahit, 'Warfare as a Tool of Diplomacy: Background of the First Ottoman-Safavid Treaty in 1555', *Turkish Historical Review* 10 (2019): 3–24.
Aydın, Dündar, *Erzurum Beylerbeyliği ve Teşkilatı: Kuruluş ve Genişleme Devri (1535–1566)* (Ankara, 1998).
Babaei, Sussan, 'Shah 'Abbas II, the Conquest of Qandahar, the Chihil Sutun, and Its Wall Paintings', *Muqarnas* 11 (1994): 125–42.
Babaei, Sussan, *Isfahan and Its Palaces: Statecraft, Shi'ism and the Architecture of Conviviality in Early Modern Iran* (Edinburgh, 2008).

Babayan, Kathryn, *Mystics, Monarchs, and Messiahs: Cultural Landscapes of Early Modern Iran* (Cambridge, MA, 2002).

Babayan, Kathryn, 'The Safavid Synthesis: From Qizilbash Islam to Imamite Shi'ism', *Iranian Studies* 27, No. 1/4 (1994): 135–61.

Bacqué-Grammont, J.-L., and C. Adle, 'Quatre lettres de Šeref Beg de Bitlîs (1516–1520). Études turco-safavides XI', *Der Islam* 63 (1986): 90–118.

Bacqué-Grammont, J. -L., 'Un rapport de Fîl Ya'ḳûb Paşa, beylerbey de Dîyâr Bekir en 1532', *Wiener Zeitschrift für die Kunde des Morgenlandes* 76 (1986): 35–41.

Bart'old, V. V., 'K istorii orosheniya Turkestana', in V. V. Bart'old, *Sochineniya*, vol. 3 (Moscow, 1965).

Baysun, M. Cavid, 'Aḥmad Pas̲h̲a, Ḳara' *Encyclopaedia of Islam*, 2nd edition (Leiden, 1960–2005).

Bhalloo, Zahir, 'Shāh Ṭahmāsp's Narrative of Safavid-Ottoman Relations from 938–969/1531–1562', Unpublished MPhil thesis in Oriental Studies, University of Oxford, 2008.

Blair, Sheila, 'Invoking God's Protection: The Iconography of the Qur'anic Phrase *fasayakfīkahum allāh*', in *Farr-e Firouz, vol. 5 of Distinguished Scholars of the Cultural Heritage of Iran, Special Edition in Honour of Dr Firouz Bagherzadeh*, ed. Shahin Aryamanesh (Tehran, 2019), 191–206.

Bockholt, Philip, 'Shah Ṭahmāsp and the *Taẕkira*: A 16th Century Ruler's Justification of His Politics', in *Rulers as Authors in the Islamic World: Knowledge, Authority and Legitimacy*, ed. Maribel Fierro, Sonja Brentjes and Tilman Seidensticker (Leiden, 2024), 635–59.

Boyar, Ebru, 'Ottoman Expansion in the East', in *The Cambridge History of Turkey. II. The Ottoman Empire as a World Power, 1453–1603*, ed. Suraiya N. Faroqhi and Kate Fleet (Cambridge, 2013), 74–140.

Brittlebank, Kate, 'Accessing the Unseen Realm: The Historical and Textual Contexts of Tipu Sultan's Dream Register', *Journal of the Royal Asiatic Society* 21 (2011): 159–75.

Calmard, Jean, 'Une famille des sādāt dans l'histoire d'Iran: les Mar'aši', *Oriente Moderno* 18, No. 79 (1999): 413–28.

Canby, Sheila R., *The Shahnama of Shah Tahmasp: The Persian Book of Kings* (New York, 2011).

Csirkés, Ferenc Péter, 'A Messiah Untamed: Notes on the Philology of Shah Ismāʿīl's Divan', *Iranian Studies* 52, Nos. 3–4 (2019): 339–95.

Dale, Stephen, 'Steppe Humanism: The Autobiographical Writings of Zahir al-Din Muhammad Babur, 1483–1530', *International Journal of Middle East Studies* 22, No. 1 (1990): 37–58.

Dale, Stephen, 'Autobiography and Biography. The Turco-Mongol Case: Bābur, Haydar Mīrzā, Gulbadan Begim and Jahāngīr', in *The Rhetoric of Biography: Narrating Lives in Persianate Societies*, ed. Louise Marlow (Cambridge, MA, 2011), 89–105.

Dávid, Géza, 'Ulama Bey, an Ottoman Office-Holder with Persian Connections on the Hungarian Frontier', in *Irano-Turkic Cultural Contacts in the 11th-17th Centuries*, ed. Eva M. Jeremias (Piliscaba, 2003), 33–40.

Dehqan, M., and V. Genç, 'Reflections on Sharaf Khān's Autobiography', *Manuscripta Orientalia* 21 (2015): 46–61.

Dickson, Martin, 'Sháh Tahmásp and the Úzbeks: The Dual for Khurásán with ʿUbayd Khán 930–946/1524–1540', PhD dissertation, Princeton University, 1958.

Dirayati, Mustafa, *Fihristagan-i Nuskhaha-yi Khatti-yi Iran* (Tehran, 1334).

Emecen, Feridun, 'İbrahim Paşa, Makbul', *Türkiye Diyanet Vakfı İslam Ansiklopedisi* (Istanbul, 1988–2016), vol. 23, 333–5.

Emecen, Feridun, *Kanuni Sultan Süleymân ve Zamanı* (Ankara, 2022).

Echraqi, Ehsan, 'Le Dār al-Salṭana de Qazvin, deuxième capitale des Safavides', in *Safavid Persia: The History and Politics of an Islamic Society*, ed. Charles Melville (London, 1996), 105–15.

Floor, Willem, 'The ṣadr or Head of the Safavid Religious Administration, Judiciary and Endowments and Other Members of the Religious Institution', *Zeitschrift der Deutschen Morgenländischen Gesellschaft*, 150 (2000): 461–500.

Floor, Willem, *Safavid Government Institutions* (Costa Mesa, 2001).

Floor, Willem, and Hasan Javadi, 'The Role of Azerbaijani Turkish in Safavid Iran', *Iranian Studies* 46, no. 4 (2013): 569–81.

Floor, Willem, and Mohammad Faghfoory, 'Shah Esmail, Deputy of the Hidden Imam?' *Zeitschrift der Deutschen Morgenländischen Gesellschaft* 171 (2021): 375–88.

Fragner, Bert, 'Ashrafi', *Encyclopaedia Iranica*, II/8, 797–8.

Ghereghlou, Kioumars, 'Chronicling a Dynasty on the Make: New Light on the Early Ṣafavids in Ḥayātī Tabrīzī's *Tārīkh* (961/1554)', *Journal of the American Oriental Society* 137, No. 4 (2017): 805–32.

Ghereghlou, Kioumars, 'Ġaffāri Qazvini, Aḥmad', *Encyclopædia Iranica*, online edition, 2016, available at http://www.iranicaonline.org/articles/ghaffari-qazvini.

Green, Nile, 'The Religious and Cultural Roles of Dreams and Visions in Islam', *Journal of the Royal Asiatic Society* 13, No. 3 (2003): 287–313.

Haneda, Masashi, 'The Evolution of the Safavid Royal Guard', *Iranian Studies* 22, No. 2/3 (1989): 57–85.

Hinz, Walter, 'Zur Frage der Denkwürdigkeiten des Schah Ṭahmāsp I. von Persien', *Zeitschrift der Deutschen Morgenländischen Gesellschaft* 88 (1934): 46–54.

Hinz, Walter, *Irans Aufstieg zum Nationalstaat im fünfzehnten Jahrhundert* (Berlin, 1936).

Ivanow, Wladimir, *Concise Descriptive Catalogue of the Persian Manuscripts in the Collection of the Asiatic Society of Bengal* (Calcutta, 1924).

Johnson, Rosemary Stanfield, 'The Tabarra'iyan and the Early Safavids', *Iranian Studies* 37, No. 1 (2004): 47–71.

Karakaya-Stump, Ayfer, *The Kizilbash-Alevis in Ottoman Anatolia: Sufism, Politics and Community* (Edinburgh, 2020).

Karamustafa, Ahmet, 'In His Own Voice: What Hatayi Tells Us about Şah İsmail's Religious Views', in *L'Ésotérisme shi'ite, ses racines et ses prolongements: Shi'i Esotericism: Its Roots and Developments*, ed. Mohammad Ali Amir-Moezzi, Maria De Cillis, Daniel De Smet and Orkhan Mir-Kasimov (Turnhout, 2016), 601–11.

Kasheff, Manouchehr, 'Gīlān v. History under the Safavids', *Encyclopaedia Iranica* X/6, 635–42.

Kırzıoğlu, M. Fahrettin, *Osmanlılar'ın Kafkas-Elleri'ni Fethi (1451–1590)* (Ankara, 1998).

Krotkoff, G., 'Abjad', *Encyclopædia Iranica* I/2, 221–2.

Lambton, A. K. S., '*Pīshkash*: Present or Tribute?' *Bulletin of the School of Oriental and African Studies* 57 (1994): 145–58.

Marlow, Louise (ed.), *The Rhetoric of Biography: Narrating Lives in Persianate Societies* (Cambridge, MA, 2011).

Marlow, Louise, *Medieval Muslim Mirrors for Princes: An Anthology of Arabic, Persian and Turkish Political Advice* (Cambridge, 2023).

Matthee, Rudi (ed.), *The Safavid World* (London, 2022).

Matthee, Rudi, *Angels Tapping at the Wine-Shop's Door: A History of Alcohol in the Islamic World* (London, 2023).

Melville, Charles, 'The Chinese-Uighur Animal Calendar in Persian Historiography of the Mongol Period', *Iran* 32 (1994): 83–98.

Mitchell, Colin P., 'The Sword and the Pen: Diplomacy in Early Safavid Iran, 1501–1555', PhD dissertation, University of Toronto, 2002.

Mitchell, Colin P., *The Practice of Politics in Safavid Iran: Power, Religion and Rhetoric* (London, 2009).

Mitchell, Colin P., 'Tahmasp I', *Encyclopaedia Iranica* available online at https://www.iranicaonline.org/articles/tahmasp-i (accessed 1 November 2023).

Mitchell, Colin, 'Custodial Politics and Princely Governance in Sixteenth-Century Iran', in *The Safavid World*, ed. Rudi Matthee (London, 2022), 79–110.

Moin, Azfar, *The Millennial Sovereign: Sacred Kingship and Sainthood in Islam* (New York, 2012).

Morimoto, Kazuo, 'The Earliest 'Alid Genealogy for the Safavids: New Evidence for the Pre-dynastic Claim to Sayyid Status', *Iranian Studies* 43 (2010): 447–69.

Newman, Andrew J., 'Daštakī, Ġiāt̲ al-Din', *Encyclopaedia Iranica*, VII/1, 100–2.

Newman, Andrew J., 'The Myth of the Clerical Migration to Safawid Iran: Arab Shiite Opposition to ʿAlī al-Karakī and Safawid Shiism', *Die Welt des Islams* New Series 33, No. 1 (1993): 66–112.

Newman, Andrew J., *Safavid Iran: Rebirth of a Persian Empire* (London, 2006).

Özcan, Abdülkadir, 'İskender Paşa', *Türkiye Diyanet Vakfı İslam Ansiklopedisi* (Istanbul, 1988–2016) vol. 22, 565–6.

Parsadust, Manuchihr, *Shah Tahmasp-i Avval: Padishahi Azmand, Zirak, Ba Siyasat-i Khas-i Mazhabi* (Tehran, 1377).

Pinder-Wilson, Ralph, 'The Persian Garden: Bagh and Chahar-Bagh', in *The Islamic Garden*, ed. E. B. Macdougall and R. Ettinghausen (Washington, DC, 1976).

Posch, Walter, *Osmanisch-safavidische Beziehungen 1545–1550: Der Fall Alḳâṣ Mîrzâ* (2 vols, Vienna, 2013).

Quinn, Sholeh, 'The Dreams of Shaykh Safi al-Din and Safavid Historical Writing', *Iranian Studies* 29 (1996): 127–47.

Quinn, Sholeh, *Persian Historiography across Empires: The Ottomans, Safavids and Mughals* (Cambridge, 2021).

Quinn, Sholeh, and Charles Melville, 'Safavid Historiography', in *Persian Historiography*, ed. Charles Melville (London, 2012), 209–57.

Ray, Sukumar, *Humāyūn in Persia* (Kolkata, 2002, 1st edn, 1948).

Rebstock, Ulrich, 'Weights and Measures in Islam', in *Encyclopaedia of the History of Science, Technology, and Medicine in non-Western Cultures*, ed. Helaine Selin (Berlin: Springer, 2008), 2255–67.

Reynolds, Dwight F. (ed.), *Interpreting the Self – Autobiography in the Arabic Literary Tradition* (Berkeley, 2001).

Rizvi, Kishwar, *The Safavid Dynastic Shrine: Architecture, Religion and Power in Early Modern Iran* (London, 2011).

Rota, Giorgio, 'The Man Who Would Not Be King: Abu'l-Fath Sultan Muhammad Mirza Safavi in India', *Iranian Studies* 32, No. 4 (1999): 513–35.

Şahin, Kaya, *Peerless among Princes: The Life and Times of Sultan Süleyman* (New York, 2023).

Savory, Roger, 'The Principal Offices of the Ṣafawid State during the Reign of Ismāʿīl I (907–30/1501–24)', *Bulletin of the School of Oriental and African Studies* 23, No. 1 (1960): 91–105.

Savory, Roger, 'The Principal Offices of the Ṣafawid State during the Reign of Ṭahmāsp I (930–84/1524–76)', *Bulletin of the School of Oriental and African Studies* 24, No. 1 (1961): 65–85.

Savory, Roger, and Ahmet T. Karamustafa, 'Esmāʿil I Ṣafawi', *Encyclopaedia Iranica* VIII/6, 628–36.

Schmitz, Barbara, 'On a Special Hat Introduced during the Reign of Shāh ʿAbbās the Great', *Iran* 22 (1984): 103–12.

Schmucker, W. 'Mubāhala', *Encyclopaedia of Islam*, 2nd edition (Leiden, 1960–2005).
Soufi, Denise L. 'The Image of Fāṭima in Classical Muslim Thought', PhD dissertation, Princeton University, 1997.
Steingass, Francis Joseph, *A Comprehensive Persian-English Dictionary, Including the Arabic Words and Phrases to Be Met with in Persian Literature* (London, 1892).
Storey, C. A. *Persian Literature: A Bio-Bibliographical Survey*, I. 2 (London, 1936).
Storey, C. A. *Persidskaya Literatura: Bio-Bibliograficheskii Obzor*, translated into Russian and revised with additions and corrections by Yu. E. Bregel (Moscow, 1972).
Sümer, Faruk, *Safevi Devleti'nin Kuruluşu ve Gelişmesinde Anadolu Türklerinin Rolü* (Ankara, 1992).
Szuppe, Maria, *Entre Timourides, Uzbeks et Safavides: questions d'histoire politique et sociale de Hérat dans la première moitié du XVIe siècle* (Paris, 1992).
Szuppe, Maria, 'La participation des femmes de la famille royale à l'exercice du pouvoir en Iran safavide au XVIe siècle (deuxième partie)', *Studia Iranica* 24 (1995): 61–122.
Szuppe, Maria, 'Kinship Ties between the Safavids and Qizilbash Amirs in Late Sixteenth-Century Iran: A Case Study of the Political Career of Members of the Sharaf al-Din Oghli Tekelu Family', in *Safavid Persia: The History and Politics of an Islamic Society*, ed. Charles Melville (London, 1996), 79–104.
Teufel, F., 'Šâh Ṭahmâsp I. und seine Denkwürdigkeiten', *Zeitschrift der Deutschen Morgenländischen Gesellschaft* 37, No. 1 (1883): 113–25.
Trausch, Tilman, *Formen höfischer Historiographie im 16. Jahrhundert: Geschichtsschreibung unter den frühen Safaviden, 1501–1578* (Vienna, 2015).
Turan, Şerafettin, *Kanuni'nin Oğlu Şehzade Beyazid Vak'ası* (Ankara, 1961).
Turan, Şerefettin, 'Mustafa Çelebi', *Türkiye Diyanet Vafkı İslam Ansiklopedisi* (Istanbul, 1988–2016), vol. 31, 290–2.

Toukin, Sergei, 'The Horoscope of Shah Tahmasp', in *Hunt for Paradise: Court Arts of Safavid Iran, 1501–1576*, ed. Jon Thompson and Sheila R. Canby (New York, 2003), 327–31.

Vasilyeva, Olga, *A String of Pearls: Iranian Fine Books from the 14th to the 17th Century in the National Library of Russia Collections* (St Petersburg, 2008).

Waines, David, 'Tree(s)', *Encyclopaedia of the Qur'an* (Leiden, 2005).

Walsh, John R., 'The Revolt of Alqās Mīrzā', *Wiener Zeitschrift für die Kunde des Morgenlandes* 68 (1976): 61–78.

Yamamoto, Kumiko, 'Naqqāli', in *Encyclopaedia Iranica Online*, © Trustees of Columbia University in the City of New York. Consulted online on 2 September 2023, http://dx.doi.org/10.1163/2330-4804_EIRO_COM_363720.

Yıldırım, Rıza, 'Turkomans between Two Empires: The Origins of the Qizilbash Identity in Anatolia', PhD thesis, Bilkent University, Ankara, 2008.

Yıldız, Leyla, *Safevi Döneminde Tebrîz: Kentsel Mekânda Dönüşüm Süreçleri (1501–1736)* (Ankara, 2021).

Zhukovsky, V. A., review of P. Horn, 'Die Denkwürdigkeiten des Šāh Ṭahmâsp I. von Persien', *Zapiski Vostochnogo Otdeleniia Imperatorskogo Russkogo Arkheologicheskogo Obshestva* 6 (1891): 377–83.

Index

Note: Figures are indicated by page number followed by 'f'. Footnotes are indicated by the page number followed by 'n' and the footnote number e.g., 20 n.1 refers to footnote 1 on page 20

'Abbas, Shah 33, 36
'Abdallah Khan Ustajlu 56, 67 n.82, 70 n.92, 95, 110
'Abdi Beg Shirazi 24, 35
Ab-i Tutun 115 n.66
Abisaab, Rula Jurdi 18 n.34, 63 n.66
Abraham, Prophet 83 n.139, 104 n.26
Abu Bakr 108 n.43
Abu Sa'id b. Abi'l-Khayr 120 n.83
Abu'l-Fath al-Razi 75 n.114
Abu'l-Fath Sultan Muhammad Mirza 37, 38f, 39f, 60 n.48
Abu'l-Husayn 'Ali b. Abi Talib 50
Abul Aldi Aqa 70
Achih Sultan 72
Adham Beg Rumlu 132
Adham Khiyarji Qazvini, Mawlana 53
Āfat-i Tekellū 66 n.80
Agha Muhammad Ruzafzun 57 n.38
Agha Rustam 57 n.38
Aghricha 141 n.8
Aghzıvar Khan 76 n.116, n.117
Ahar 111, 112, 113
Ahlat 70 n. 94, 95, 115, 125
Ahmad Aqa Chavushlu 58, 147 n.iv
Ahmad Khan 141
Ahmad Sultan Afshar 54, 55 n.30, 56, 66, 134
Ahmed Pasha 116 n.67
Ahsan al-Tawarikh 12 n.23, 13 n.26, 24, 32 n.77, 51 n.10, 55 n.32
Akhi Sultan Tekellu 58, 59 n.47, 59–60
Alexander (the Great) 76
Ali Ağa 32, 138, 142, 144 n.22
'Ali al-Riza
 shrine in Mashhad 74 n.110

'Ali Aqa 98, 140
'Ali b. Abi Talib 4, 6, 19, 22, 50 n. 8, 62, 86 n.149, 105 n. 28, n.32, 107 n.40, 108 n.43, 120, 124 n.5, 125 n.9
'Ali Beg 60–1, 63 n.64, 66
'Ali Karaki 20, 63 n.66, 64 n.73
'Ali Khan Beg Tekellu 57
'Ali Riza Abbasi 36
'Ali Sultan Chepni 101 n.7, 114, 148 n. xxiv
'Ali Sultan Taqioghli 115
'Ali Sultan Zulqadar 53, 55
'Ali-Quli Beg 111
Allah Quli Beg 111, 112
Allah Verdi Aqa 138
Allouche, Adel 7 n.13
'al-Mubahala' ('the cursing') 105 n.29
Alqas Mirza 78, 80, 96, 97 n.2, 99, 100, 103, 76, 118, 120, 139
 support of the Qizilbash 14, 15 n.28, 114–16
Amasya 15, 17, 71, 137
 see also Ottoman-Safavid Treaty
amīr al-umarā' (commander-in-chief, 'military wakil') 51 n.13, 53
Amir Beg Rumlu 73, 76, 93
Amir Ghiyath al-Din Muhammad 8
Amir Jamal al-Din Sadr 54
Amir Khan Mawsillu 8, 61 n.55, 111, 132
Amir Qiwam al-Din, *see* Mir Buzurg al-Mar'ashi
amīrākhur 76 n.118
Anatolia 5–6, 9f, 12, 67 n.84, 103 n.22, 126 n.13

Index

Āqā-yi jilawdār 60 n.49
Aqquyunlu 5–6, 5 n.9, 54 n.29
Arab Mehmed 142 n.13, 142–3
Arabgirlu 94 n.26
Ardabil 3, 12, 18, 33, 36, 37, 58, 92, 96, 98, 111
Ardanuç 123 n.2
Ashrafis 103 n.22
Aslan Beg Pazuki 117 n.74
Astarabad 60, 143
Astarabadi, Mir Jamal al-Din 52
Ayas Pasha 132
Azerbaijan 5, 58 n.42, 67 n.84, 85, 114, 116, 133, 141
   campaigns against non-Muslims in 4
   dialects 25, 26
   Safavid governor of 12

Babayan, Kathryn 6 n.10, 19 n.36
Babur 21, 22, 27–8, 29
Baburnama 21
Badiʿ al-Zaman 119
Badinjan Sultan Rumlu 58, 147 n.iv
Bagh-i Jannat 142
Baghdad 15, 61, 62, 63, 66, 71, 85, 89, 116, 118, 119, 133, 138, 139
Bahram Beg Qaramanlu 58
Bahram Mirza 10, 64, 65 n.75, 72, 76, 78, 80, 93–6, 99 n.10, 111, 112, 113, 117 n.72, 118, 119, 143
Bayazid Bayat 28
Bedir Beg 55 n.33
Beyazid, Sultan (son of Süleyman) 16, 30, 31, 33, 137–9, 142–4
   audacious plan 141 n.12
   deal with defectors 139
   defeat 137
   disrupt relations 140–4
   Tahmasp's letters to 140 n.5
Beyazid II 26, 67 n.84
Bisharat Kelle 133
Bitlis 29, 69, 70, 114
Bitlisi, Sharaf al-Din 70 n.94

Budaq Khan 93
Burhan ʿAli Sultan 117 n.76
Burun Sultan Tekellu 53, 55, 57
Būzakhāna 81 n.136

Caucasia 4, 123 n.2, 135 n.44
   campaigns against non-Muslims in 4
Çavuşbaşı Ali Ağa 138
Celâlzâde, Mustafa Celebi 67 n.84, 96 n.31
Chaldiran, Battle of in 1514 7, 81
Charandab Sultan 111–12
Charkhaband 78 n.127, 80
Charkhjīs 95 n.28, 132
Chayan Sultan 52 n.15, 64
Chekirge Sultan Shamlu 60
Chemishkezeklu 94 n.26, 114–15
Cherken Hasan Tekellu 64
Chiragh Sultan 79 n.130, 111, 118
Chuha Sultan 10, 11, 12 n.23, 53, n.21, 54 n.27, 58, 59 n.45, 64 n.68, n.69, 66, 67 n.84
Chukhur-i Saʿd 71 n.100, 113, 117, 123 n.2, 138

Damri Sultan Shamlu 59–60, 76 n.116
Darius 76
dārūghā (city prefect) 67 n.85, 86
Darvish Beg 58–9
Dashtaki Shirazi, Mir Ghiyath al-Din Mansur 63 n.65, n.66, 64–5 n.73
Dav İli 125 n.11
dawlatkhāna (Royal Precinct) 12 n.23, 59 n.46, 65, 73
Delü Efendi 133
Delü Qaytmaz 133 n.38
Delü Sayyid Hasan Abdallu 130
Div Sultan 9, 11, 51 n.12, 52 n.14, n.19, 53, 54 n.24, n.27, 55 n.32, 58 n.43, 59 n.45
dīvānkhāna (Audience Chamber) 142 n.14

Diyarbakır 6, 61 n.55, 70 n.95, 71, 96, 115, 123 n.1, 133, 139
   see also Kara Amid
Durak Ağa 139
Durmish Khan Shamlu 53, 54 n.30, 67 n.82, 81

Egypt 103 n.22, 123 n.1
   Mamluk empire in 7
Engli Cayı 96 n.30
Erciş 70, 94, 95, 96, 113, 125
Erzincan 6, 116–17
Erzurum 15, 113, 117, 123, 125, 131, 132, 133, 139

Farid al-Din 99 n.8
Fars 53, 64, 65, 66, 69, 111 n. 54, 118
Fathi Beg 74
Ferruh Beg 141 n.7
Fil Pasha 70–1
Firdawsi 26, 93 n.18
Firuzkuh 60
Floor, Willem 6 n.10, 25 n.57, 52 n.18, 58 n.41

Ghadir Khumm 105 n.31, 106 n.34
Ghaffari Qazvini 24
Gharchistan 73
Ghazi Khan 14–15, 76, 79, 83, 86, 96 n.31, 97 n.2
   escaping from Tabriz with Ulama 89
   link between Ulama and Alqas 14
Gilan 56, 63, 141, 143
Gökche Sultan Qajar 95, 117 n.76
Gulbadan Begam 28

Habib al-Siyar 51 n.10
Habil Beg 69
hadith qudsi (divine speech) 108 n.44, 112 n.58
Hafiz 26, 44, 84, 102 n.21, 112 n.59, 134 n.42
Hajji Beg 93 n.24

Hajji Lor 70
Hajji Tarkhan 141 n.9
Hamza Beg Hajlu-yi Turkman 58–9
Hamza Sultan Chemeshlu Zulqadar 55, 64
Hasan Beg Yuzbashi 93, 95, 121, 130–1, 138, 141–2
Hasan Kashi 118
Hasan Rumlu 1 n.1, 12 n.23, 24, 32, 43, 55 n.32, 147
Haseki Sultan 126 n.14
Hashtad Juft 55
Haydar 4–5, 92
Herat 58, 64, 65, 71–73, 76, 83, 84, 86, 114
Hijaz 135 n.44
Hınıs 114–15
Hinz, Walter 5 n.8, 30 n.72
Horn, Paul 41 n.93, 42 n.98, 45
Humayun 28, 143
   Tahmasp's support to 2
Hürrem Sultan 126 n.14, 137 n.1
al-Husayn 50 n.8
Husayn ʿAli Beg Qajar 93 n.19
Husayn b. Sultan ʿAli b. Musa al-Riza 57–8
Husayn b.ʿAbd al-Samad al-Harithi 62 n.62
Husayn Khan Shamlu 10, 11, 13, 53, 53 n.22, 54, 64 n.69, n.70, 65, 66–7, 69, 73, 76 n.116, n.117, 149 n. xxviii
Husayn-jan Sultan 123 n.2
Hüsrev Pasha 32

Ibn Malik 108
Ibrahim Aqa-yi Burbur 116 n.68
Ibrahim Khalifa 66
Ibrahim Khan Mawsillu 61 n.55
Ibrahim Khan Zulqadar 112 n.56, 113, 118, 121
Ibrahim Pasha 13, 68–9, 75, 77, 79, 89, 94, 96 n.32, 99, 101, 148 n. xiv

Ibrahim Qutbshah 34
Iesse 132 n.31
Ij, Fars 111 n.54
ijtihad 62 n.62
Imam Abu'l-Hasan 'Ali b. Musa al-Riza 73
Inanoghli 116
Iraq 7, 90 n.3
  amirs of 118
  Arab 61 n.55, 62
  and Iraq border 116 n.70
  Ottoman campaign against 68 n.87, 116
  Persian 63
  western part 91 n.11
'Isa Khan 132
Isfahan 2, 53, 59 n. 46, 61 n. 55, 64, 65, 91
Isfahani, Ahmad Beg Nur Kamal 55 n.31, 63 n.64, 75 n.113, 82
ishīk-āqāsī (Chamberlain) 59 n.44, 67, 135
īshīk-aqāsī-bāshī (grand chamberlain) 13, 59 n.44
İskender Pasha 15, 121
  Ottoman governor of Erzurum 123–135
Isma'il Mirza (son of Tahmasp) 5, 70 n.93, 113, 117 n.76, 125
Isma'il, Shah 5 n.9, 6, 7, 52 n.17, 61 n.55, 79 n.131, 120 n.81
Istanbul 15, 57–8, 71, 75, 92, 99, 100, 125, 126, 138, 139

Ja'far al-Sadiq 124 n.7
Ja'farabad 78 n.126
Jahan-ara 51 n.10
Jahangir 28
Jalal al-Din Muhammad Tabrizi 52 n.17, 52–3 n.19, 53 n.20
Jani Khan Beg 62
Jilawdar Muhammad Yuzbashi 116 n.68
Junayd, Shaykh 4, 5 n.9

Kahramanmaraş 71 n.98
  see also Mar'ash
Kaikhosro II 132 n.29
Kanlu Çimen 133
kapıcıbaşı (chief of the palace guards) 142 n.13
Kara Ahmed Pasha 116 n.67
Kara Amid 115 n.64
  see also Diyarbakır
Kara Uğurlu 141
Kars 113, 138
Kazan 141
Kechel Pir 'Ali Hajjilar 91 n.9
keshik (royal bodyguard) 65 n.78
Khanum, Pari Khan 24, 128
Khaybar 98 n.4
Khoy 70, 83, 92, 94, 110, 128
Khulasat al-Tawarikh 35
Khurasan 3, 6, 17, 18, 53, 54, 58, 60, 62, 67, 72, 102
Khurshah b. Qubad 1 n.1, 10, 11 n.22, 12 n.23, 13 n.25, 24, 34 n.82, 35, 43, 57 n.38, 126, n.15
khutba (sermon at Friday prayers) 99
Khwaja Habiballah Savaji 54
Khwaja Sahib 54 n.30
Kirman 56, 111, 118, 141
Konya 137
Köpek Sultan Ustajlu 9, 11, 51–2, 52 n.14, 53, 54 n.27, 55 n.32, n.34, 58, 59 n.45, 111
Kuchkunji Khan 62
Kuduz Ferhad 143 n.18
Kur Shah Suvar 95
Kurdi Beg 55
Kurdistan 133
Kurds 29, 60–1, 69
Kurtkale 134

lala (tutor) 8, 51, 53, 60 n.48, 61 n.55, 90, 96 n.31, 117 n.76
Levan, King of Kakheti 132 n.32
Lumsden manuscript 37, 39f

Ma'mun Beg 29
Mahdi Imam 92
Mahidasht 61 n.56
Mahmud Beg 125, 126
Mahmud Khan 111, 113
Mama Hatun 116
Mamluk empire 7
Man la Yahduruhu al-Faqih (Ibn Babawayh) 44
mann (Unit of weight) 109 n.47
manuscripts of the *Memoirs* 54 n.30, 148 n.xxii
    Berlin 41
    Gulistan 33, 51 n.10
    Lumsden 37, 39f
    Memoirs' composition and 30
    St Petersburg 33
Maqsud Beg Inan Oghli 116 n.68
Mar'ash 71
    see also Kahramanmaraş
Mari Sultan Shamlu 58
Marv 62, 64, 73
Marwan, Umayyad caliph 86
Mashhad 18, 53, 81, 141
Matthee, Rudi 22 n.47, 81 n.135
Mazandaran 56, 57, 141, 142
Mehmed Pasha 119
Membré, Michele 19 n.35, 90 n.6, 101 n.17, 142 n.14
Memoirs of Tahmasp
    Berlin manuscript 41
    composition and extant manuscripts 30
    Gulistan manuscript 33, 51 n.10
    Hebrew script 149 n.xxx
    in historical context 3
    in literary context 23–30
    Lumsden manuscript 37, 39f
    Memoirs' composition and 30
    Ottoman ambassadors 30
    St Petersburg manuscript 33
Mentesha Sultan 63, 70, 71, 73, 76, 78, 86, 90, 93, 148 n. xiv
mihmāndār 69 n.90, 138

Minorsky, Vladimir 54 n.28, 60 n.49, n.50, 67 n.85, 76 n.118
Mir 'Abdallah and Sayyid Zayn al-'Abidin 57
Mir Buzurg al-Mar'ashi 56–7
Mir Hasan Beg Yuzbashi 138
Mir Hasan Razavi 54
Mir Ibrahim Isfahani 98
Mir Ja'far Savaji 54
Mir Murad Khan 5
Mir Qiwam al-Din naqīb-i Isfahani 52, 56–7, 62, 63
Mir Sayyid Muhammad 81, 82 n.137
Mir Shahi ibn 'Abd al-Karim ibn 'Abdallah 56, 57
Mir Shahsuvar Kurd 90
Mirza Baqir 119
Mirza Haydar Dughlat 29
Mirza Husayn I 52
Mirza Qasim Miraki 54–5 n.30
Mitchell, Colin P. 4 n.6, 8 n.15, 17 n.32, 52 n.17, 53 n.20, 56–7 n.37, 139 n.4
Mongols 51 n.9, 90 n.6
Mosul 71
Muhammad Aqa 116
Muhammad Beg Mawsillu 60–1, 132
Muhammad Beg Sharaf al-Din Oghli Tekellu 60 n.48
Muhammad Husayn Damavandi 36–7
Muhammad Khan Sharaf Oghli 60 n.48, 66 n.81
Muhammad Khan Zulqadar 56 n.36, 63, 66, 79 n.131, 85 n.148, 87
Muhammad Mahdi Khan Shirazi 35
Muhammad Qazvini 44
Muhammad Shaybani Khan 6
Muhammad Sultan Afshar 78
Muhammad Sultan Sharaf al-Din 'Ali Tekellu 60, 63
Muhammad, Prophet 4, 31 n.76, 76, 107, 124, 129 n.23
Muhammadi Beg 58, 133

muhtasib 82
Mujtahid al-Zamān 62 n.62, 64–5 n.73
mujtahid 62–3 n.62, 64
Mulla Hasan 93
Mulla Muhammad 93
Mulla Shams Ilchi 138
Mulla Vazir Qazvini 138
Murad Sultan 55
Murad III, Sultan 21
Musa al-Kazim 50 n.8
Mustafa Sultan 51–2, 60
Mustafa Yasakçı 141
Muzaffar Sultan Gilani 56 n.35

Nakhchivan 58, 125, 127, 130
naqīb al-ashrāf 58 n.39
Narin Beg Qajar 54
Nasir al-Din Shah II 29
Newman, Andrew J. 3–4 n.6, 18 n.34, 63 n.65
Ni'matallah Hilli 62–3, 64–5 n.73
Ni'matallah, Sayyid Shah 120
Nishapur 62
Nizami 26, 83, 102 n.20, 117 n.75, 125 n.8
Nogai Horde 141 n.11
Nuh Pasha 138
Nukhud Sultan 60–1

Oghlan Qasim Pazuki 117
ordu (royal camp) 131
Osman Pasha 116 n.71
Ottoman Empire (c. 1300–1922) 1, 3, 6, 126
Ottoman(s) 1, 7, 11, 12, 14–15, 18, 23, 61 n.57, 66 n.81, 67 n.84, 71 n.99, 85 n.145, 99 n.7, 101, 103 n.23, 109, 113, 114 n.62, 115 n.64, 116–17, 123
  envoys 36
  war against Tahmasp 96 n.31
  wars with Safavid 1–3, 7 n.13
Ottoman-Safavid Treaty 135 n.44
  see also Amasya

Parikhan Khanum 128
parvānachi 74 n.111
Pasinler 114, 129
Persian
  administrators 7
  chronogram 11
  historiography 29
Pervane Beg 66
Phillott, D. C. 41 n.95
pīshkāsh 91 n.10

Qadi-yi Jahan Qazvini 52 n.16, 54 n.24, 56
Qal'a-yi Kurt 134 n.40
Qapūchīs (gatekeepers) 93 n.22
Qara Isma'il Qurchi 95
Qara Khan 56
Qaraja Beg Ustajlu 54
Qaraja Sultan Tekellu 53, 55
Qasim Ghani 44
Qaya Beg Shukroghli 93
Qazvin 33, 56, 59 n.47, 63, 138 n.3, 141
  Sayfi sayyids of 52 n.16
Qilij Bahadur 61–2
Qizilbash Amir Khan 8
'Qizilbash interregnum' 8–9, 12
Qizilbash tribes 4–5, 7–8, 43, 59 n.45
Qubad Sultan 66
Qudurmush Sultan 66
Qur'an 31 n.75, 83, 102 n.18, n.19, 105, 124, 127 n.20, 140
qūrchībāshī 54 n.28, 55 n.33, 76, 83, 93, 117–18
qūrchīs 55, 61, 65, 70, 73, 76, 80, 85, 93, 95–6, 111, 114, 116–17, 128
Qutb-shahi dynasty 34
Qvarqvare 132 n. 29

Rasht 56 n.35, 58
Rayy 56, 58 n. 40, 72 n. 101, 77
Riza, Imam 18, 74 n. 112, 81, 97
Roemer, H. R. 3 n.6
Rukn-i Saltana 54 n.28

Rumlu, Hasan, *see* Hasan Rumlu
Rüstem Pasha 99 n.11, 100, 115, 119, 126, 139

Saʻdi of Shiraz, Muslih al-Din 26, 55, 90, 99 n.9, 100 n.14, 101 n.16, 110, 143 n.19
Sadr al-Din Khan 80, 93
ṣadr 8, 52 n.17, n.18, 62, 63
Safavid state
  administrative terminology 10 n.18
  foundation of 5
  historians 21–2
  historiography 24 n.53
  non-muslims in 4
  pilgrims 135 n.44
  revolution 18
  Safavid dynasty of Iran 1
  Shiism 18 n.34
  territory 135 n.44
'The Safavid Synthesis' 18 n.34
Safi al-Din, Shaykh 3–4, 21–2, 36, 50 n.8, 112 n.57
Saksanjak 55 n.34
Sam Mirza 14 n.27, 26, 53, 54, 64 n.70, 65 n.75, n.77, 76 n.117, 87, 89, 90
  as rebellion 14 n.27
Samarqand 21, 62 n 61, 74
Samtskhe-Saatabago 132 n.29
Saru Qaplan 130
Sarulu 68 n.86
Sarupira Ustajlu 55 n.33
Sava 60
Savaji, Habiballah 54 n.29, 55 n.30
Savory, Roger 7–8 n.14, 51 n.12, n.18, n.19, 54 n.27, 59 n.45, 62 n.62, 67 n.83
Şavşat 132
Savuj Bulagh 58 n.40
Sayfi sayyids 52
Sayyid Fakhr al-Din 57
Sayyid Muhammad 93 n.20, 95

Sayyid Nasir al-Din 57
sayyid 4, 56–7, 72, 90, 120, 124, 126
Selim I, Sultan 7
Selim, Sultan (son of Süleyman, future Selim II) 16, 26, 126 n.15, 126, 140, 144
Sevinduk Beg 78 n.124
Shabankara 111 n.54
Shah ʻAli Sultan Chepni 101 n.17, 114, 148
Shah Nur al-Din Niʻmatallah Baqi Yazdi 120 n.81
Shah Qubad 66 n.79
Shah Quli Aqa 135
Shah Quli Khalifa 78, 93, 113, 124, 132, 138, 148 n.xxiv
Shah Verdi Sultan 94, 131
Shahgeldi Beg 132
Shahrazur 29, 71, 94 n. 24
Shahrukh 97
Shahzada Sultanum 126 n.16
Shamlu tribe 8, 11, 55 n.30, 60 n.53, 65 n.78, 67 n.83
Shams al-Din Khan 77, 125, 126 n.17
*sharābkhāna*s 81 n.136
Sharaf al-Din Khan b. Shams al-Din Bidlisi 67 n.84, 137 n.2
Sharaf al-Din 117 n.74, 85 n.148, 97
Sharaf Beg 69 n.89, 72
Sharaf Khan 29, 77
Sharafnama 29
Shaybanid dynasty 6
  see also Uzbeks
Shihab al-Din Mahmud Ahari 112
Shiism 1, 2, 5, 12, 19, 20, 86
  in Iran 18 n.34
  in Safavid domains 65 n.73
  theology 104 n.26
Shir Hasan 93
Shiraz 26, 53, 55, 65, 76, 79, 93, 111, 112, 118, 141
Shirvan 96, 97 n.2, 117 n.76, 118, 123 n.2

campaigns against non-
  Muslims in 4
Shirvanshah dynasty 97, 117 n.76
Sinan Beg 133 n.36, 134–5, 138–9
Sistan 64, 141
Sivas 71, 101, 108
siyar 27, 101 n.15
Sufi Khalil Mawsillu 63 n.63
Sufi spiritual guide (*murshid*) 4
Sufism 21
Sufraji 93 n.21
Suhrawardi, Shihab al-Din 112 n.57
Sulayman Sultan Rumlu 94, 95
Sulayman, Safi II 37
Süleyman, Sultan ('the sultan') 13–17,
  31–2, 68 n.87, 69 n.91, 90 n.3, 91
  n.11, 92 n.15, 96 n.31, 114 n.62,
  123 n.1, 126 n.15, 130 n.27, 135
  n.43, 137 n.1
Sultan Ibrahim Mirza 128
Sultaniyya 55, 79, 80, 91, 94
Sunnism 12, 103 n.23
Surkhab Sultan 119–120, 120 n.80
Syria 7

Tabatadze, K. 30 n.73, 41–2, 132 n.30,
  n.32, 149 n.xxxvi
Tabriz 5, 7, 13, 17, 28, 67–8, 71, 75,
  79, 86, 89–90, 91, 112 n.57, 138
Tahmasp, Shah 1, 56 n.35, 85 n.148,
  97 n.2, 105, 139 n.4, 140
  and affair of Ulama 49
  and Alqas Mirza 97
  and Beyazid 16, 137
  defectors from 12
  dreams 21–2
  envoys from Ottoman empire 3
  fighting at Saksanjak 55 n.34
  Georgian allies 133
  genealogy of 50 n.8
  and Ghazi Khan 14, 89
  and İskender Pasha 15, 123
  manuscripts, *Memoirs*'
    composition and 30

Memoirs in historical context 1, 3
  negotiations with Ottomans
    127 n.18
  protect society from false
    mujtahids 62–3
  Uzbeks and 72 n.102
  victories over Ottomans 74 n.110
  victory of Rumlu and Tekellu 58
tāj ('crown') 100 n.12
Tajlu Begum 65 n.75, 90 n.4
Takmilat al-Akhbar 24, 35
Tarikh-i Ilchi (Khurshah b. Qubad)
  24, 34, 123 n.2, 126 n.16
Tarkhan Beg 132
Tavernier, Jean-Baptiste 108 n.46
tawḥīd-khāna 120
'Tekellu calamity' (*āfat-i Takallū*) 11,
  12, 13, 14, 66 n.80
Tekellu tribe 7, 10–11, 58 n.42, 66
  n.81, 67
Timur Kurd 76, 97
Timurid dynasty 5, 24, 25
Tipu Sultan 21
Tiyūldar 60 n.50
Transoxiana 64
Treaty of Amasya in 1555 15,
  135 n.44
Tuhfa-yi Sami 26
Turkey 7, 29, 44, 81 n.136, 123 n.2
Turkmen 4, 5, 7, 68, 85, 95, 141
Turko-Mongol tradition 8

'Ubayd, *see* 'Ubaydallah Uzbek Khan
'Ubaydallah Uzbek Khan 17–18, 60
  n.52, 61 n.59, 62 n.61, 72
Ujan 53, 80, 90 n.6
Ulama Sultan Tekellu 13, 49, 67, 67
  n.84, 69, 72, 75–6, 85, 86, 111,
  113, 129
  and Ahmad Pasha 94–6
  and Alqas 14
  defection of 61
  and Ghazi Khan 86, 91–2
  Ibrahim Pasha and 94

as Ottoman governor of Erzurum 123–135
and Rustem Pasha 115
and Zulqadaroghli 91
Ulang-i Nishin 73 n.105
Ulughkhan Beg Sa'dlu 132
Umayyads 124
Ustajlu 9, 51 n.12, 53–4, 55, 58 n.42, 63–4, 66, 95, 116–17
Uzbek Khan, see 'Ubaydallah Uzbek Khan
Uzbeks 6, 10, 17, 53, 58, 60 n.53, 62, 64, 72 n.101, 84
   campaign against 58 n.42
   Tahmasp's wars with 3, 9
   see also Shaybanid dynasty

Van 15, 32, 68, 86, 87, 92–95, 101, 102, 111, 113–114, 128, 133, 138, 139, 148 n. xxiv
vakīl 10, 11, 13, 53 n.20

wilāya 105 n.32

Ya'qub Sultan Qajar 61, 93, 95
Yadgar Beg ibn Mansur 137 n.2
Yadgar Beg Pazuki 137
Yadgar Muhmmad Sultan 95
Yadgar Rojaki 70
yasāvul (aide-de-camp) 12–13, 15, 67, 93, 129
Yazid, Umayyad Caliph 74 n.109
yūzbāshī (centurion) 70 n.96

Zafarnama 97 n.1
Zanjan 78, 79, 80, 91, 148 n xiv
Zawiya 93, 120 n.85
Zayn al-'Abidin 57
Zayn al-din Tabrizi 36
Zaynal Khan Shamlu 60, 73 n.106, 78
Zaynash Bahadur 60 n.52
Zhukovsky, V. A. 30 n.72, 41
Zu'l-fiqar ('The splitter') 108 n.45
Zulfiqar Beg 60–1, 61 n.57, 63 n.64
Zulqadar 66, 79, 95
Zulqadaroghli, see Muhammad Khan Zulqadar

Plate 1 The opening of Tahmasp's *Memoirs* in the short recension, in a manuscript made for Shah 'Abbas in the handwriting of Riza 'Abbasi. National Library of Russia, St Petersburg, MS Dorn 302, fol. 2b.

Plate 2 Shah Tahmasp and the Ottoman ambassadors. National Library of Russia, St Petersburg, MS Dorn 302.

Plate 3 Opening of the long recension. British Library, MS Or 5880, fol. 1b-2a. Courtesy of the British Library Board.

Plate 4 Opening of the long recension in the Calcutta manuscript made for Lumsden. By kind permission of the Asiatic Society, Kolkata, MS PSC 87.

www.ingramcontent.com/pod-product-compliance
Lightning Source LLC
Chambersburg PA
CBHW052123300426
44116CB00010B/1773